Scribe Publications
BEHIND THE EXCLUSIVE BRETHREN

Michael Bachelard is an Australian journalist and author whose first book, *The Great Land Grab: what every Australian should know about Wik, Mabo and the Ten-Point Plan*, was published in 1997. In 1998, he joined *The Australian* to work in its Melbourne bureau, where he was the workplace relations writer and, later, the Melbourne business and finance editor, and the Victorian political reporter. In 2005 he was awarded a Jefferson Fellowship in journalism, and travelled to the US, China, and Japan for a study tour into China's growth and burgeoning influence.

Michael Bachelard became part of *The Age*'s investigative team in 2006, and he now writes for *The Sunday Age*. In 2008 he won a Quill award for the best news report in print.

This book is dedicated to those people, both within and outside the Exclusive Brethren, who have suffered, and who suffer now, under the doctrine of separation.

BEHIND THE EXCLUSIVE BRETHREN

Michael Bachelard

SCRIBE
Melbourne

Scribe Publications Pty Ltd
PO Box 523
Carlton North, Victoria, Australia 3054
Email: info@scribepub.com.au

First published by Scribe 2008
Reprinted 2009
This edition published 2010

Copyright © Michael Bachelard 2008

All rights reserved. Without limiting the rights under copyright reserved above, no part of this publication may be reproduced, stored in or introduced into a retrieval system, or transmitted, in any form or by any means (electronic, mechanical, photocopying, recording or otherwise) without the prior written permission of the publisher of this book.

Typeset in Dante by the publishers
Printed and bound in Australia by Griffin Press.
Only wood grown from sustainable regrowth forests is used
in the manufacture of paper found in this book.

National Library of Australia
Cataloguing-in-Publication data

Michael Bachelard, 1968–
Behind the Exclusive Brethren

New ed.

9781921640230 (pbk.)

Plymouth Brethren. Plymouth Brethren–Australia–Political aspects.
Religion and politics–Australia. Political planning–Australia.
Australia–Politics and government–21st century.
Australia–Religion–21st century.

289.9

Australian Government

This project has been assisted by the Australian government through the Australian Council for the Arts, its arts funding and advisory body.

www.scribepublications.com.au

Contents

A Note on Terminology	vi
Introduction	1
PART I: HISTORY	
1 The Making of a Cult	7
2 The Australian Succession	27
PART II: PEOPLE	
3 Life in the Brethren	47
4 The System	81
5 The Alderton Family	115
6 Albury	144
PART III: POLITICS	
7 Persuasion	173
8 Schooling	215
9 The Family Court	246
10 Silencing Criticism	272
Conclusion	290
Acknowledgements	297
Notes	299
Index	311

A Note on Terminology

Throughout this account I refer to the Exclusive Brethren, and use the term 'the Brethren' as a convenient abbreviation. But this group is just one of many different shades of Brethrenism, whose nomenclature varies in different parts of the world. All of the different groups sprang from the early movement that began in Ireland and England in the late 1820s, which became known as Plymouth Brethren. But successive splits divided the movement into two broad camps: the Open and Closed Brethren. There are many subsets of these different movements, which go by different names, usually denoting when they split. There are the Kelly–Lowe–Continental Brethren, the Darbyites, the Tunbridge Wells or Natural History Hall Brethren, and others.

This book is about the sect known in Australia and New Zealand as the Exclusive Brethren, and elsewhere variously as the Taylorites and the Raven–Taylor–Hales Brethren, The Jimmies, The Connexional Brethren, and Plymouth Brethren Number 4. They have traditionally resisted adopting a name themselves, but have done so more recently. The most powerful sign of this is that, when they set up their own website at www.theexclusivebrethren.net, they described themselves as The Exclusive Brethren Christian Fellowship.

Introduction

On 7 August 2007, the long era of John Howard, Australia's prime minister and the member for Bennelong, was drawing to its close. It was a Tuesday, and a very busy one for the man who was staring down the barrel of an election he was about to lose.

Just the night before, Howard's dramatic intervention in Aboriginal affairs in the Northern Territory had passed the Lower House. That morning, Newspoll had released another terrible set of numbers for Howard, and the Reserve Bank had decided to hike the official interest rate to a 10-year high of 6.5 per cent. Howard's policy to directly fund the Mersey hospital in Tasmania was beginning to unravel, as was his lavish WorkChoices advertising campaign.

Yet, in the midst of this pre-election political frenzy, the prime minister found space in his schedule to meet up with some old friends. 'I was in Canberra and I greeted Mr Howard and enquired from him whether Mr Hales could meet him for a short discussion,'[1] recalls the Exclusive Brethren's main man in Canberra, Warwick John.

Howard gave him the nod, and John immediately phoned the Sydney-based world leader of his sect, Bruce D. Hales, aka the 'Man of God,' the 'Elect Vessel,' 'Mr Bruce'. Hales donned his tie, collected his security guard, and went to the airport to board his private jet. Also aboard were his brother, millionaire pump-supplier Stephen Hales, and another Sydney pump salesman, Mark Mackenzie. The three Exclusive Brethren elders and political lobbyists flew to Canberra where, that same afternoon, they were signed through security, probably by Stephen Hales using his special parliamentary pass, and they walked into Howard's office for a meeting.

The Exclusive Brethren is a conservative Christian sect whose members do not vote. Even if they did, these votes would have little impact. The church has just 15,000 members in Australia, and about 43,000 worldwide – a number that would be dwarfed by the crowd on a quiet day at the Melbourne Cricket Ground. (Trade unions, which Howard declared irrelevant, have 1.8 million members in Australia.)

'There was no agenda for the meeting and nothing critical was discussed, only economic matters in general,' Warwick John explained. 'Mr Howard is always interested in how small business is faring, and there was a brief discussion about TV shows concerning the Brethren. Mr Howard did not approve of the public vilification of the Brethren as a Christian church.' There was 'general talk regarding interest rates', and the Brethren also confirmed that they were praying for Howard.

What they really talked about will probably never be known. But burning questions remained: who is this sect, and how did it come about that they had such a close relationship, such an open door, to the most powerful man in the country?

Before 2005, very little was known in Australia about the Exclusive Brethren. During that year, Greens politicians on both sides of the Tasman uncovered some unusual activity surrounding the election campaigns of Howard in 2004 and the National Party's Don Brash in New Zealand in 2005. Investigations by politicians and journalists into those campaigns revealed the hidden hand of a tiny, well-heeled religious group whose members dressed conservatively, and spoke politely and persistently to politicians – but who, behind the locked gates of their assembly halls, preached a radical doctrine of separation from the world. They also discovered how close to the boundaries of legality the Brethren had been prepared to walk in order to mask their involvement in these campaigns.

These investigations uncovered the fact that the Brethren's leader, Bruce D. Hales, made soothing comments in public that they were 'committed to being decent, law abiding and contributing citizens of Australia'[2] but, behind closed doors, told his flock, 'We have to get a hatred, an utter hatred of the world'.[3] It emerged that the Brethren's lobbying of politicians had been decades-long, and very successful – they had carved out a number of exemptions for themselves from the laws that govern others, by making special requests on the grounds of religious conscience. Also emerging was a hidden community of former sect members, damaged and devastated by the loss of their families to a group that they insisted was an oppressive cult.

My first interest in this group emerged from an innocent-enough question from my editor in September 2006: would the Exclusive Brethren be participating in the Victorian state election? The answer, I quickly discovered, was 'Yes'. My initial story in Melbourne's *The Age* prompted a blizzard of correspondence from people desperate to tell their personal stories of heartbreak and hardship at the hands of the religion they had grown up in. It led to many more questions, and answers.

Since then, I have met dozens of ex-Brethren members. Most have been highly intelligent and articulate people. Since leaving the Brethren, some say they have found God for the first time, and some have lost Him forever, but all of them still struggle with the psychological scars left by their Brethren upbringing. Their experience is summed up well by Tim Twinam, a former English Brethren member now living in the United States, who set up a website, peebs.net, to act as a clearing house for ex-Brethren stories: 'One of the side effects of a cult is that they suck you out of you and replace you with a template. And these empty people come in, they're angry and they don't even know why, and gradually they find themselves. It's not a religious concept, it's a psychological one.'[4] I hope this book adequately conveys to the world what these people have been trying to tell us.

I have also met a number of current Brethren members, who are equally intelligent and articulate, but who are very careful about what they say. This book is not intended to vilify any of these individuals nor, in fact, the sect in general; it is, rather, an attempt to dig out the truth.

It's important to note that scrutiny is not vilification. The Exclusive Brethren will not see it that way, of course, but every religious or cultural group that plays a part in national life should accept that who they are and what they do is a legitimate topic of discussion in the public domain. This is particularly true of a group that, without voting, and without being candid about itself, seeks constantly to influence the political process.

Changes are afoot in the Exclusive Brethren under Hales. Some of these changes seem to move in the direction of greater personal freedom for his followers. But others, such as setting up a comprehensive Brethren school system, move decisively in the opposite direction.

This book is intended to inform the public about these issues, to expose what has remained hidden about this sect, and something of its history and background. It is also intended to forewarn those in political life about the background of those respectful, conservatively dressed men who knock at their doors seeking special exemptions and privileges.

Part I
History

CHAPTER ONE

The Making of a Cult

The sect that we now call the Exclusive Brethren was 141 years old when its world leader travelled to the picturesque Scottish town of Aberdeen in July 1970 to address the faithful.

In those meetings, which lasted for three days, the fatal weaknesses that had been built into the sect from its earliest days suddenly came together and split the Brethren in two. What became known as the 'Aberdeen Incident' cost the exclusive branch of Brethrenism about 8000 members worldwide, one-fifth of the total flock, and starkly illustrated how the ambitions of their founder to return to a simpler, Bible-based life had, by the latter third of the twentieth century, become hopelessly corrupted.

In the view of Robert Stott, one of the senior members who quit at the time, those who stayed attached themselves to 'a system where man had replaced Christ, where persons took precedence over principles, and where conscience had become valueless'.[1] Some believe it remains as bad today.

James Taylor Junior, called 'Mr Jim', or JT Junior, had, by 1970, been the sect's 'Elect Vessel', or 'Man of God', for 11 years. He was the fourth of what the Brethren call the 'unbroken line' of 'Ministers of the Lord in the Recovery' of the truth, who claim direct spiritual descendance from the Apostle Paul, and whose founder was the dour Irish intellectual John Nelson Darby. Taylor presided over a flock that, during its history, had already split a dozen times over issues of theology and church administration, over power and politics. With each division, its followers had become more isolated from the rest of society, and more power had been conferred on the leader of the day. In Taylor they had a leader who was an alcoholic, and whose affliction had gained a firm grip on his mind.

The cardinal rule of this church, its founding principle, is the doctrine of separation. Under this doctrine, the wider world and its system is considered morally corrupt and to be avoided as much as possible. The separation doctrine rests on an idiosyncratic application of Darby's own translation of some Bible verses in the Second Letter of the Apostle Paul to his protégé Timothy.

The central verse, the Exclusive Brethren 'charter', is the sentence in Darby's translation, 'Let everyone who names the name of the Lord withdraw from iniquity.' (In the King James' version, it is 'depart from iniquity'.) In the years leading up to 1970, this separation had become vastly stricter and more fanatically adhered to. Taylor Junior had already alienated thousands when he first came to power in 1959. He began by excommunicating rival leaders, discrediting them as 'compromisers', and then he introduced his own hard-line edicts that banned all members of the Brethren from eating or socialising with outsiders.

James Taylor Junior himself was charismatic and entertaining. His meetings attracted attention and devotion from younger members whose faith, until then, had been entirely joyless. But he was also erratic, cruel, and unpredictable, and by 1970 he had pushed the limits of what his long-suffering flock could tolerate, by introducing hundreds of new rules for living.

Under his regime, families were always under the threat of being excommunicated, or 'withdrawn from', for some infraction or other. This carried with it the threat for individuals of being removed from their families, their belief systems, and their hope of salvation, instantly and irrevocably. According to psychologist and writer Louise Samways, 'Cults often have large numbers of rules, so there can be plenty of opportunity to punish members who break them inadvertently.'[2] There is little doubt that, at this point in Brethren history at least, it was indistinguishable from a cult.

In this God-fearing group, the most important theological events were three-day meetings, where local leaders from around the world gathered together to receive both their spiritual nourishment and their marching orders. The transcripts of the Aberdeen meeting never made it to the official Brethren record because of the scandal that immediately followed. But the recording itself is available, from which an unofficial 14-page transcript of the afternoon session on 25 July has been made. This is a small excerpt:

(Loud laughter)
James Taylor Junior: What the 'ell are we doing here? You so and so, what are you saying?
Thomas Matthew Bennett: This will get us somewhere, this will get us somewhere, I don't know where.[3]
JT Junior: George, what do you think of this here? George Brown, what do you think of this here?
George Strang: I'm sorry I didn't hear your question.[4]
JT Junior: I wasn't talking to you, boob. George!
George W. Brown: Yes, Mr Taylor?[5]
JT Junior: What was the answer?
George Brown: I don't quite know, Mr Taylor, what to make of it.
JT Junior: Anybody know that. Is your wife here?
George Brown: Yes, she is.
JT Junior: And she's mad.
George Brown: No, she isn't, Mr Taylor.
JT Junior: She is so. All going to have a good time here. Oh, yes. We're going to ... you nut! ... we're going to have a good time here.

And you, you dear, dear, dear, dear, dear boob, what do you want to say?'

For almost an hour, the Elect Vessel carried on in this vein as he drank periodically from his customary glass of Scotch whisky. The meeting was in uproar. The recording reveals loud laughter, stamping, and hooting. Taylor Junior harangued people, called them 'stinking bum' and 'sons of bitches', asked, 'Why didn't you bring some toilet paper with you?', and constantly repeated an apparent pun on the word 'ell (hell) or El (God). He gesticulated, thumbed his nose, and made the sign of the Cross – which, in Brethren terms, is Papist blasphemy.

Amongst all this, his constant refrain was, 'You never had it so good', apparently referring to the spiritual nourishment he was providing. It appears from later correspondence among the Brethren that this kind of behaviour had become Taylor's norm in meetings of his home assembly in New York, as his slide into alcoholism worsened. A letter from Brethren man William T. Petersen later related that, in the lead-up to Aberdeen and afterwards, 'filthy, blasphemous speaking proceeded in the assembly almost daily'. But this bitter reality was, until the events in Aberdeen, not well known elsewhere in the Brethren world.[6]

What transpired in the meeting hall might have been shocking to his flock, but what was going on at the house where Taylor was staying that weekend was as bad. The doctrine of separation means that travelling Brethren do not stay in hotel rooms. Instead, visiting Brethren are billeted with locals. Well-regarded leaders in a locality ('the approved') host the leaders. On this trip to Aberdeen, Taylor was put up by James Alec Gardner, a high-ranking man in the local Brethren assembly. A number of others were also staying at the house, including a young couple, Alan and Madeline Ker, whom Taylor had specifically requested be accommodated there.

A long letter about the incident written later by Gardner reveals that, for much of the three days of his sojourn, Taylor stayed in his room, alone with Mrs Ker, with the door shut, after she had been led there by her husband.[7] After Madeline Ker had spent the Thursday and Friday nights in Taylor's bedroom, Gardner writes that he tried on Saturday morning to barricade the route to the room, because 'we were disturbed and unhappy as to the length of time they were spending together'.

But the Kers were not satisfied at being kept from the Man of God. According to Gardner's letter:

> Mr and Mrs Ker tried to break down the door so that she could reach Mr Taylor's bedroom. In the process a large glass panel in the door entrance was cracked. When our other visitors left for the meetings Mrs Ker managed to slip through to Mr Taylor's bedroom, staying there alone with him for some time, so that we were again late for the afternoon meetings. When she came out of the room she said that she had been told to tell me that I was a 'son of a bitch and a bastard'.

The afternoon meeting referred to is the one partially transcribed above. On Saturday evening after dinner, Gardner wrote:

> [I] felt I had to find out what was happening in my house. I went through to Mr Taylor's bedroom and found Mrs Ker undressed and in bed with Mr Taylor. He only had on his pyjama top, which was open down the front ... I remonstrated with Mr Ker and asked him to get his wife out of there.

Gardner called in a witness, Stanley McCallum, from Detroit, who was at the house for dinner. McCallum told Taylor what he was doing was 'unsuitable, uncomely and not morally right', and asked what his wife would think. 'I suppose you would tell her!' countered Taylor. Gardner then turned the Kers out of his house, prompting the insistence from Taylor: 'She is my woman.' Taylor's son, James the Third, was called for, as was his doctor, a Brethren man, Bill Thomson, who had been treating him for his alcohol-related illnesses. Gardner relates Thomson saying that 'medically he was a sick man, but the moral side is a matter for the priests'.

On Sunday 26 July, Taylor left Aberdeen, abandoning the final day of the meeting, and was led back to his New York home by his son, who had flown into the city from the south of England in the early hours of Sunday morning. The following Tuesday night, Gardner and others revealed what they had witnessed in their home to the Aberdeen assembly. All but two families from the entire congregation of that town – over 200 people – accepted his account. They collectively confessed that they should have protested against Taylor at the meeting, and then they repudiated him.

Following normal Brethren procedure, Gardner and the other leaders of the Aberdeen church then sent the account of events to Taylor's home church in Nostrand Avenue, New York. In doing so they were suggesting that New York should discipline Taylor himself, almost certainly to excommunicate or 'withdraw from' him, and the church continue on without him. In the Brethren, to withdraw from someone is to put them outside the church globally, but the 'judgment' is always carried out by the individual's local Brethren assembly.

For a sect that emphasised high moral standards, no charge could have been clearer cut: it was a case of sexual misbehaviour, 'corrupt language', and treating the assembly with contempt. There were credible witnesses by the hundred, even tape recordings available.

In the days following the events at Aberdeen, Taylor attempted to mount a defence by taking the argument public in the English tabloids. 'We are not ashamed, says Big Jim', the London *Daily Express* shouted from its front page. The story was accompanied by a picture of him with his arm draped over Mrs Ker's shoulder, his hand hovering over her left breast, and a glass of whisky in his other hand. But if the Aberdeen leaders believed they could win this battle, they underestimated the power that the 'Man of God' had come to assume in their own church, and what he and his supporters were prepared to do to keep it.

At stake was what, in the Exclusive Brethren, is known as 'the position'. This is simultaneously a theological and administrative concept, which refers to both the theological state of 'walking in the path of separation' from the world, as well as the structure of the church itself, including the ownership of property, and how the various meeting halls around the world interact and are kept together under one supreme leader.

The events at Aberdeen quickly became a power struggle over what really was the 'position': would Taylor be the one excommunicated and would the Exclusive Brethren continue under a new leader? Or would his supporters close ranks around him and retain control?

It was a momentous choice for a church that had spent the previous decade building their leader up into 'the Paul of our day', a man whose power and purity were supposed to rival that of Christ, and whose leadership was considered to be the only way to prepare for the second coming.

Taylor's camp moved quickly to provide a cover story. Taylor denied the accuracy of the tapes of the meeting, claiming they had been tampered with. He said in a letter of 7 August that Mrs Ker had merely been washing his feet, rubbing his head and massaging him, at the suggestion of her husband.[8] He instructed the Detroit Brethren to withdraw from witness Stanley McCallum – so that, by the time McCallum got home, he was locked out of his own assembly meeting, and could not officially inform them of what he had seen. McCallum was then accused by four members in Detroit of trumped-up charges of homosexual molestation – charges that were never brought to a court, despite several attempts by his enemies who stayed within the Brethren.

Taylor told his followers in a letter in August 1970 that Gardner's house was 'leprous', and his testimony therefore unreliable, and that the Aberdeen Brethren were 'criminals'. 'The charge made by that bastard [F. David] Waterfall [leader in the Brethren stronghold of Birmingham] that I was in bed with another man's wife is a dastardly lie,' Taylor wrote in a letter about the incident. 'If I wanted to sleep with another man's wife would I go to Aberdeen – costing about $1000? Brooklyn would be cheaper. Some brethren have shown themselves to be boobs.'

Brethren around the world were required, under threat of excommunication, to swear 100 per cent loyalty to Taylor. Members were told in meetings that they had to affirm that he was a pure man. In some assemblies, married men were asked to declare publicly that they would allow their wives to 'administer comfort to Mr Taylor'.

In Scotland, the upheaval cost the Exclusive Brethren all but about 200 of its 3000-strong flock. In England, the effect was more diluted, but the large and influential London meeting split in half. In New York, Taylor himself was eventually forced to walk out of the meeting after one of his hitherto strongest supporters, Billy Petersen, challenged him and then refused to leave. When Taylor quit the meeting he took only about half its attendees with him, and even one of his own sons and both of his daughters-in-law initially refused to stand by him.

But still Taylor's supporters refused to relinquish 'the position'. It took them a month after the original events to come up with the final version of the cover story. It emerged in a letter dated 21 August 1970 from Magnus Dawson. The letter, which was circulated widely, claimed that Taylor's actions in Aberdeen were a cunningly devised test of loyalty, an ambush to identify those who were insufficiently faithful, and to root them out. The church was now 'rid of the drag' of those people. 'Dear George, It is too near the rapture to turn back', the letter begins:

It is nearly a month nearer than it was at the time of the incident you write about and the revival goes on in vigour. What a change to have the Supper in conditions purified from conflicting spirits, silent opposition and rivalry ... Many a time we have admitted to each other that some drastic test would need to be applied, especially in Scotland – it surely has come! ... He [Taylor] ... drew all into the one ambush. There, to demonstrate purity and to expose every kind of impurity, he put himself into a position which jeopardized the honour of his manhood (and what it cost him to do it). It was a test no one could possibly understand save those who had kept close to him in incorruption. There was no immorality, it was all done so openly.[9]

Despite the importance invested in the Man of God, in 1970 thousands of traumatised people did leave Taylor's branch of the Brethren. They emerged from their separate lives questioning their entire belief system, wondering if their lives had been lived in the service of a lie at the hands of an erratic alcoholic. The suddenness and ferocity of the split was unprecedented, and it caused untold trauma, splitting families forever.

Just three months after the 'Aberdeen Incident', on 14 October, Taylor Junior, still defiant and unapologetic, died of an alcohol-related disease. His loyalists continued to prosecute his case. But those who opposed what had happened also had their voice. Robert Stott of Brighton, who was also a trustee of the Brethren publishing house the Stow Hill Depot, gathered the facts from witnesses, collated the evidence, and then, in November, printed and disseminated them. His document, *If We Walk In the Light*, included a transcript of the meeting and letters to and from disgruntled members. Stott pointed out that, 'JT Junior and those who supported him violated almost every principle governing assembly action in an attempt to prevent the true facts from reaching the brethren.'

'Those who supported JT Junior justify his behaviour on the

ground that the man of God is pure and can do things which would be corrupt for us to do,' Stott wrote. This was 'heresy'. The Brethren, whose forebears had themselves withdrawn from the established church because they had become corrupted by Popery, were now victim to precisely the same kind of personality cult, Stott wrote.

For those who remained in the Brethren, possession of this document immediately became an offence punishable by excommunication, and the faithful were ordered to destroy it. Severely battered, its reputation ruined, 'the position' survived. About 80 per cent of the Brethren's worldwide flock bought the cover story, or were prepared to live with it. Diminished, made poorer by the loss of a large number of its properties, and with a decided shift in numerical influence towards Australia and New Zealand (where the effects of the split were barely felt), the sect continued, found a new 'Man of God', and the events of Aberdeen became just another part of its fractious history.

Aberdeen was the worst single crisis that the Exclusive Brethren had faced. But, almost from its inception, this had been an argumentative sect, subject to fights, divisions, and clashes. These disagreements, it seems, are built into its structure. Its founding doctrine of separation divides the world into good and evil, splitting the 'gold and silver vessels' from the 'wooden and earthen'. It builds judgmentalism into the very structure of the church, which has often divided the assembly itself.

The man who founded the Brethren movement, John Nelson Darby, was what we would recognise today as a charismatic evangelist. He was the strongest personality, and soon became the leader, among a small group of like-minded men and women who had grown sick of the traditional church. In 1827, four of these men gathered in Dublin to break bread for the first time, and in 1829 they set up a new assembly where any man could preach the gospel, and where the Bible was read thoroughly and taken literally.

Darby described himself in an 1832 letter to the Brethren at Plymouth, where the movement first took off, as 'a man of contentions', a description amply borne out by his own history and the early history of the church.

Darby was not, by one account, an attractive physical specimen. Francis William Newman, one of the group of earnest young men who formed the original Brethren assembly in Plymouth, described his 'bodily presence' as 'weak'. Newman wrote of him thus:

> A fallen cheek, a bloodshot eye, crippled limbs resting on crutches, a seldom shaven beard, a shabby suit of clothes, and a generally neglected person, drew at first pity, with wonder to see such a figure in a drawing-room. It has [been] reported that a person in Limerick offered him a halfpenny, mistaking him for a beggar; and if not true, the story was yet well invented.[10]

Newman went on to say that this unkempt young man 'rapidly gained an immense sway over me'.

Another disciple, Walter Scott, also recorded that it was 'the experience of most men brought into personal contact with Mr Darby that the influence exercised over them has been almost overwhelming'.

Darby was the youngest son of a wealthy establishment family who was born in 1800 and grew up in a reputedly haunted house, Leap Castle, in King's County, Ireland. The castle's bloody history included a rift between two brothers, which led one to murder the other while he was conducting mass in the chapel. Darby was a brilliant scholar, educated at Westminster and Trinity College in Dublin. He graduated a gold medallist from university in 1819, and became a barrister. But, eight years later, his religious bent soon found expression in the Church of Ireland, part of the Anglican

Church, where he became a minister.

Darby was assigned a parish in the wild mountain lands of Ireland among the Roman Catholic peasants of the parish of Calary, near Enniskerry, in County Wicklow. But even on this unfriendly ground, Darby's talent for evangelism found early success, and he later claimed to have won hundreds of converts among the people he described as 'almost as wild as the mountains they inhabited'. Despite his success, though, Darby wrote in a later letter that he was, at the time, 'governed by the feeling of duty towards Christ, rather than by the consciousness that He had done all and that I was redeemed and saved'.

This attitude changed in 1827 after Darby's horse threw him against a doorpost. He was laid up in bed, giving him uninterrupted time to ponder. 'During my solitude, conflicting thoughts increased; but much exercise of soul had the effect of causing the Scriptures to gain complete ascendancy over me,' he later wrote.

Darby came to believe that the established church was 'associated with the world', and some of its believers were 'merged in the very world from which Jesus had separated them'. For evidence of this, he needed only to turn to an 1827 ruling by William Magee, the Archbishop of Dublin, that his clergy should petition the British House of Commons for protection against the Roman Catholics who harassed them during their parish work. This order greatly distressed Darby, who, like the biblical character Ezra, was ashamed to ask for horsemen from the worldly king, believing it made God subservient to the government. He wrote a long paper on the subject in which he summoned all his barrister's ability to argue, and his newfound theological enthusiasm, and then had it printed and distributed to the clergy in the diocese.

The thesis of the paper, which gives an insight into Darby's hardline views, was that any clergyman worth his salt would not seek protection from worldly evil, but would 'enter into conflict with the power of darkness'. The place of the clergy was 'the kingdom and patience of Jesus Christ, their business, to endure hardness as good soldiers of His'.[11] The Roman Catholic Church and 'Papacy', which was the source of the harassment, was 'the organised system of Satan for keeping men's souls, where the light of Christianity had entered, as far as he possibly can, under the same bondage in which he held them under heathenism'.

The process of writing this missive appears to have convinced Darby that he had no place in the established church, and that he had to separate and strike out on his own. He gave up his parish and began looking for an alternative kind of Christianity – one that would better suit his non-conformist ideas. It was a time when a great many young people were leaving the established churches; and, in Dublin, Darby found a small group who had also grown dissatisfied with ritualism and clericalism. One of these radicals was Francis Newman, the younger brother of John Henry Newman, who was later to become the renowned Roman Catholic Cardinal Newman. Francis Newman invited Darby to go to Oxford to meet his friend Benjamin Wills Newton, a Fellow of Exeter College. Newton later returned to his home in Plymouth, in the south of England, taking Darby with him.

In Plymouth, the pair began to attract a following, established a chapel, and started preaching a gospel that quickly hardened into a distinctive doctrine. According to sociologist Bryan R. Wilson:

> Twelve of the earliest Brethren were, or were training to be, Anglican clergymen (in England and Ireland), and five were ministers in nonconformist churches. A number of them were men of private means, including five titled gentry; and eight of them were, or had been, commissioned officers.[12]

By 1832, with Darby and Newton its leading lights, the group had formed into an assembly. They simply referred to themselves as brethren. Others identified them as the Plymouth Brethren.

Their doctrine, like that of a number of strains of non-conformist theology growing up at the time, encouraged any of the male members of the group to preach, instead of relying on the whole theatre of a formal clergy, who were viewed as standing between God and the flock. They also promoted the close reading of the Bible, whose every passage was to be known and adhered to. While biblical literalism is a familiar concept now, it was new and exciting in the 1830s.

Darby, a highly intelligent man, worked from early morning, reading and writing. He has been described as the most voluminous theological writer of the nineteenth century. His theological musings are relentlessly earnest. His friend William Kelly, who edited his 34 volumes of writings, described Darby as being 'delighted in a concatenated sentence, sometimes with parenthesis within parenthesis, to express the truth fully, and with guards against misconception'. Kelly admitted that, to the uninitiated, this made for 'anything but pleasant reading, and to a hasty glance almost unintelligible'.

Despite this, a number of Darby's doctrines survive today, and not just among the Brethren. In 1832, he was at the centre of a newly developing theology in the non-conformist churches: the doctrine of the 'secret rapture'. This was God's ultimate test, in which true believers would be swept up by Christ and taken out of the world, and the rest left behind. Whether Darby actually came up with the doctrine, or went along with a wider movement started by another refugee from the established church, Edward Irving, is a moot point. These two, who were bitter rivals for the souls of English fundamentalists, began preaching it at around the same time. It is clear, though, that Darby brought the doctrine to the United States, where it took root in the popular imagination and was adopted by dozens of different strains of evangelism.

Darby was, and the Brethren remain today, 'pre-millennialists' and 'dispensationalists'. This means they believe that the 'saints', those who have found God through Christ, are swept up into heaven, secretly, before judgment day. According to Kelly, 'the righteous shine out, not on the earth, but as the sun in the kingdom of their Father'. A period of chaos ensues, after which Christ appears to reign for 1000 years, working with the 'faithful Jewish remnant' to ensure their conversion. Then comes the final Judgment Day, when the devil is cast into hell and the dead judged before the Great White Throne. A new heaven and earth are created, where all tears and crying and pain have passed away. To this day, in Exclusive Brethren theology, the Rapture is regarded as imminent, though they do not put a date on it.

This story and its variations are based on various biblical teachings read together. In the twentieth century it prompted a series of popular novels, known as the 'Left Behind' series, and even a movie, which painted a doomsday scenario for those not spiritually prepared for the coming of Christ. Some children brought up in these religions report their terror at being abandoned on earth for their sins, of returning home from school to find their parents out, and thinking that they have been left behind. Others say that, as children, they regarded the Rapture as something wonderful, eagerly looked forward to.

Also fundamental to the early belief-system of the Brethren was that the world must be kept at bay. Darby wrote that 'business, politics, education, governments, science, inventions, railroads, telegraphs, social arrangements, charitable institutions, reforms, religion and all, are of the world-system'. Scientific progress, he believed, was no more than 'the worldly element developing itself'. Democracy made the poor into masters, and 'the effect on the masses and on the active minds of the country will be infidelity, exalting man (over God)'.

According to Darby, the world system was 'becoming more and more perfect every day', and therefore more frightening. 'Will it surprise anyone to hear that Satan is the god of this world, the prince of the power of the air, and manager of this stupendous system? His is the energy, his the presiding genius, he is its prince,' he wrote.

The good Christian 'must needs be in contact with the world-system to some degree', to the extent of following the law and earning a living, 'but this contact is never to be one of fellowship; what concord can there be between Christ and Belial?' Darby asked. Voting, for example, was too close an interaction with the world: government was 'of God', and the Brethren should pray for it to do good work, but should not help to choose it.

Darby, the self-confessed 'man of contentions', who, from the beginning of his religious career, had chosen the hardest road, was creating around him a faith that expressed this desire to maintain a constant argument with the world. The only way to achieve true Christianity, to become a candidate for being swept up in the Rapture, was to remain aloof. 'God's unity is always founded on separation, since sin came into the world. "Get thee out" is the first word of God's call,' he wrote in 1845.

In practice, this also meant that the assembly had to separate from evil-doers by excommunicating them. In 1880, Darby wrote, 'The assembly purges itself.' The judgment of who should be purged, also known as being 'withdrawn from', or 'put out', was made by the assembly itself. Only those who truly repented could be admitted back.

From very early in the church's history, the doctrine of separation caused problems for its adherents, and adverse public comment. An 1869 article by religious writer James Grant in a religious magazine of the time, the *Sword and Trowel*, related the story of a Plymouth Sister 'whose family do not share her views':

> [She] cannot help expressing her dissent from any and every act of worship in the family. She even turns away her face when the head of the house asks the divine blessing on the meals of which they are all about to partake. Is not this sad?[13]

In his personal dealings, too, Darby was argumentative. A contemporary, Walter Scott, describes him as a 'keen and able controversialist':

> His critical acumen in detecting principles where others, perhaps, would have dealt only with details, was truly marvellous ... The weakness of an opposed argument was soon apparent, and the truth got more firmly established.

The spirit that this engendered was commented on by Grant, who wrote that argumentativeness was the sect's 'universal characteristic':

> This controversial feeling, often degenerating into something resembling regular quarrels, is the chronic condition of Plymouth Brethrenism. They are in a state of constant antagonism with (another sect) the Bethesda party; and ... when they have no one of the opposite party to quarrel with, they will disagree among themselves ... So great, indeed, is their disposition to engage in controversy ... that it would be a thing quite new to see two of their number remain together for many minutes without a decided disagreement on some one point or other ... Insinuations, slanders, insolence, threats, and violence are resorted to for the maintenance of their position.

Darby appeared at times to question his own propensity to disagree with others, writing in 1832, 'God is my witness whether I loved it or not.' But, from the beginning, the Brethren faith was shaped around his singular and firmly held beliefs. These views were quickly disseminated among believers, wherever they lived, by the enthusiastic use of the printing press. Darby also wrote copiously – letters, lectures, and sermons – and others also made reports of the meetings he led. The printing and distribution of these teachings led to an unusually high level of conformity between different Brethren assemblies.

In 1837, Darby began a punishing set of travels throughout Britain and Europe, often going by foot. Wherever he took his fierce form of evangelism, he sowed the seeds of new Brethren assemblies, some of which still adhere to the faith today. But it was not long before division entered into the very heart of the growing church in Plymouth. While Darby was away for an extended period in Switzerland, one of the group's other founding members, Benjamin Wills Newton, Darby's junior by seven years, began preaching what the older man believed to be unauthorised doctrine.

Returning from his travels to Plymouth in 1845, Darby objected. The differences were over a number of issues, theological and administrative. Most were arcane, but Darby appeared particularly to object to the formal appointment of elders to take a more active role in the services, believing it was creating a system a little like the priesthood. It is hard to escape the conclusion that, as with many later splits in the Brethren movement, the underlying cause of the argument was about power. Newton, described by one contemporary as 'autocratic and controlling', had been the leading light of the Plymouth assemblies for almost a decade as Darby travelled. When his co-founder returned, and wanted changes made to church administration, the men irrevocably fell out.

The struggle was conducted in words and pamphlets. In an 1845 letter to an unknown recipient, Darby, typically hard-line, wrote that 'purity is better than unity':

> Or is the doctrine of the unity of the body to be made a cover for evil? That is precisely the delusion of Satan in Popery, and the worst form of evil under the sun ... Now, I believe myself, the elements of this have been distinctly brought out at Plymouth; and I cannot stay in evil to preserve unity. I do not want unity in evil, but separation from it.

At Plymouth, Newton prevailed over the majority, and Darby quit the assembly, taking fifty or sixty members with him. Other assemblies around the country and the world were also forced to choose sides.

It was the assembly's first major split and, out of it and a number of later divisions, emerged the cleavage that remains to this day within the Brethren movement, between open and closed assemblies. Darby and his followers formed the 'closed', 'exclusive', or 'Darbyite' brethren, adopting a more centralised structure, particularly for the purposes of theological teachings and discipline. As a result of this split, when a member of the exclusive branch is under assembly discipline – particularly being excommunicated, or withdrawn from – they cannot simply go to another meeting house and be accepted there. Once out of the church, a member is out of all its halls until such time as he or she is accepted back centrally.

The Open Brethren, on the other hand, consider meeting halls to be independent units. Discipline and administration are the responsibility of the local gathering, and they in turn have no right to interfere in the management of a neighbouring assembly. If somebody is withdrawn from at one meeting, they can simply go down the road and join another. The obvious result of this is the fracturing of views among the Open Brethren, which has led to the existence of hundreds of different versions of openness, from the liberal to the evangelical – and to some, at the extreme, which have been described as 'Exclusive Brethren-lite'.

The 1845 split may have been the first, but it was followed by a dozen others. Among the Exclusives there was the 'Kelly trouble' in 1879, the 'Grant division' in 1883, the 'Stuart division' in 1885, and the 'Bexhill division' (also known as the 'Lowe division') in 1890. More followed in the twentieth century – each disagreement splitting off individuals or whole meetings, and often sending them into the arms of various parts of the Open Brethren, which would sometimes split further, and sometimes try to reunite.

Once a member had split from Darby's group, he viewed them as worse than any ordinary outsider. He wrote in 1845 that those who had left the Plymouth assembly had lost their place entirely at 'the table of the Lord', and, 'I should think worse of them than of sectarian bodies, because having more pretension to light [sic]'.

This attitude survives to this day. Those 'outs' who have been abandoned by the Brethren, or who have voluntarily left, often find that, to compound the loss of their faith and, sometimes, their family, their former friends and intimates cross the road to avoid them.

After the 1845 split, Darby moved to a meeting in London. As he grew older, he continued to write copiously and to travel, making at least five missionary journeys to North America between 1862 and 1877, mostly to New England, Ontario, and the Great Lakes Region. But he also took one extended journey from Toronto to Sydney by way of San Francisco, Hawaii, and New Zealand – a considerable undertaking in the late nineteenth century. During his life he also translated the Bible into a number of languages from the original texts – translations still used by the Brethren. In 1882, aged 81, Darby died or, in Brethren-speak, became 'with Christ'.

CHAPTER TWO

The Australian Succession

For such a centralised and hierarchical organisation, it is unusual that the Exclusive Brethren has no apparent method for appointing a successor when a leader dies. There are two reasons for this: first, they believe that the leader is chosen by God and, second, they never expect to need a new one, because each leader is convinced that he will see the Brethren through to the Rapture. In reality, the method of transfer of power is quite opaque. The official Brethren explanation for this, contained in a recent document, is simply that 'moral leadership and authority become evident'.

When John Nelson Darby died, a few years of uncertainty and rival claims followed. Among the contenders was a leading light in the Greenwich meeting, the 45-year-old Frederick Edward Raven. But before he could become the undisputed leader of the sect, Raven prompted a cataclysmic split of his own – over one of his own obscure theological points. According to theologian Eryl Davies, the 'Bexhill' (or 'Lowe') division was prompted by Raven's musings about whether true believers in God had eternal life 'as a present possession'. The doctrines were described by one internal enemy as 'an intricate maze'. Raven himself later admitted that he had made 'defective statements ... on the road to light'. But the practical effect of the split, according to Brethren historian W.R. Dronsfield, was that Raven's enemies quit the church, and he 'was established as the teacher and leader of the dominant faction in London. From that time until his death nobody could challenge his supremacy, although some of his doctrinal statements became wilder and more suspect.'[1]

Raven is said by Brethren historian Gordon Rainbow to be the 'least known of those used in an outstanding way in the recovery of the truth'.[2] His father, Samuel, was a solicitor's clerk and a devout member of the Church of England. Raven was born in 1837 and brought up in the Church of England. In 1865, at the age of 28, he left the church to join Darby, though his parents stayed members of the Anglican Church until their death.

Raven was described as a short man with piercing eyes who was unusually careful about his dress. For most of his working life, he was a public servant – an occupation that would not be allowed in the modern Brethren. A father of nine, he was employed at the Royal Naval College in Greenwich, and became secretary in 1873. He retired at 60 on a public pension in 1897, and refused a knighthood for services rendered to the British Admiralty. He explained to his flock that 'the Christian should refuse to be renowned or distinguished in a scene where Christ has only been dishonoured'.

Raven was quite unlike other Brethren leaders. His three daughters, for example, were educated as well as their brothers. One daughter, Jessie, studied at Bedford College, was awarded a Master of Arts, and subsequently became a lecturer at Westfield College, where she wrote standard monographs on French medieval literature. In the modern Brethren, tertiary education of any kind is discouraged, and women are second-order citizens who are unable to take an active role in church services (apart from suggesting which hymns should be sung), and who cannot seek employment after marriage.

Raven also seems to have been more compassionate than many

of his successors. He was often quoted saying that if he had not been a Christian, he would probably have been a communist. Like his predecessor's, Raven's preaching, his 'ministry', was collected and disseminated, making 20 volumes. A further volume of letters is also available. Some of it, like Darby's, is complicated and convoluted. Other ministry is simply odd.

'I get the millennium in my house but not in my garden,' he said in one flight of fancy:

> Christians ought to have a millennium in the house. Many who have not got it in the house, try to have it in the garden, while there is a great deal of moral confusion in the house. The Lord does not care a bit about your garden, but He cares a great deal about your house.[3]

In 1902, Raven made his second visit to America, but was very ill on his return in November. In August the following year, suffering from what his doctor diagnosed as a 'thickening of the lung', he died.

Another period of uncertain leadership ensued, during which there was growing tension between the leading men in London and the younger Irish–American, James Taylor Senior. It is Taylor, the father of James Taylor Junior, who has been recognised by the Exclusive Brethren history writers as the next Elect Vessel.

Taylor was born into a Brethren family in County Sligo in north-western Ireland in 1870. At 18 years of age, and already working for a linen-importing company, Mills and Gibb, he emigrated to Newfoundland (then a British colony and now part of Canada). The following year, 1889, he moved to the cultural melting-pot of New York. He was by no means a wealthy man in his early years there. He and his wife Estelle had six children in the first nine years of their marriage, of which James Junior was the fifth. The fast-growing family lived in lower Manhattan in an upstairs flat over the 51st

Street meeting room where, according to a contemporary, Mary Markham, 'all the fresh air they could get was to go downstairs and walk up and down the crowded street a few times'.[4] Estelle died, along with her sixth child, in 1901. James remarried in 1913, but had no more children.

Taylor was one of the minority in New York who stood by Raven during the Bexhill division, and was one of the eight signatories to an 1890 letter rejecting Bexhill's actions. Taylor had also been to London in 1902 to visit Raven in his last illness. Brethren legend, as reported by Mrs Markham, records that it was at this time that 'Mr Raven's mantle fell on Mr Taylor'.

But it was not until 1910, seven years after Raven's death, and after another theological contretemps, that Taylor's leadership became undisputed. The trouble had started as a result of Taylor's addresses to meetings in Chicago in 1904 and 1905, during which he had controversially stated that salvation was to be found in the assembly. Many of the English Brethren took this to be an error that downgraded the role of God in saving souls. The transcripts of that meeting, the 'Chicago notes', generated much controversy and, according to Mrs Markham, there was 'quite a tense atmosphere' when Taylor visited England in 1910 to represent his company and to preach.

However, in a packed assembly hall on a hot night in the south London suburb of Kennington, Taylor sufficiently impressed the sceptics with his testimony on the Spirit of Christ in the Book of Esther that he won the crowd over. He was to remain undisputed leader for the next 43 years.

During the years in which Taylor was trying to establish himself, another defining theological split occurred. In 1908, the Glanton division divided the assembly over the question of which assemblies had the power to judge another. The argument was typically convoluted, but the result for those who stayed in the Brethren was the establishment of a stricter hierarchy by which discipline would be imposed. Ostensibly, local leaders would deal with matters arising in their localities; but, in effect, everything was subordinated to a hierarchy that, in 1908, was centred in London. The practical effect was to centralise ultimate administrative responsibility and power over all assemblies and individuals who were in fellowship. It was another step down the road to the cult of personality that prevailed by the time of the events at Aberdeen.

Under Taylor, the locus of this power moved to New York, and he began to direct the affairs of his followers from his new home in Brooklyn. Taylor was described by Mrs Markham, an ardent admirer, as 'marked by boundless hospitality, and almost endless patience and grace if there was any hope of saving a brother'. However, 'if the truth was in question he was inflexible'.

Mrs Markham paints a picture of a man maintaining an iron grip over his organisation: 'While carrying the burden "of all the assemblies" he had individual care and interest for each one in his locality,' she wrote. As long as this power was wielded reasonably, this moderated the Brethren tendency to divide, and no significant division occurred after 1908 for the rest of Taylor Senior's life.

In 1919, Taylor made a move that was to change forever the Brethren's approach to earning a living. He left his employer, Mills and Gibb, and went to work in the business that his youngest son, JT Junior had set up, making and selling linen. From then on, following the Taylors, a man with ambitions to attain a position of leadership must be in business, not an employee. In the modern Brethren, business matters have become a particular preoccupation.

Taylor also began introducing the notion, further developed by his son, JT Junior, that when a spiritual man said something in an assembly, the Holy Spirit was present. This meant that the words of the Exclusive Brethren leaders provided continuing revelation, or 'new light', which was equivalent to biblical scripture. One of Taylor's addresses was entitled, 'The Assembly: Its Heavenly Character' and, shortly before his death in 1953, he declared: 'The greatest thing that I know of at the present time on earth is the presence of the Holy Spirit in the assembly.'[5]

This doctrine greatly freed the church's leaders from the close biblical readings and the heavy, convoluted intellectualism of Darby, and allowed them to lay down edicts in the name of one branch of the Holy Trinity, the Spirit. The new, post-Glanton administrative mechanism could then enforce these interpretations as law around the Exclusive Brethren world.

Soon, even though Darby had envisaged a church where any brother could speak and there were no priests, the Taylorites were now accrediting certain brothers as 'Levites', or 'the Lord's servants' – effectively, untrained ministers – to interpret and propagate their ideas of biblical truths. In the modern day, these people are even known among the Brethren as 'priests'. Taylor's view was that these elders were 'vessels', selected by God to 'bring forth the truth'. He was the chief of the vessels, chosen by God – like the apostle Paul, the Elect Vessel. It was also he and his followers who first imposed on the fractured and contentious history of the Brethren the story of an 'unbroken line' of vessels – namely, Darby, Raven, and Taylor – which suggested that their ministry had divine backing.

With these changes, Taylor was rapidly gaining the power, if he chose to use it, of a cult leader. The Brethren needed to wait just one more generation for the full impact of these innovations to become apparent.

James Taylor Senior died in 1953. Even the Brethren history-makers would struggle to describe what followed as an 'unbroken' succession. For six years, according to Dronsfield, the leadership was fought for with a 'rivalry ... which resembled the struggle for power in the Kremlin after the death of Stalin'.[6] Even a sympathetic chronicler of the early period of Brethren history, Gordon Rainbow, describes those years as an 'unprecedented, relentless and extended struggle' for the leadership.[7] By 1959 the field had narrowed to two combatants: James Taylor Junior and Gerald Robert Cowell, of

Essex in England. Both parties were committed to extreme separation, but Cowell was prepared to give Brethren members some leeway, while Taylor insisted on the excommunication of anyone who did not fall into line immediately.

After years of positioning, disputes, and proxy battles in jurisdictions around the world, the defining moment came at a special meeting in London in 1959, where Cowell, in Brethren style, using scriptural allusions, chided Taylor over his devotion to rules and regulations, and his hard-line attitude.

'I suppose I am right in this ... that the greatest numerical losses we have had of late years have been through the Galatian spirit,' Cowell said, referring to the apostle Paul's opposition to the Galatians' excessive legalism. 'We have had conflicts for the truth and casualties have been limited, but the Galatian error can be a very disastrous thing.'

Taylor hit back: 'What did you say, legality was the cause of the great numbers? ... I could not accept that. I do not accept that statement.'

So controversial was this exchange in the atmosphere of the time that it was left out of the official Brethren record of the meeting.[8]

After these exchanges in London, Taylor pressed his case and was recognised as world leader. Cowell was quickly excommunicated, and his supporters either withdrew or were withdrawn from in 1959 and 1960, leaving the field to their rival. Cowell died just three years later, in 1963.

A few months after his victory, at a meeting in Manchester in July 1960, Taylor gave a clear signal of the way he would conduct himself. He issued an edict that nobody in fellowship could eat with anyone outside it, even though his father had regularly done so as part of his job as a linen importer. In a September 1960 letter, Taylor Junior explained that: 'I used to go and eat [with outsiders] but have stopped long since. If we are minded to go, it would not be the mind of the Spirit and invariably we are contaminated when we go, for the uncleanness comes out over the table'.⁹ The idea of contamination remains strong in the church to this day. Taylor made this onerous rule a 'test of fellowship' – in other words, anybody who insisted on eating with an outsider was withdrawn from.

Ron Fawkes, a former Australian leader of the sect, recalls 'chaos around the world' as a result of the edict: 'I was 17 in 1960, and I remember the pain and anguish, the awful situation of spouses who were married for 40-odd years forced to separate from their unbelieving husbands, who had before coexisted quite happily and normally.'¹⁰ Iain Gibb, a Brethren member in Scotland at the time, recalls two elderly sisters in their seventies who defied the rule: 'The sister in the meeting said she had always eaten her meals at the same table as her sister and had no intention of changing. She was summarily withdrawn from.'¹¹

'It was the start of the change from a strict, joyless form of Christianity to a brutal dictatorship,' Gibb says. 'I was 12 years old at the time, but remember the furious arguments – reports almost weekly of meetings dividing, leading men being excommunicated.'

Hundreds upon hundreds of new edicts followed from Taylor Junior. As the 1960s brought a revolution in permissiveness in the wider world, Taylor merely needed to pass a comment in a letter or a church meeting for it to be faithfully transcribed and distributed as a regulation demanding strict obedience. By the time of his death in 1970, shortly after the farcical events at Aberdeen, 'Mr Jim' had delivered some 390 directives in this way. A mixture of spiritual guidance and domestic tips, these interfered in almost every aspect of the lives of his followers, from the clothes they could wear (no shorts for men) to how they would conduct their businesses (keep small); who should take out the garbage at night (the husband); how they drove their cars ('you're going to get caught if you keep on despising signs'); what to wear to their weddings (white); and how to approach the issue of facial hair (no beards or moustaches). He banned young people from going to university, on the grounds that the lifestyle was sinful. 'It is not that directives make you spiritual,' Mr Jim said, 'But they pave the way for it.'[12]

The drift of people away from the Brethren continued as this legalism became more arbitrary and more difficult to comply with. The new rules went along with Taylor's rigid enforcement of the doctrine of separation, when husbands were separated permanently from their wives, and children from their parents. Those caught even speaking to a loved one who was 'out' were themselves subject to assembly discipline. When the Brethren come to public notice, it is usually because of some inhumane application of this doctrine of separation. Taylor referred to those people who left as 'profitable losses'.

As this book was being written, new evidence was emerging that Taylor's sexual misbehaviour might have been much more serious than had been understood until now. A former Brethren member, Alan Robertson, has written an account of how, as an 11-year-old boy, he was allegedly anally raped by Taylor one night after the Brethren leader had addressed a meeting in Kilmarnock, Scotland, in May 1970. In a vivid account, which was unpublished at the time of writing, Robertson says that, as he was being raped, Taylor told him he was expressing 'the highest form of divine love ... a special love, peculiar to those in Christ'.[13] The alleged rape, and another incident of sexual assault by Taylor the following morning, has left Robertson with post-traumatic stress disorder, and he has attempted suicide.

Then came Aberdeen. After that rout, and Taylor's subsequent death, the leadership was once again an open question. Clearly in contention was a pig farmer from Neche, North Dakota, 'Big Jim' Symington, who had been seen as a favourite of Taylor's, but he was not without rivals. George Maynard, a doctor from Barbados, was one, and another was James Taylor Junior's son, James Taylor III, who was seeking to make the Taylor dynasty last for a third generation.

In Australia, the ambitious Hales brothers, John and W. Bruce, had long harboured pretensions to the leadership, but had overreached themselves in the 1960s, and found themselves out of favour at the 'universal' level at the crucial time (see Chapter 4). Symington, declaring that there was an unbroken line of succession in the Recovery and that the seat of Paul was never vacant, reached out and grasped the prize.

Born in 1913 to Brethren parents, Symington said Taylor had indicated he would be the next leader. Symington cited a comment by Taylor the week before he died, at his final meetings in New York, when he said, 'Big Jim will take the next (universal meeting) held at Bristol.' He also said at that meeting, 'I need to change my Cabinet.'[14] Symington viewed Taylor's parting words as a clear indication that the mantle was being passed to him, and also that everyone who was prominent in the Brethren world at the time needed to be replaced.

Symington promptly excommunicated his rival, Maynard, and a purge ensued of all the talented leaders of the day in order to remove potential threats to Symington. Iain Gibb says it was done with 'ruthless brutality':

> Every leading member of the Exclusive Brethren, including all those who supported JT Junior at Aberdeen, was excommunicated or carpeted within a couple of years. Symington promoted his own men, and then got them excommunicated. And then promoted another tranche.

It was a time of ruthless internal politics as the pretenders for influence jostled to be favourite, and elbowed rivals out of the way. One prominent Australian who fell during the purges was Ron Fawkes, who was withdrawn from in 1984, and has not seen his wife and six children since. John S. Hales, an important Sydney-based leader, was kicked out for a second time in 1976, readmitted, removed again in 1979, and then 'restored' in 1984. His brother, W.

Bruce Hales, once considered world leadership material, spent most of the 1980s 'out', working as a Sydney taxi-driver.

Under Symington's leadership, the Brethren became even quicker to punish. Where Taylor Junior, for his many faults, had some scruples about separating parents from their children, Symington was ruthless in this, and families were split apart at an unprecedented rate. Like Taylor, Symington was an alcoholic. His ministry records him calling people 'old dopes', referring to their 'stinking old mugs', and saying, 'You're rotten, some of you.' He made free sexual references, and exhorted one Brethren man in dispute over a parking space to 'drive the bastard into the ground' with a law suit.

Theologically, Symington moved the sect even more closely to the worship of the apostle Paul. Naturally, given the special place in the Christian world reserved by God for the Brethren, the world leader of the sect was to be known as 'the Paul of our day'. He dismissed the Brethren forebears, saying of the writings of John Nelson Darby that 'we have no ability, hardly, to follow what he is saying', and that the Lord had 'a right to emphasise any feature of the truth that He elects to, at any time that He elects to do it'.

The making of rules continued, and the rules themselves became increasingly bizarre. Symington banned the houses of Brethren members from sharing walls or even sewer lines with their 'worldly' neighbours, lest they suffer contamination. In 1982, Symington took a firm set against technology. Radio and TV had long been banned, but he extended it to fax machines; and, towards the end of his regime, as computers and mobile phones were coming into common usage, he dubbed them all 'evil', 'worldly', and 'conduits for filth'. He preached that the 'Man of Sin' (the devil, who intends to take over the world) would use these devices to instantaneously communicate with those he would lead astray. Even automatic garage-door openers were forbidden on the grounds that they used radio waves.

Symington reduced the age at which children had to leave school – they could go no further than year 10 under his regime – and he confirmed the ban on university education. He exhorted older members who had already attained degrees to take them outside and urinate on them. Many did.

Former members recall that meetings during these years were full of sordid accusations and admissions of sins, some long past, which the flock were forced to publicly confess to and then to beg forgiveness for. Particularly highly valued were the details of sexual misdemeanours. Hundreds were punished by confinement or excommunication during Symington's period; there were no big divisions, but there was a constant flow of people out the door, and families split up. The sad legacy of this period lasts to this day. One such story is told in Chapter 4.

During his leadership, Symington was investigated by the United States Internal Revenue Service for tax evasion over his failure to declare the millions of dollars in donations that flowed to him in cash-filled envelopes from the flock around the world. The Elect Vessel was in the habit of boasting to confidantes about the tracts of North Dakota farmland he had purchased with these 'gifts'. After the investigation closed, with no charges laid, Brethren members were ordered to vary the monthly amounts of each donation given to him so it more resembled a gift, and less a form of regular income.

Symington also moved into asset protection. A split of the magnitude of Aberdeen could, as it had done in 1970, remove hundreds of buildings and land packages from the hands of the 'saints', radically reducing their extensive property portfolio. To guard against this, he centralised control in himself, instigating a change in the trust deeds, which gave the world leader and his successors a veto over any changes to the trusts that controlled meeting rooms around the world.

Symington died in 1987, aged 74. He was blind from adult-onset diabetes.

Because the events of Aberdeen had prompted the loss of so many thousand members in England and the United States, the strength of numbers in the Brethren had moved to the antipodes: to Australia and New Zealand. In the 1960s, two of the Brethren's most ambitious youngsters had been a pair of Australian brothers, W. Bruce Hales, and John S. Hales. During Taylor's time, both had travelled the world addressing meetings to help enforce the strictures laid out by the American. W. Bruce, the charismatic younger brother, had even married one of Taylor's daughters, Consuelo.

When Symington died, in 1987, John Hales, an accountant and graduate of Cambridge University, who had formerly worked at gas company CIG, was widely regarded as the inevitable leader. But, before he could be fully installed, the Brethren needed to deal with some uncomfortable matters of history. John S. Hales had been booted out of fellowship three times. His first spell outside was in 1965 when his mentor, Taylor Junior, judged him for his attempt to introduce a 'commercial system' that competed with the assembly (see Chapter 4). His brother, W. Bruce Hales, was also kicked out at this time. Both were readmitted a year later, but W. Bruce was ejected again, and spent the 1970s and 1980s out of the Brethren. He never regained prominence, despite his charisma and ability as a preacher. John Hales was withdrawn from twice more, in 1976 and 1979.

On Symington's death, the drive from the Australians to install Hales as God's new Elect Vessel was irresistible. But before he could be declared the 'pure man', he needed a clean bill of spiritual health. So a meeting in Sydney was called on 13 October 1987 to settle the inconvenient matter of his excommunications. The meeting produced a full statement of 'facts' to be distributed to the Brethren worldwide.

'There has been increasing concern over recent months regarding the ground on which we withdrew from our beloved brother Mr J.S. Hales', the statement begins. 'Enquiry into these judgments reveals that in 1976, what was presented to the assembly was both unfair and unjust.'[15] It goes on to say that, at the time, many 'malicious accusations' had been circulating against Hales, and that his accuser had made insufficient inquiry into the facts. In a candid admission about the politics of that over-heated era, Hales' accuser, who is not named, 'now admits ... (that) he saw, and seized on the opportunity he thought would gain him favour with persons then prominent universally'.

'It is therefore abundantly clear that these assembly judgments in both 1976 and 1979 in connection with Mr John Hales, and in 1981 regarding Mrs Hales have no righteous basis, and cannot stand.' Hales, his purity re-established, duly became the leader.

Hales, true to his training as an accountant, became interested in the finances of his church. He began encouraging the faithful to make a substantial donation to the sect out of their estate when they died, and also made sure that any children or relatives who were out of fellowship were given little or nothing. Taylor senior, in the early part of the twentieth century, had been the first universal leader to go into private business; but, under Hales, business became a dominant theme. Hales encouraged his flock to borrow money from each other rather than from commercial lenders – a policy that has proved of massive continuing benefit to the financial health of Brethren businesses, and of distress to their commercial competitors. Of course, having financial ties with fellow Brethren also makes a member much less likely to quit the church.

Apart from consolidating the financial wealth of the Brethren, individually and as an organisation, the main innovation of the John Hales era was to begin using some of that wealth to build Brethren-only high schools throughout the world, starting with one in the north-western Sydney suburb of Meadowbank, over the back fence from his own home, in 1992. Going into the education business meant that the Brethren can strictly limit the amount of contact that impressionable young minds have with the 'world'.

It also had the positive effect for ordinary Brethren of making education itself a matter of great interest. This was a significant change for a sect that had a strong anti-intellectual bent and in which, until the 1970s, children were not educated beyond the minimum school-leaving age.

Hales reigned over the Brethren through the change of millennium. On 12 January 2002, he died at the age of seventy-nine.

At the next Australasian Brethren meeting on 31 January of that year in Windsor, New South Wales, speculation was rife about who would take over. A clear frontrunner was John S. Hales' third and youngest son, Bruce, who was considered by his father to be the most spiritual of his boys.

Hales junior was born in 1952 and educated at Canterbury Boys' High School in Sydney, as was former Australian prime minister John Howard (though Bruce attended many years after Howard's time). Bruce was considered by his peers as the most serious of the three sons of John, but also 'more of a good-hearted type of guy; a softer type of nature than the others', said one former intimate of the Hales family, who wants to remain anonymous.[16] 'His older brother, Stephen, was more of a joker, and Daniel, the oldest, was a very obnoxious, precocious character. Bruce was a very easy guy to get on with.'

Bruce was not the perfect Brethren boy. He has admitted in his own ministry to having appeared before judges on driving charges, and to having given his teachers hell. Others recall him going to the cinema and smoking the odd cigarette as a youth. But, on the death of his father in 2002, Bruce D. Hales's 'moral leadership and authority became evident'[17] and, without serious opposition from any quarter, he was quickly installed as the seventh 'Minister of the Lord in the Recovery'. He also became the second son of a world leader to ascend to the position of 'Man of God'.

Hales junior, known as BDH or Mr Bruce, is, like his late father, an accountant. He runs Archway House, a highly successful business in the Brethren style, supplying office furniture. But his spiritual talents were, before he took on the role as guide for his worldwide flock of 43,000, less proven than his business acumen. According to one account, he had taken just one three-day meeting and one monthly fellowship in his life, at times when his father was too sick to serve.

But, to cement his leadership, Hales immediately began to address an international roster of special meetings. These travels culminated in the universal three-day meetings of all the top brass invited from all locations around the world in Leicester in June 2002, over which he presided.

The following year, Hales junior introduced his biggest reform: the 'Review', intended to increase the size of his flock in anticipation of the Rapture, to clear the assembly of past wrongs and injustices, and to put his unique stamp on the organisation. Although all Brethren leaders publicly revere their predecessors, his regime, apparently, would be a more forgiving one than those that went before. BDH published a worldwide instruction to people whose relatives had been put out during the reigns of Symington and his father to invite their loved ones back into the fold. Thousands of Brethren took advantage of the amnesty to contact long-lost relatives. All over the world, tearful reunions were made, apologies given, and 'assembly judgments' re-litigated.

Hundreds of local meetings ruled that fatal judgments made years ago had been wrong – either insufficiently investigated, misinterpreted, or misrepresented to the world leadership of the day (the world leaders themselves, of course, remained unimpeachable). Some of the local leaders deemed to be at fault for having passed on misrepresentations were themselves demoted or excommunicated as a result – how the political wheel turns. As one observer put it, the middle managers suffered 'to keep the top shelf clean; but the top shelf was filthy'.

For the Brethren themselves, the process served to clear the collective conscience. In a document called 'Suggested Approach to Administrative Reviews', the objectives were said to be to 'Clear the Assembly record as to the action taken', to apologise, and to 'establish reconciliation'.[18]

In the end, though, the Review did not bring large numbers back into the Brethren. For many of those approached and apologised to, the process simply reopened old scars. Most of those invited to return were reluctant to subject themselves again to the strictures of Brethrenism. Some thought that they could get access to their families again, some after decades apart, without having to rejoin the Brethren; but this proved too much to ask, even of the new, forgiving regime. The amnesty could not overcome the doctrine of separation; hopes were dashed, and many simply became bitter that they had been through such heartache over assembly judgments now officially acknowledged to have been unjust.

'He opened this leniency, and then some went overboard and people were visiting people and having far too much to do with them. It lasted about six months,' one observer of the time said.[19]

'Although a few "outs" took advantage of the amnesty to come back to the Brethren to be cared for by their relatives, or pick up the lucrative deals that were being made, by and large the "Review" has been a dismal failure,' said Russell Dent, a member of a Sydney meeting at the time (but since withdrawn from):

> All it has left is a festering legacy of broken hearts, wounded souls, and hurt feelings, as ex-Brethren come to grips with the stark reality of the broken marriages that need not have been, the children lost in the stranglehold of Brethrenism, and the short-lived moratorium on 'compromise' which re-opened healed wounds and gave a false glimmer of hope to those cut off from their loved ones.[20]

Theologically, BDH is no Darby in terms of his analysis and explication of the scriptures. His ministry leans heavily on that of his forebears, but he has elevated them even further in the constellation of world religious teachers. Hales now preaches that the Brethren leaders had all enjoyed personal visits from Jesus: 'These men, I have no doubt that they had corporeal appearings from Christ,' he said at a meeting in Perth in 2002. 'We've been in the presence of the greatest service that you could ever measure, and you're never going to be in the presence of anything greater, I can tell you that much,' Hales told the flock in another meeting. 'Even when you're in heaven you're not going to get any closer to Christ than you've been this last 20 years.'

Under Hales, other aspects of Brethren life have shifted quickly, however, as he preaches that the Lord has 'turned a corner', or 'moved on'. While Darby ruled out participating in government at all, believing it was part of the 'world system', Hales incited his flock in 2004 to become active politically, supporting conservative parties worldwide.

However, the political involvement instigated by Hales has rebounded on him. It has prompted unwelcome scrutiny by the media and opposition figures into every aspect of the life of the church, and the creation of some powerful enemies, including the current prime ministers of Australia and New Zealand. Kevin Rudd has described the Brethren as a 'cult'.

Internally, under Hales, the rules of the Brethren have been substantially relaxed (see more in the next chapter). The dress code is breaking down, access to technology is widely allowed, and it now takes a significant effort to be excommunicated. The focus of Bruce Hales's administration has shifted from the religious to the 'worldly' concerns of business and politics. Business success, not theological obscurantism, is now sufficient to promote a Brethren man to the front ranks of the assembly. Hales himself travels the world – not, as Darby did, on foot, but in a chartered Cessna Citation executive jet at a cost of up to $5000 per hour.

For the Brethren's 43,000 members worldwide, John Nelson Darby's hard road has become a lot easier to tread in recent times.

PART II
People

CHAPTER THREE
Life In The Brethren

Looked at through unfocused eyes, the Exclusive Brethren could almost represent the ideal human society. It has a strong family ethic, where having children is encouraged and supported, and the divorce rate is negligible; it provides a cradle-to-grave welfare system for its adherents, including its very own low-fee private schools in towns and cities throughout the world; there is little or no unemployment, because Brethren businesses offer almost guaranteed work to young brothers and sisters leaving school; and for those interested in striking out on their own, there is interest-free start-up capital, business advice, and ready-made suppliers and customers for their goods.

This is an old-style society – like a country town in the 1950s – where everybody has large families who know each other, and where people eat together regularly. Sin is watched for and punished, children live at home until marriage, business success is warmly encouraged, men dominate, women are married early and have plenty of children, homosexuality is abhorred, and everyone goes to church. It is little wonder that this small sect has proved so attractive to conservative and authoritarian politicians such as John Howard.

Yes, it bans its adherents from watching TV, using the internet, and going to nightclubs and restaurants, but it is not just Brethren who are concerned about the excesses of modern life, the predation of the marketing industry, and the lurking dangers of the internet, drugs, and unsafe sex. Many in mainstream society might look enviously at the bans they are able to impose on these pursuits, and the control they exercise over their offspring – what they wear, what they watch, what they ingest, how they entertain themselves – and the protection this affords from the worst of popular culture.

Of Brethren schools, one teacher told me: 'It's a bit old-world and churchy. Things are a bit more segregated, a bit more disciplined, like I imagine going to school in the 1950s. There would never be boys and girls kissing around the corner – there is something sweet and special about it.'[1]

One young woman, 'Janie' (not her real name), was in the process of leaving at the age of 20 when she spoke to me. She said: 'The thing is, if you're prepared to be a good Brethren and commit yourself to that, it can be happy ... Most girls my age, they would be married or getting married, they don't want to leave. They're all pretty happy.'[2] In 2007, Exclusive Brethren world leader Bruce D. Hales issued a statement called *Living Our Beliefs*, describing his followers as 'peaceful, law abiding, contributing citizens of Australia' who 'deserve to have our beliefs respected by the community'.[3]

But there is a severe cost for maintaining this enclave of old-worldliness in the midst of modern life. It is called the doctrine of separation; and the coercive way it is applied to those who cannot, or will not, toe the party line, is, for some, a recipe for misery and despair. In *Living Our Beliefs*, Hales is unapologetic about the doctrine, saying, 'the practice of separation represents a moral distinction between what is right and what is wrong, what is righteous and what is unrighteous, and what is good and what is evil'. 'Good and evil are incompatible and any recognition of God must necessarily and instinctively recognise the absolute distinction,' he writes.

The doctrine of separation is based on Brethren founder John Nelson Darby's translation and interpretation of the Bible, including a verse in Paul's second letter to Timothy, chapter two, which requires Christians to 'withdraw from iniquity'. But while most Christians would interpret this to be a metaphorical requirement, the Brethren take it literally. In 1960, world leader James Taylor Junior made the doctrine radically stricter than it had been until that point, banning his church's members from eating, drinking, or socialising with any outsider.

The doctrine means two things in practice. The first is that the Brethren erect a wall between themselves and the outside world. The eating rule means that there are no friendships, no social intercourse whatsoever with outsiders, and sect members are encouraged to behave with an air of being impervious to the outside world and aloof from it. This contributes to the innocence and unworldliness of Brethren, but it also makes them fearful of what lies beyond the confines of their small community.

At their churches, the walls are literal ones. Their meeting rooms are windowless, and surrounded by high wire-fences and locked gates. In any locality, when the time comes to let the Brethren in to worship, a senior member of the faithful mans the gate and denies entry to any outsider. For public consumption, it is explained that these precautions are for 'security reasons'. When I tried to enter a meeting in 2006, I was denied entry on the basis that I 'could be the most corrupt man in Melbourne'. I was told by the gatekeeper that I would need to make an appointment for an interview with some senior people who would check my motivations, but they refused to give me any contact details. When I persisted in trying to enter, I was confronted by four burly men, threatened with the police, and then, the following day, sent a legal letter spelling out the law suits, professional complaints, and apprehended violence orders I would receive if I tried again to enter a meeting. Yet on these premises, as we shall see later, the Brethren are granted a rate exemption which, in many jurisdictions, requires them to be places of 'public worship'.

The second implication of the doctrine of separation is that once a person is 'withdrawn from', thrown out for some infraction, or decides to leave, he or she is no longer considered to be 'walking in the light' of fellowship. In practice, this means they are kept separate from anybody who stays inside the sect, including their spouses, their children, and all their other relatives. The human consequences of having the gates shut on you in this way by the people you love and the only society you know are immense and inter-generational.

Former members say that life inside the Brethren is defined by three powerful forces that protect people and bind them. These are the 'three Fs': fear, family, and finances. The strongest of these three is family. Bruce D. Hales, in *Living Our Beliefs*, wrote that 'the preservation and protection of the family unit is fundamental to the Brethren' and that 'the conception of children is prized as a blessing from God'. While you are in the Brethren and your family remains with you, this is true. Divorce and family break-up are severely frowned upon and, all going well, a happy life is possible – within the bounds of the conformism demanded of you.

But take the fatal step of leaving the sect, and all of this changes instantly. Those who leave the sect at a mature age are commonly men, because women often cannot bring themselves to abandon their family, and also because, being unable to work, the women have had much less contact with the world through business. But if a man who wishes to leave cannot convince his family to join him in the outside world, and he is 'withdrawn from,' he will be separated entirely from his loved ones. Once the elders are convinced that the deserter's decision is final, and that convincing him to repent and 'get right' with the sect is impossible, they may play a role in convincing his wife, children, parents, and other relatives that he is evil and dangerous. Some men are required by the elders to sign pro-forma quasi-legal 'separation agreements'. Women and children have, in some cases, simply been moved out of the family home during the day when the husband is at work.

Commonly, family members will then refuse to have any further contact with him. So deeply ingrained is the belief in the doctrine of separation that, heartbreakingly, its continued enforcement is performed by the man's loved ones themselves. Separation in practice means that the phone is hung up in his ear, doors are shut in his face, his letters and gifts are returned unopened, and court orders are sought against him.

In a number of cases in Australia, family members have sought and won apprehended violence orders through a court to enforce separation. Only the flimsiest evidence of violence, or the threat of violence, is required to obtain such an order, but it can restrain one party from approaching another – putting a legal barrier, backed by the police, between family members. Importantly for the Brethren, it buys time for the elders to help confirm the family in their resolve to stay apart, and sometimes to move them permanently to a different location.

In some cases, the fact that a loved one has decided to leave is taken by other families in the area as an indication of general contamination in the household. A woman whose husband has left can find herself treated like a pariah, particularly if he decides to speak publicly about his experiences in the Brethren. Alternatively, those who might seem to be on the brink of following their close relative to the outside world can find they are feted, paid special attention, placed on a pedestal, and treated like martyrs. It is not uncommon for women and young people to be offered gifts of money, houses, expensive medical procedures and, particularly, travel to keep them within the sect.

Those men who wish to try for access rights to their children (as is encouraged in Australia under the Family Law Act) can expect a long fight through the courts against a sect with relentless resolve and bottomless pockets, funded from donations paid into a 'fighting fund' for precisely this purpose. The Brethren are likely to brief a senior barrister to fight every inch of the way, appeal orders, call upon judges to disqualify themselves on the grounds of bias, and then appeal again (see Chapter 9).

If the court does grant the husband access, he may see something of his children, but they are likely to be encouraged strongly by the Brethren elders to believe that their father is 'of the Devil', and they may refuse to come to the car to be picked up. The Brethren insist that, from the age of eight, their children are able to make their own decision about whether to see their 'withdrawn from' father or not. Children are sometimes coached to write hurtful letters such as those received by one former member, Mark Humber, a musician. His 12-year-old daughter, Clara, wrote to a Tasmanian newspaper after an article had appeared there, saying of her father, 'Obviously his trombone meant more to him than Mum and us kids.'

Ex-Brethren members fighting for access in the Family Court are often worn down by these tactics, mentally and financially, and end up abandoning their litigation.

When challenged about the apparent hypocrisy of claiming a strong belief in family while strictly enforcing the doctrine of separation, the Brethren have two replies. The first is that it is sin, not the sect, that breaks up families, neatly transferring the blame to the 'sinner' (the one who leaves the sect or breaks its arcane rules in some way). The second reply is to simply deny that the Brethren have a problem with broken relationships. To do this, they quote a copy of a 2006 report by Monash University sociology professor Gary D. Bouma, called 'The Brethren: an investigation into marriage and family relations among the Exclusive Brethren in Australia'. They cite a figure, based on a survey run by the sect itself, that their divorce rate is just 0.8 per cent, compared to 10.8 per cent in the general population.

It is true that the divorce rate within the Brethren is minuscule.

For one thing, the sect does not accept any valid reason for divorce apart from the 'biblical basis' of admitted or proven adultery – the notion of no-fault divorce has not penetrated into this sect. The low figure is also partly explained because not all of the Brethren couples who are separated are divorced, and they therefore do not show up in the statistics – some women remain married to a spouse outside the sect whom they never see. Such women become known as 'widows for the truth', and are supported by the Brethren charitable fund, the 'Australian relocation and poverty fund'. A particularly low divorce rate can also be seen as evidence of coercion and control: people feel unable to divorce their partners, no matter how bad the situation.

In the triumvirate of 'fear, family, and finances', 'finances' refers to the dark flipside of the help that young starters are given in the world of business. The Brethren are extremely well off, boasting in a 2004 document that they are 'found in the middle to upper levels of the socio-economic group'.[4] And they are very generous with their money, as long as it stays within the sect.

But any businessman (there are no businesswomen) who leaves or is kicked out of fellowship stands to lose the contacts, the suppliers, the access to funds, and the Brethren staff to which they were formerly entitled. Others have been 'encouraged' to sell their businesses. Brethren businesses are reluctant to deal with the companies of the 'outs', former members, who come to be seen as pariahs. Those contemplating leaving the sect are therefore also contemplating potential financial ruin.

These financial bonds are growing in strength under Bruce Hales. The sect is increasingly encouraging young men to set up companies that are closely related to other, larger Brethren-owned family concerns. For example, Bruce D. Hales' older brother, Stephen, owns a very successful pump business called All Pumps. In recent years, Brethren members in various states of Australia have set up All Pumps franchises to piggyback off his success. Bruce Hales himself is very successful in the office-equipment supply business, and he encourages 'vertical integration': encouraging other Brethren families to open businesses which do the steel cutting, the powder coating, or the making of desktops to supply him.

This is a very efficient way for larger Brethren businesses to expand and also spread the financial largesse to smaller ones. But, according to former Brethren member Len Joyce:

> The devilish thing is your business depends on you being in fellowship. It's all tied up. If you want to leave, you can't get rid of your staff, so someone else takes it over. The business employs the wife and children, and you end up with nothing.[5]

'Fear' refers to the horror engendered in the Brethren of quitting this secure but stifling society. This is both specific – the very real fear of the financial and family consequences of leaving – and general. It is a fear of society, of outsiders and their motives, of the contamination of the outside world. This fear is instilled from birth, and fostered by constant repetition throughout life. Members of the Brethren are brought up believing that the world is a place of evil motives, where few can be trusted and where you are likely to come to harm.

In *Living Our Beliefs*, Bruce Hales wrote that Brethren had 'regular contact with non-Brethren neighbours and fulfil a commitment to live and reside in peace and friendliness with their environment'. But behind closed doors, in his ministry to his members, the language is quite different. At a reading at Hutt, in New Zealand, in April 2006, he spoke of the evil in the world:

> See, you come in touch with worldly people, if you get a little too close to them, you'll have some sense of defilement ... Don't talk to them about anything else except what the subject you want to talk to them about.[6]

He added that the Brethren needed 'badgers' skins' to keep them impervious:

> So there's something in your demeanour, there's something in your face, there's something in your whole bearing, that makes you really proof. And they can detect it, and they won't, they won't bring up something defiling, they'll have felt forced back ... and you're in control, you're superior, I mean morally.

In Sydney in the same year, he said:

> [T]he whole principles of the world have to be scorned and disdained and just hated, really, hated. We have to get a hatred, an utter hatred of the world. Unless you've come to a hatred of the world you're likely to be sucked in by it, and seduced by it. You must hate the world, every feature of the world.[7]

According to former Brethren member Janie:

> Even after I realised that I didn't want to be a Brethren, it still took me a long time to actually stop believing that the people out there weren't bad people who were going to hurt you – I don't know how to explain it – to trust people. You're told that you go out there, that you're going to get into trouble, no one's got your best interests in mind, you'll be lonely, you'll be miserable, you'll come back.
>
> You hear the horror stories of people who married murderers, or had three abnormal children. You don't know the truth of these things, because they control the information.[8]

But, more than that, some Brethren are also told to fear what God might make happen to them if they have the temerity to leave. One former member said people were told that they would be struck down by lightning, or die in some way:

One mother said to her daughter as she was leaving, 'I hope you are raped before you reach the end of the street so you know that this is a place of safety'. And the minute something happens to a person, that's how they interpret it.[9]

At the very least, the Brethren believe that those who leave the sect will not be saved. In Sydney in 2002, Hales said that, while you could be a 'true believer' if you belonged to another Christian grouping, you could not if you had left the Brethren:

> Someone that goes out of fellowship and deliberately despises the light of the assembly, they've cut themselves off from the truth, they can't claim to be believers, they can't claim to be real believers, they can't claim to have a real link with Christianity.[10]

(In modern times, the Brethren do not officially believe that they are the only Godly people, though that is the message that some rank-and-file Brethren still take out of the meetings. The endorsed position is that all Christians are true believers and can be saved, and that the bulk of those in heaven will be Catholics, but that the Brethren are the 'saints' who have 'received greater light'. They will have the front-row seats next to Jesus after the world's end.)

Some flirt with leaving the Brethren and then come back to the fold. Some who are wavering are offered glittering prizes as incentives. One young woman was asked, 'What exactly would it take to get you back?'

From a purely anthropological point of view, there are sound reasons for so assiduously guarding the boundaries of the faith. A sect that does not recruit and convert people from outside (and the Brethren have not done so since JT Junior banned eating together in 1960) must survive and grow by other means. Its members must have large families, and most of the children must be kept inside the sect, despite the rebellious tendencies of youth. The sect's leaders must erect high walls of separation, by coercion if necessary, until its young people settle down, marry, have children, buy businesses and, thereby, become subject to the same ties that bind their parents.

For the Exclusive Brethren, there is no sense of religion being a part of life – it *is* their life. Even those who do obey the rules feel the threat of separation hanging over them. And, as with any closed system, the pressure and stress can eventually build to an unbearable level: alcohol use, and abuse, is rife (the favoured drink is Scotch whisky), and anti-depressants have replaced Valium in recent years as the drug of choice for those who cannot cope without medication.

The excessive consumption of alcohol has played a significant role in the history of the Brethren. At least two world leaders, JT Junior and Jim Symington, were probably alcoholics, whose deaths were partly contributed to by drink. Brethren members imbibe freely at home and at mealtimes. Scotch whisky is still the drink of choice, but other spirits are popular, depending on what the local favourite is. Janie says:

> I know people who, whenever they're stressed, they'll have a brandy. I know plenty of people like that: women who have a house full of people and cook them a roast dinner, they will have themselves a drink just to calm their nerves and make everything go smoothly. A lot of people have terrible nerves, that's what I'm trying to say, and they need drink to get over that.

But being visibly drunk, or acting badly in public under the influence, is frowned upon. The rate of alcoholism is unmeasurable, but probably high, although people have also been 'put out' or 'withdrawn from' for being alcoholics.

Drinking is common among young Brethren, too. Hales allows it, but tries to control it by making children drink in the home rather than in public. Asked his opinion on the subject in Leicester in 2006, he said, 'We try and make a rule not to drink away from your father's house'. And regarding the amount children should be allowed to drink: 'We won't be excessive, but we're not going to be mean'.[11]

A former school principal from Queensland attested that one school child had boasted to him about the bar-fridge in his bedroom – which was presumably there so he could store the mixers for his Bundaberg Rum. According to Janie, in the country town where she lives, 14-year-olds go out drinking, particularly on a Friday night, sometimes returning home vomiting: 'It's a problem that kids start drinking pretty young because there is not much else they can do to have fun.'

The Brethren are best known by the general public for the large number of odd rules and regulations they enforce on their believers regarding technology, as well as their harsh treatment of those who leave the fellowship. But it's important to note that, at this point in its history, under the leadership of 'Mr Bruce', the sect's seventh 'Man of God', there are some rapid changes being made. Rules taken as articles of religious faith since the 1950s or earlier are being shed willy-nilly, or watered down, and recent developments suggest that the harsh enforcement of assembly discipline is also easing.

Until 2005, the ban on all modern technology meant that people were excommunicated simply for owning a fax machine, computer, or mobile phone. This prompted the ludicrous situation in which Brethren businessmen would pop next door to their worldly neighbours' establishment, or to the local Brethren school (which was allowed to own fax machines), to conduct their business. Then, suddenly, in 2005, almost everything was allowed – even computers.

There remain restrictions, of course: the computers must be for business purposes; they must be supplied by a Brethren company, National Office Assist; and they must be cut-down versions called 'Wordex machines', which come equipped with email, but no access to the internet, which the Brethren believe is the 'pipeline of filth'. The Brethren now even have an in-house computer guru and a website of their own. Brethren children now use these computers on school campuses, under strict supervision.

Since late 2005, the Brethren have also equipped themselves with mobile phones. In a meeting in Perth just 12 months earlier, in 2004, Bruce Hales described mobile phones as a 'tool of the devil ... an instrument of hell,' saying 'I could prove it'.[12] The fear, as with all modern communications equipment, was that the 'Man of Sin', the devil, would use them to instantaneously communicate with the masses, misleading them to death and destruction. In the same meeting, Hales threatened to excommunicate anyone who owned one, saying that, 'If everyone in this room is not prepared to be subject to the authority, authority in the assembly, well, it's sad to say, but finally there won't be a place for you here.'

Two years later, the senior Sydney Brethren men who form Hales' inner sanctum were putting their mobile phone numbers on their public communications.

Another outward manifestation of change is in the Brethren 'uniform'. Until now, women have been expected to keep both their hair and their skirts long, to use no make-up, and to wear headscarves, regarded as 'protection' against the world. Men have been permitted no shorts or facial hair, and their uniform usually consists of dark pants; a white, open-necked, short-sleeved shirt; and a bomber jacket. They are urged to keep their shoes shiny.

This dress code now appears to be more loosely interpreted. The hemlines of women's skirts are creeping up towards knee level. Women were once humiliated for cutting their hair at all, after Taylor Junior pronounced it an 'affront to God', but they are now being seen with somewhat shorter styles. Some are even said to be using make-up. Men have been seen in some localities wearing shorts to work in the garden (despite the preaching that 'The Lord takes no pleasure in the legs of a man'). And, these days, the men occasionally even wear jeans, as long as they are dark, to the meeting hall. Wider changes are also afoot. Swimming in the presence of outsiders is acceptable (it has not been at times in the past); pets are reportedly being kept for the first time; and some Brethren are even bold enough to be seen eating in restaurants.

These adjustments in the outward appearance of difference point to much deeper changes afoot. In 2003, when Hales instituted the 'Review' of old punishments meted out by his predecessors, ex-Brethren who had been out of the sect, sometimes for years, were contacted, and even visited by long-lost relatives. Some very limited contact has apparently continued. In most cases this has not resulted in anything more than a single visit, and nothing approaching a normal family relationship. But some people are, quietly, and without drawing attention to themselves, hopeful that more contact may follow.

Even the most contentious of all Brethren activities, the imposition of assembly discipline, appears to be easing marginally. Brethren assemblies have two main forms of discipline available to them: 'shutting up' and 'withdrawing from'. A person who is shut up is under virtual house arrest, cut off from all contact with any other members of the sect except the designated elders who are assigned to 'handle' the case. They are also not permitted to attend church.

For the person under discipline, being 'shut up' cuts off any human contact whatsoever, except for the 'priestly visits' from the local elders. In these visits, they are quizzed about their 'sin', told what they need to do to 'get right', and assessed as to whether they have repented sufficiently to be readmitted to the sect. Repentance usually means admitting wrongdoing and begging for forgiveness – in other words, submission. The period of detention can be indefinite, and the priestly visits sporadic. Some who have undergone it refer to it as 'humiliation'.[13] A person who is withdrawn from is simply excommunicated, cut off entirely from all family, church, and social ties, and regarded as a pariah. There is very little hope of returning from such a position.

At times in the past, leaders of this sect have meted out the ultimate punishment capriciously and cruelly. But recent testimony from inside the Brethren reveals that members are increasingly unlikely to be withdrawn from. It now reportedly requires something tantamount to criminal activity, or trenchant disagreement with the Man of God, to suffer excommunication.

In a meeting in October 2007, Hales told the faithful that he would prefer to work-through disciplinary problems rather than impose instant punishment:

> It's easy just perhaps to shut people up, withdraw from them ... there's much more exercise required to work with persons, carry it, see if you can bring about healing ... I don't want them shut up, and have to go and visit them once a fortnight. We've got difficult young people, we know that. But when they come out with their sins, and come out in transparency ... that's a breakthrough ... healing is within reach.[14]

These rapid changes present some tricky theological challenges for a group that believes the old rules were handed down by the Holy Spirit speaking in past years through 'these great men' in the assembly. In the very recent past, the Brethren had been insisting that, 'In a changing world, we maintain that God is the same and does not change his standard.'[15] Fortunately, though, the intimacy that the Brethren leaders share with God allows them to notice when the Almighty does change his position. As explained by Bruce Hales: 'The Lord might turn a corner, and we might miss it. See, He can make a turn at any time, a turn in the testimony. Will I be alert? Will I be close enough to be in touch with it, recognise it?'[16]

Under Hales' leadership, the Lord has 'moved on' or 'turned a corner' quite often. Hales teaches that while the Bible might be the

Scripture, it needs to be 'completed' by the testimony of the apostle Paul. And as the Brethren's leaders are considered to be the 'Paul of our day', they have the continuing prerogative to interpret and, if necessary, change the rules. These changes can lead to quite substantial confusion, and Hales's ministry shows that he is regularly asked to clarify the latest theology on an issue. Digital cameras, for example, were described by Hales in 2003 as 'highly sophisticated scientific instruments' and 'a trap morally' that was 'leading to moral degradation at large'.[17] Now, they are in free use.

But it is important not to overstate how far the sect has moved on issues of separation and discipline. Hales is still fully committed to these doctrines, and he still regards the infractions of his flock as sins that require the 'sinner' to bow down to the rules of the assembly before they can be forgiven. He is adamant that the world must be despised and that the Brethren must remain aloof from it.

Importantly, those who have been excommunicated in past years for breaking rules that are no longer enforced are still 'out'. God might move on, but 'You can't go ahead of the Lord', according to Brethren doctrine.

Former Brethren also report that they are still being denied access to their families in the sect. In a new development, they are particularly shunned if they are seen to speak against the sect publicly: then they are considered to be 'opposers'. Some of those labelled in this way have been warned by their families not to speak against the Brethren, for fear of having even limited contact curtailed. They are also warned that family members still 'in' will suffer pressure, or will be ostracised as a result of being related to an 'opposer'. This fear explains why a number of the people who have spoken to me for this book want to remain anonymous, even when they have been out of the sect for decades.

As Hales is easing some of his application of the rules, he is reinforcing a number of new institutional structures that increase the separation between the sect and the rest of the world. The construction of schools is the best example of this. As the reach of the private schools has spread, Brethren children of high-school age are not just encouraged, but required, to attend Brethren-only schools instead of local public schools. This removes children from any external influence and friendship with 'worldly' playmates, and also from teachers who might encourage them to go on to tertiary education, or to follow their hearts into a career in the arts or music rather than in business. The teachers' contracts explicitly preclude them from entering into such conversations.

These schools stop young people from having contact with anyone who might help them with accommodation, advice, or counselling, if they do want to escape. The full effect of this increased separation will only be exacerbated as the Brethren roll out new primary schools. Children educated in seclusion from the age of five will have no insight at all into the wider world.

Indoctrination in the ways of the Exclusive Brethren starts from just eight days after birth. Unlike most of the non-conformist churches that sprouted in the mid-1800s, the Brethren under John Nelson Darby believed in infant baptism because he could not deny to a child the salvation he himself had found. Among one of the hundreds of rules and regulations laid out by James Taylor Junior was a stricture handed down in 1963 that babies must be baptised 'in eight days'. Baptism involves full immersion; an order in 1964 stated, 'Be sure the head goes under'.[18]

Under Taylor's rules, the baptism is conducted in the home, with little ceremony, by a Brethren man of the family's choice, and with only the immediate family present. A baby cannot attend the assembly before baptism, but afterwards is expected to be brought to begin his or her spiritual education. Other branches of Christianity hold a 'confirmation' ceremony in a child's teens, when the child celebrates first communion and affirms that he or she wishes to be a member of the church. But the Brethren give first communion when the child is about six months old – the earliest opportunity to hold a cup of wine to the infant mouth.

As children grow, they come to realise that a very high premium is placed on their compliance with the authority of the church. 'I can remember being 10 and realising if I wasn't a good Brethren my parents wouldn't love me. It was not a question of whether what I was doing was good or bad, but whether you get caught,' one ex-Brethren member said.[19]

Another member has related some of the stock phrases used with children by their Brethren elders to increase obedience and prevent the asking of difficult questions. 'If you don't understand it, don't oppose it,' children are told. Another phrase acts as a catch-all: 'Even if the Brethren are wrong, they're right.' Worldly teachers who have taught Brethren children report them to be courteous, compliant, and unquestioning of authority.

Once they have finished school, young Brethren are not permitted to study at university. The Brethren see the student lifestyle as sinful, a threat to the authority of the church, and far too tempting for the sheltered young adults turned out by the sect. In the words of one Brethren publication, it is 'detrimental to the pursuit of our Christian beliefs'. Another publication states that by studying full time and adopting a 'campus lifestyle', young people are 'joining another fellowship and this would put them in conflict with their church fellowship'.

Besides, for children whose religious and family leaders want nothing more than for them to work in their successful manufacturing and light-industrial businesses, a technical education is quite sufficient, and this is amply supplied by the Brethren education system, and if necessary, TAFE.

However, the university ban has led to a severe shortage of Brethren with professional qualifications, and some in the sect are now reporting that a plan is being hatched to set up further training courses to turn out, for example, accountants and tax planners, so that advice on these sensitive areas can be kept in-house, and the separation from the world more complete. There is also a dearth of Brethren qualified in the medical and legal professions, but no current plan to address this. Only a handful of qualified Brethren doctors are left — all trained in the days before the university ban of the 1960s — and all legal expertise needs to be bought at commercial rates from outsiders.

Once they have left school, most Brethren young people are given work in a Brethren firm – the girls in the offices, or as telemarketers, and the boys on the factory floor. For the girls, this will be their only taste of the workplace, and they will only ever be in a junior position because in no way are they permitted to be in 'a position of authority over a man'.

Under Hales, young people have also been offered ample opportunities to travel, often overseas, to attend fellowship meetings and to meet other young Brethren. In a relatively small gene pool of just 43,000 worldwide, it makes good sense for the health of the population to have children meeting partners from around the country, if not around the world. These trips have become much-sought-after diversions for the young Brethren, who have all-too-little entertainment in their lives. But they have also led to some problems of discipline.

'It appears from confirmed reports that this increase in the Brethren coming together has led to a setting on and promotion of worldliness and substandard activity,' Bruce Hales wrote in a stern letter to Brethren worldwide in 2003. This letter, known among the Brethren as 'The Letter of May the Fifth', was hung for years on the fridges of Brethren families as a warning. Problems listed by Hales included excessive drinking, sometimes at the meeting rooms, attending 'venues of worldly entertainment including restaurants', worldly dress, 'exposed midriffs, faded jeans ... short skirts', unsuitable hairstyles including 'sideburns and long hair' for men and 'brothers, hair tinting', CDs, pre-recorded music, and 'corrupt language and talk'.

'In addition to the above there have been substantial reports of unsuitable behaviour and liaison between younger Brethren including illicit conduct (drugs/physical contact) that even the world regards as unacceptable and dangerous,' he wrote. If it did not stop, and the Brethren did not 'accept the need for control', the program of 'increased Fellowship contact' would also need to stop.

'Do not provoke the Lord to jealousy,' Hales ended the letter, adding that it should be read out at every assembly worldwide, and that the Brethren were to reaffirm publicly that they would toe the line.

As Brethren grow older, they are encouraged to settle down; when women reach their early twenties, there is mounting pressure for them to get married. A decade ago, women were married younger, perhaps in their late teens. These days, according to Janie:

> Once you get to an age that could be, like, 23, you're considered to be quite an old maid. I expected to be married around 21, and the grandmothers would be saying, "Are you getting married soon, have you got any good news"?

But even that decision is not entirely in the hands of the lovestruck young couple. 'We're putting these marriages off a bit,' Hales said in 2005:

> I tell you what, it's interesting, it's interesting. They all come up, you know, twenty, twenty and a half, looking for the big OK, you know, and bliss, just bliss shining out of their eyes, as though that they're just floating up on a cloud to heaven. Twelve months later, after waiting, they've been through a bit of exercise, they're actually thinking a little bit differently, they've, you know, suddenly found rock bottom.[20]

For those who are finding it difficult to locate a marriageable partner, or for those who leave it too late, help is also at hand. In each state in Australia there is a match-maker. This is a senior man who will trawl through the available singles among the flock worldwide to find an appropriate bride or groom. 'He works with the blokes that leave it too long to get a good bride, and who are sitting on the shelf — maybe aged between 25 to 30. And then he trawls through all the available old spinsters to get them hooked up,' says one young man who recently left the sect. Women from 23 or 24 onwards were considered to be at risk of staying single, he said; by the time they were 28, they were 'old spinsters'.[21]

The wedding ceremony itself is not simply a statement of faith and love for the betrothed, but also a promise to the church. The vow that the young couple makes in front of the Brethren assembly says: 'I take thee to be my lawful wedded wife/husband, being committed to uphold in our Household scriptural principles as held amongst Brethren with which I am in complete agreement.'[22]

Once married, a woman is encouraged to begin having children, and large families are usual. Five children are considered normal. Once a young woman has children, of course, her entanglements within the sect are much stronger, and it is much harder for her to leave. Janie left the Brethren as soon as she had finished school because the reality of her future prospects had hit her:

> I got very very depressed in year 11 and 12, and it was only when I realised I could leave did the depression lift. It was the lack of life prospects, the fact that I had nothing to look forward to but kids, marriage, husband, church, that made me so desperate.

Abortion is not allowed except in medical emergencies, and contraception is frowned upon, but IVF is, apparently, used quite extensively by those having trouble fulfilling the large-family dictum. The worst possible sin is homosexuality, and Brethren make no effort to conceal their distaste for the 'wickedness' of gay sex. Bruce Hales has said it is 'unnatural against the anatomy', and when the (gay) Australian Greens senator Bob Brown met three senior members of the Brethren in June 2006, one of them, David Thomas, said of homosexuality, 'We repel it because it's against God's word ... people get themselves so perverted and they just can't think morally.'

Young men who are sufficiently motivated have the hope of being set up in their own businesses. These have been almost exclusively of the light-industrial type, as befits a group of people with a technical education whose ban on 'worldly' entertainment precludes them from being involved in the service or hospitality industries. Brethren companies are most often found in the industrial estates on the outskirts of major cities and country towns – manufacturing, assembling, or importing and reselling goods such as pumps, sheds, car accessories, playground equipment, and homes.

Hales writes, though, that with the decline of manufacturing industries, the typical profile of a Brethren business is changing in favour of 'occupations that focus on marketing, sales, accounting, warehousing, workplace safety and technical and management skills'.

These businesses, on the whole, are very successful, partly because, apart from religion, there are very few distractions from work, and partly because of the natural advantages conferred by living in a tight-knit community of people whom you can trust to give you advice, interest-free loans, staff, and support. But business is also the area where Brethren come into closest contact with worldly people, and therefore the potential for corruption. To guard against 'defilement', Hales, in a 2006 meeting, recommends ruthlessness:

> If you're going to visit a customer, don't ask him about his business, it is of no interest, all you want to tell him is about your business. You don't want to buy his goods, do you? It's a dreadful trap ... you

want to tell them about your business, and then you want to get the order.[23]

Young men contemplating entering business are told, 'If you look after the Lord, the Lord will look after you' – that is, they will be given financial help as long as they adhere to the Brethren line on theology and lifestyle issues.

When a young Brethren couple come to buy or build a house, there is another rule: it must be free-standing. Flats and semi-detached dwellings are considered to provide 'mixed conditions' and to be 'unclean'. There are no TVs, CD, or DVD players, and no radios in these houses. The 'Wordex' computer is only linked to the internet for email. Those seeking wider internet access are confronted with an 'Install Block' dialogue box. Dogs, cats, birds, even goldfish are absent from Brethren homes since JT Junior decreed 'no idols or pets', though there is news in some quarters that this rule has softened. Novels are banned, and theatres and cinemas are likewise out of bounds – fiction generally is regarded with great suspicion. Newspapers and magazines are allowed, within reason, as Brethren, in JT Junior's words, want to be 'cognisant of things in the world without stuffing yourself with the newspaper'.

Brethren houses, particularly in Australia, where the flock are relatively wealthy, tend to be more comfortable, more luxuriously furnished, and more likely to be air-conditioned than average. Come Christmas and Easter, there is no celebration; they are just normal days of worship. Darby preached that Christmas had simply been the establishment church's attempt to appropriate a heathen festival that it could not stop. As for Easter, the Brethren say that they 'celebrate the Lord Jesus dying for us every Lordsday (Sunday) morning at 6am'. There are also no birthday parties for the children.

A Brethren person cannot join a club or society that includes anybody outside the Brethren. Trade unions are particularly hated, and the sect has managed to lobby to install 'conscience' clauses in government legislation around the world to exempt their businesses from the need to deal with unions.

Central to the Brethren way of life is, of course, the assembly meeting: there is one every day, and several on Sundays. The assembly is held by the Brethren to be the place of heavenly judgment, where the Holy Spirit attends and fills the faithful with knowledge. There are different kinds of assemblies. The smaller ones are held in meeting halls that are like suburban houses with the internal walls removed; the larger gatherings are held in purpose-built meeting halls with banks of seating around a central area, where the preachers stand. Hymns are sung, unaccompanied by any instrument, at the beginning and end of the service. The only formal task that the women perform is to 'give out' the hymns: that is, to choose and call out the number of the hymn to be sung from the 'Little Flock' hymn book. While women are expected to attend every service, they are not permitted to speak.

Sunday, which is called 'Lordsday', begins at 6.00 am with the Lord's supper and worship in small groups. All people, including tiny children, are expected to participate in the smaller groups of thirty to forty people. Children still wearing nappies are woken, their dummies are taken out of their mouths, and they are helped to their feet by their fathers to pray. Then, at 9.00 am, the Bible study meeting is held in the large hall, where one of the leading men, the 'priests' or 'elders', will suggest a subject and scriptures to be read, and the other men will enter the discussion.

Following that service is 'break', where people are sent to the homes of their fellow Brethren for a meal. The man of the household is handed a note on a small piece of paper at the Tuesday meeting each week, informing him which families he and his wife will entertain the following Sunday, or which household their family will go to. The roster for the 'break' is worked out by a pair of men in each locality who are specifically assigned the delicate task of keeping warring families apart, or putting a loyal family into the midst of a gathering that is showing signs of rebellion.

Particularly to be avoided is the impression that one is developing 'special friends' because, according to a pronouncement by Bruce Hales in 2004, they 'work against the fellowship'. It has been a long-held view, but Bruce's father, John S. Hales warned that 'we shouldn't allow the natural thing to assert itself, cater to special friendships, special affiliation'. In the past, though not in recent years, Brethren have been excommunicated for socialising with people deemed to be their special friends. The organisation of social activities within the Brethren, including the big meal between services on Sunday, is done on a strict basis of rotation because, as Hales has said, he wants 'an equality of outlook towards all the saints'.

Up to 18 or 20 people are fed in the lounge room at this weekly occasion, depending on the size of the house, where food and drink, in ample quantities and of high quality, is expected to be provided and served by the woman of the household. Poorer Brethren families are not exempted. Women who have left the sect testify that the social pressure and scrutiny they felt at those gatherings were one of the most significant contributors to their considerable load of stress.

After 'break' on Sunday there is more gospel preaching, which continues through the day until about 6.00 pm. The prayer meetings, services, and Bible study meetings are held every night of the week. On a Tuesday night, promising young men are expected, when they reach a certain age, to 'speak as personally exercised' on a scriptural subject.

This constant church attendance is not the only religious observance performed by the dutiful Brethren. The utterances of the most senior Brethren men, particularly Hales, are taped and transcribed by the Brethren publishing house in the UK, the Bible and Gospel Trust. The resulting 'ministry' is then bound between white covers and distributed worldwide. Having a paid subscription to the 'white books' is compulsory, and a $90 subscription in Australia lasts about six months. And it's not just one subscription per household that is required, but one per person: men, women, and children.

White books are regularly grouped together and reissued between more robust brown covers ('brown books'), and it is expected of every Brethren that they read them thoroughly. Quoting a recent piece of scripture, or quizzing a rival or a less senior member on some recent utterance by the Man of God, are favourite pastimes of those hoping to show off or catch their neighbours out.

In 2005, Bruce Hales made it clear that he viewed the Bible, and the teaching of Brethren ministers, as the saviour of the sect's youth, saying, 'If young people are going to be anything worthwhile in the testimony, they have to addict themselves to reading the Scriptures and the ministries'. Historically, Brethren have also been expected to preach the Gospel on street corners. This street preaching is the one claim that Brethren have to be spreading the Gospel to the general public rather than just within their closed society, but they do not seek to make converts: they just leave the word of God hanging in the air as a general comfort and guide.

Once a month, on a Saturday, is the 'care' meeting, where the elders of the church in each locality get together to work out the finances. Here the 43,000-or-so worldwide Brethren do their 'levitical giving': that is, they make their donations to the world leader and other senior elders of the church. These sums, amounting to millions of dollars per year, are carried across national borders in cash, and borne in white envelopes, to be received, tax free, as gifts.

This money only goes to the most senior 'priests', including Hales and a few others, who have, in Brethren-speak, 'carried an exercise', or borne a spiritual task or burden in the service of the church. Hales encourages donors, where it is legal under the law of their country, to claim tax exemptions for these amounts as a gift to a charity. Brethren will also spontaneously hand wads of cash to Hales and other elders when they travel to preach. The Brethren world is a strictly hierarchical one, its members ranked in what is effectively a class system. Those in the ruling class are the ones sitting in the front row of seats in the meeting hall. In the modern Brethren, those in the front row are the financially well off who also might carry some 'priestly' responsibilities. There is some mobility within this system – a man can climb up the ranks if he achieves money and success, if he shows some leadership qualities, and if he is prepared to discharge the responsibilities of being an elder.

However, as with most class systems, there are some families who are simply considered aristocracy, and others, for reasons of history and politics, who will never make it to the front rank. The further back the male of the family is in the seating plan, the less important the family is considered.

Apart from the potential tax-free financial benefits of taking on a leadership role, and the regular worldwide travel to meetings, becoming an elder, or 'priest' confers great responsibility over the lives of a man's neighbours – an officially endorsed right to know about their private business – and a direct line to the Man of God. Matters of assembly discipline are, in the first instance, dealt with locally. Priests from each assembly are able to impose discipline on church members, putting transgressors in a 'shut up' position, and then counselling them and seeking their repentance.

If something remains a problem, matters are referred to a senior person in the 'interchange'. In Australia, the interchange is the group of assemblies within a three-hour drive, who meet regularly at the large group meetings on Sunday and some nights during the week. The leader speaks regularly to 'Mr Bruce' or some member of his inner circle in the north-western Sydney suburb of Ermington, from where he and his senior colleagues conduct their own businesses and the big operation of their religion.

Being a local priest confers enormous influence, but it also carries risks. In past purges, priests have become targets for younger, ambitious men seeking to take their position. This kind of political manoeuvring was particularly rife in the regime of Jim Symington.

Ambitious youngsters trying to make their way in the Brethren world, but who are thwarted in their own city or town, can also take the path of relocation. The Exclusive Brethren have been assiduous in establishing assemblies in new localities; in his early years, at least, Bruce Hales was keen to spread assemblies further afield, setting up three-person 'relocation commissions' to try to control the flow of people.

For the ambitious, or the thwarted, relocation offers the lure of being able to move to a new place and to exercise assembly leadership there. This policy has meant that Brethren have moved into small country towns at the same time as many others have been leaving them. Their businesses, which also employ non-Brethren people, have become the mainstay of some small local communities.

But there are also forced relocations. In 1998, the Brethren decided, en masse, to abandon South Africa because of a number of incidents of street violence and carjacking against Brethren members. Whether they wanted to or not, Brethren were told to move to other countries where the 'saints' were already living. The cost for those individuals and families in terms of lost jobs, reputations, and dislocation were, according to some who were involved, enormous.

But no matter what class or position the husbands achieve in this hierarchy, their wives will always be second-class citizens. In the modern era, they are educated to the same standard as their male counterparts, and when they leave school they can work, usually in reception or administration in Brethren businesses. But for those who stay within the Brethren, that is as far as their careers will ever progress. A woman cannot put herself in a 'position of authority' over a man and, once married, she cannot seek paid work. Women become volunteers in the schools, or work at home as helpmeets and partners in their husbands' businesses.

Bruce Hales clearly spelled out the official attitude in his document, *Living Our Beliefs*: 'The husband is regarded as the chief provider and is looked to for stability and as the breadwinner; the wife's important role is to care for the husband and any children.'

Among friends, he reveals his deep belief that women are incapable in business. At a Brethren business seminar in 2005, Hales was informed by a man that his business's accountant was a woman, and a partner in the firm. Hales advised him to sack her:

> Nothing wrong with lady accountants, but when they are running businesses, they can't handle it. That's the truth – they are excellent book-keepers and accountants – but when they've to do the management as well it is too much for them mostly.[24]

Nutritionist Rosemary Stanton, whose family left the Brethren when she was 17, described the sect as 'absolutely male-dominated':

> (Women) always had to sit at the back, they had to be quiet. Women were not allowed to be teachers. They were not allowed to have too much education because then they might have some authority over a man. And you also had to wear a ribbon in your hair to signify that you accepted that the man was the head of the woman ... it's not like Muslim women wearing a scarf as a sign of modesty. The scarf for the Exclusive Brethren ... is actually a sign that you accept that the man is the head of the woman.[25]

The scarf is worn only in the meetings and when the woman is out in the world. The Brethren teach that the scarf ensures God listens to your prayers, and that the angels look after you and protect you when you go out, helping make you 'proof' against the world's defilement.

The silencing of women at the meetings also extends to large social events in the home. At the big weekly social gathering between Sunday services, the host husband is expected to speak to the group at large, and women are expected to take a back seat. If they speak on male subjects such as business or the scripture, they run the risk of getting a reputation as a 'loudmouth'.

If a married couple in the Brethren get into financial trouble, they are likely to attract the support of their church. A decade ago, going bankrupt was an offence justifying excommunication, but that rule also appears to have softened. An enormous advantage of being a member of the Brethren is that all the funds of the sect remain within it. No 'worldly' charities benefit from the profits of these businesses, and the only donations made are to Brethren schools, Brethren charities, and Brethren priests.

Investment decisions are easy, too: the only investment vehicles allowed are superannuation funds and other Brethren companies or charities. Brethren are not permitted to invest in worldly markets, as Hales made clear in May 2006:

> Boy, it would be a great day when the whole share market system collapses totally and absolutely ... great fall of Babylon. That will include all the share markets, and the bond markets, and the futures markets, all built up on rotten filthy crookery. The smartest brains employed throughout the world to build up a system of utter, absolute, unadulterated crookery, and God is going to bring it down. What a day, what a great day! So don't put your trust in it.[26]

But one aspect of the world system that the Brethren are very keen to participate in is the lobbying of governments. Though they do not vote because they believe governments are chosen by God, they regularly attempt to sway governments to their views on the grounds of 'conscience'. In the late 1940s, they successfully argued that their Australian businesses should be granted the right to claim a conscientious objection to any union activity, because a union represents a fellowship outside their own (see Chapter 7).

The Brethren are also assiduous about collecting whatever welfare payment, tax concession, or government subsidy is due to them. There is no suggestion that they act illegally in doing so, but it is clear that they are encouraged to structure their affairs to reap as much cash from these payments as is legally possible (see Chapter 4). This is known within the sect as 'spoiling the Egyptians' (a reference to the book of Exodus that tells of God diverting the wealth of the wicked oppressors, the Egyptians, to the righteous escapees, the Jews).

In their personal habits, the Exclusive Brethren are opposed to vice, with the exception of alcohol. Gambling is prohibited, as is smoking, with James Taylor Junior saying of the habit that it 'brings in what smoke is – darkness and blackness. It is filthy and against the spirit of God'.[27]

But this does not mean that they never appear in courts. Bruce Hales and his brother Stephen have both admitted that, in their younger days, traffic offences had them answering to magistrates.

The Brethren relationship with the courts and justice system is a complicated one. On the one hand, they can be relentless litigants, particularly against those who have ceased to 'walk in the light'. Any lawyer, particularly one plying his or her trade in the Family Court, would be happy to take on a Brethren client because of the typical length, complexity, and expense of their cases.

These cases are paid for by a 'fighting fund', collected for precisely this purpose. On the other hand, if any Brethren member is placed under a court order such as a bond, he or she can be 'shut up' or withdrawn from for being subject to the authority of a worldly court. When it comes to hiring lawyers, the Brethren will appoint a Jew first, followed by a Catholic, because both, they believe, have experienced persecution.

Civil disputes within the Brethren are sorted out internally, without recourse to the courts. And, as for criminal matters, the Brethren are strongly discouraged from reporting to police anything that involves another 'saint'.

'They do believe that the Brethren is higher than the courts,' Janie says, 'and they do believe that if you confess something to the Brethren then the matter is finished.' In 2003, Bruce Hales said it was 'a very great matter, I think, to know that this place, the assembly, is the highest court. It's the area of God's direct dealings, and it's got the power to overrule other judgments if there's a righteous basis for it.'[28]

But this position has been shown to be inadequate when dealing with cases of child abuse. Reluctance to report a fellow Brethren member delayed by some months the reporting of one child sexual-assault matter in Australia, despite laws that those in positions of responsibility or influence (including priests) are required to report allegations of abuse as soon as they hear them. In this case, the Brethren mother, whose daughters were saying they had been abused by a man they were staying with, was told by senior women in her locality, 'It would better for a millstone to be hung around your neck and for you to be cast into the depths of the sea rather than go to the police'.[29] A man is now serving a jail term for these offences (see Chapter 6).

In recent years, another case of alleged abuse has been uncovered – this one in New Zealand – where an elderly Brethren man has been arrested and charged with indecent assaults that took place over a number of years. A former Brethren school trustee in rural Queensland has also been charged with indecent treatment of children.

There is no evidence that this kind of abuse is more prevalent within the Brethren than in any other part of society, but some argue that the habit of separating children from their parents and then lodging them with other families is a recipe for child-sex abuse

– and a number of documented cases have occurred under these conditions.

Brethren elder Chris Shore told me that the recent cases had made the sect leaders aware of the dangers of sexual abuse, and that they had adopted a firm policy, in consultation with other religious denominations, to deal with it: 'The way we have approached this whole exercise is [to ask] what does the law require ... because we must fulfil the law,' Shore said.[30]

In the future, as members of the Exclusive Brethren grow older, they, like most Australians, will be relying more heavily on their superannuation savings. But those who do not have their own savings are looked after partly by using government pensions and partly by charitable giving from within the sect. JT Junior told the Brethren to look after young people spiritually, and old people physically.

According to Bruce Hales in *Living Our Beliefs*, old people are cared for as long as possible in their own homes, or those of extended families. Nursing homes are a last resort. 'Feasibility studies are been (sic) undertaken' into the possibility of the Brethren opening their own, separate, nursing homes, he wrote.

In their wills, Brethren are encouraged to leave a substantial contribution in assets or cash to the church itself, and to minimise or eliminate the bequest to any 'withdrawn from' children. But even death does not end the Brethren's requirement to separate from the world. Funerals are performed by Brethren members who are trained and licensed as undertakers, and who are based in the larger cities. To avoid allowing a deceased Brethren to fall into worldly clutches at any point, there are a number of people in each small town whose job it is to prepare the body for the coffin. Men prepare the bodies of men, and women do the job for women. The coffins are open, so these ordinary, untrained people must do what they can to prepare the body for viewing.

This can be a traumatic process, particularly if the body is of a relative, or has been damaged by a traumatic death. According to Janie, the Brethren 'seem to have such a heartless approach to death and grieving':

> Plenty of Brethren have had to go to the hospital to pick up their wife or child in a body bag. Family members are often expected to help with getting the body ready, and if an autopsy has been done it just makes it so much worse for the family. When a young man ... died a few years back, I remember Aunty E going around to visit his mum. The brothers were in the bedroom getting his body ready for the coffin and she found his mum vomiting over the laundry tub. The washing machine was full of blood-soaked clothes (from the autopsy), which she was expected to wash.[31]

Funerals are large affairs, held in the main meeting hall of the locality, and then there is another graveside service. Relatives of the dead person who are out of fellowship, and who attend, tell horrific stories of being abandoned with the coffin at the church if they go there; or, if they go to the graveside, they are shuffled away from the grave by the assembled Exclusive Brethren.

When the service is over, enforcing separation to the last, the brothers themselves take up shovels and fill in the grave.

CHAPTER FOUR

The System

Bruce David Hales might be the ultimate spiritual leader of a worldwide religious sect of 43,000 people, but it is clear that his heart, and his special talent, lies in business. Hales, like his father and his father-in-law before him, was trained as an accountant; and, for 12 years from 1970, he worked as one. After that, he went into business for himself, building a large and prosperous office fit-out and furniture-sales business, Archway House.

After Hales became the religious leader of the Exclusive Brethren in 2002, his sect, too, became big business. Hales boasts in his self-penned guide to the sect, *Living Our Beliefs*, that the gross annual turnover of all Brethren businesses in Australia is $2.2 billion.[1] This is $170,000 for every Australian man, woman, and child who follows his teachings. He writes:

> Over the past 40 years the Brethren have gradually left the employ of non-Brethren companies and institutions and moved into our own businesses. This trend greatly accelerated during the 1970s and 1980s due to a desire to reach a closer accommodation with the Scriptures.
>
> There are now over 1000 Brethren businesses in Australia

employing about 3500 Brethren and 4000 non-Brethren employees.

It is difficult to underestimate the emphasis now put on business success within the Brethren. The Man of God's brother, Stephen Hales, a businessman, made the point in 2005 when he used the history of his sect to emphasise the role of business:

> The great men of the recovery have all been very, very good salesmen. At least the majority of them: we all know that JND [John Nelson Darby] was a lawyer, FER [Frederick Raven] was in the admiralty, but as to J.T. [James Taylor], JT Jr [James Taylor junior], JSH [John S. Hales] and our brother currently [Bruce D. Hales], they have all been very, very good salesmen and I think if we go back through some of their ministry, we can actually get some very good ideas and clues of how to about being successful, trained, disciplined salesmen without going the worldly way.[2]

Behind the closed gates of this group, Bruce Hales has used the enforced conformity of his followers, as well as his flock's ability to disseminate information and advice quickly, to form a huge, loosely linked cooperative of smaller businesses to both enrich his flock and bind them together with strong financial ties. And, through new companies such as One Fund, Onefuel, Onefleet, and Logistics One, as well as National Office Assist, the modern Exclusive Brethren is a buying group of considerable clout, a loyalty program with huge benefits for Brethren families and their businesses, and a self-help group with Hales as the financial guru.

But the transformation has not just been at the organisational level. He has also overseen a micro-level restructuring of Brethren family businesses, recommending that they be run through family trusts. This structure maximises the individual financial returns for families as well as their Centrelink payments from the government, while minimising their tax liabilities, and allows them to significantly increase their tax-free contribution to their own Exclusive Brethren school system.

The money saved by paying donations to the schools from before-tax, rather than after-tax income, is then used to increase the dollar amount of school donations, or it can be returned to the Brethren system – perhaps going to the priests and elders in the form of income tax-free 'gifts', or in the form of loans and start-up capital for young businessmen, or into a network of other tax-free charities that distribute money only within the Brethren.

This move is the culmination of a push by Hales and his equally mercantile right-hand men, particularly the Victorian leader John Gadsden, to rationalise Brethren business practice. It began in 2005 when they established and ran 'Business Seminars' to push, at a price, the latest Brethren commercial orthodoxies. The innovations were geared solely towards boosting the incomes of individual Brethren businesses. The entry fee to attend these seminars went to a company set up to channel funds to Brethren schools.

Hales has firmly established the combination of business and charity in Brethren daily life. Brethren members testify that the best way into Hales's good books is to run a successful and wealthy business, and to donate significant funds to the world leader's pet projects. Hales's long-term objective appears to be to guide all Brethren businesses to greater success, more wealth, and less reliance on the outside world. In this, he is simply following, in a subtler fashion, a path trodden by his father, John S. Hales, the former world leader of the sect, in the 1960s.

In that period, John S. Hales and his dynamic and charismatic brother, W. Bruce Hales, were a supremely powerful pair of Australian leaders – Brethren 'aristocracy' under the world leadership of James Taylor Junior. W. Bruce, armed with a gift of oratory that one observer of the time said 'could really move a congregation', was widely fancied, particularly in Australia, as the next world leader.

W. Bruce's older brother, John, was more reserved and aloof, and was seen 'as a tremendous support [to W. Bruce] with a great training in matters financial'.[3]

This was the period in history when the world leader, Taylor Junior, was most rigidly exercising control over the lives of the Brethren. Already under Taylor, the faithful were being harangued, pressured, and kept in a constant state of vigilance over potential transgressions of the growing list of rules for living and believing.

The Hales brothers' contribution to Brethren life was to expand this level of control and conformity from the social realm and into the financial. With the help of the Melbourne leader Alan Gadsden, the father of John, they radically expanded the scrutiny of the financial affairs of ordinary members of the Brethren. The new strictures, which they began making in the late 1950s, but which came into full force in 1964 and 1965, became known as the 'Commercial System' or, simply, 'the System'.

Under the System at its height, the Brethren were expected to work constantly, keep close account of their time, and even to provide the financial accounts of their businesses to the Hales brothers and their acolytes. The benefit for the church was that elders could keep an eye on exactly how much people were donating to the church, and put pressure on for more. For the Hales brothers, the pay-off was power and control.

In places where the System was most strongly enforced, including Australia, Brethren were told to write little dicta from the Hales brothers into their Bibles. W. Bruce's phrase was the Orwellian line, 'Inefficiency equals unholiness'. John S's, drawn from his studies of Keynesian economics, was, 'Wealth is the result of circulation'.

The other facet of this micro-control was the instruction that everybody must fill in notebooks, a little like lawyers' timesheets, accounting for the minutes per day spent in particular pursuits. Starting at 6.00 am, the Brethren were ordered to record their every activity and to submit the completed tables to the local priest or elder. Even school children were expected to comply, submitting the papers to their parents.

Personal and business accounts could be scrutinised by fellow Brethren, or the sect's leaders, and businesses were required to use Brethren accountants. Details of those accounts were then sometimes publicly aired in the assembly meetings.

'Essentially, these guys were control freaks,' said one former Brethren member who lived through the System days. 'They said lots of good things and did lots of good things, too, at times, but overall it was a strange and quite evil administration. What you did, where you lived, what you drove, who you married plus heaps more were all very much under their scrutiny.'[4]

To further their influence, the Hales brothers began a policy of holding meetings outside assembly hours, in people's private homes or farmhouses. These 'seminars' had no other purpose than to advise the Brethren how best to run their businesses. It was made clear that attendance was strongly recommended, and full disclosure of financial information was strongly encouraged.

Attendees recall that the Hales brothers really knew their stuff, and that the seminars were useful, even if slightly invasive. The Hales brothers, they say, had a knack for financial management. But the brothers used the information they collected to compile a global list of Brethren businesses. Those whose enterprises were most lucrative were promoted to the front rank of the assembly. There were even plans to establish a global Brethren bank, to complete the sect's financial separation from the world.

It was at this time that the idea for separate Brethren schools was first mooted; and, in fact, John Hales began the process of taking his three boys, Bruce Junior, Daniel, and Stephen, out of the public school system in Sydney to educate them privately at home. This attracted the strong opposition of Taylor Junior, who insisted that state government schools were a suitable venue for education, and that the role of young Brethren was to shine as a testimony of Christian witness. This ban on private schooling was maintained by the next world leader, Jim Symington, who believed that Brethren children 'must rub shoulders with the world' to toughen them up.

Even under normal circumstances, donations in the Brethren assembly are collected in open baskets and are therefore publicly on display, and generosity is expected within the individual means of the giver. But under the 1964 and 1965 System, this scrutiny became much more overt and public. Ex-members recall the fear and humiliation of meetings, during which one of the Hales brothers might go around the room asking how much brothers earned. Those deemed to be earning too little, or too much, or contributing too little, were ridiculed.

Peter Flinn, a former Brethren member living in Australia, tells the story on a website for ex-Brethren of one meeting in the Camberwell 'roundhouse', the main meeting hall in Melbourne, in 1964.[5] W. Bruce Hales was 'in full flight (and) the System was at its zenith'. On this occasion, a local man called Robin Bradnick defied him.

'I went home that night confused and indignant,' Flinn writes:

> I was 16, and I had seen my father humiliated in public. I cannot remember whether he or Robin Bradnick was stood up first. What I do remember was WBH asking my father to stand up, feigning pleasantries, then making the outrageous and grossly untrue statement that he (my father) had 'had it easy all his life'. I could not believe my ears. Life was a painful struggle for my poor father in many ways. Yet he just stood there in his quiet gentlemanly way and smiled.
>
> Then came the sudden question from WBH: 'How much did you put in the box last Lord's Day (Sunday)?' My father took the microphone and quietly said, 'Twice the amount I put in the previous week'. WBH was nonplussed for a moment, then told

him to sit down. I thought my father's response was terrific. For all Bruce knew, it could have been twenty quid instead of ten. But it was more likely four shillings instead of two!

'Robin Bradnick's response to the same question was certainly more spectacular,' Flinn writes. Bradnick, a well-regarded architect who had designed the building in which these humiliations were being meted out, was asked how much he earned in a year. He responded '250,000' – a fortune in 1964. Then he was asked how much he had contributed to the collection. He replied '2/6'. It was taken by all present to be an expression of dissent and defiance.

The reach of this commercial System varied in different parts of the world, depending on the local influence of the Hales brothers. 'Charles', a former Brethren member from the Isle of Wight, who wishes to remain anonymous, recalls that, in his city, the System was 'not given universal support'.[6]

'The elders/leaders did not criticise it, nor did they encourage it, so in January 1965 WBH spent three weeks in London to try to educate and convert us.'

Under the System, Charles says that, 'Everyone was frantically working every minute of the day'. For him, this meant that, as soon as he arrived home from work on his bicycle, he would go to the home of an old couple to mow their lawn, a paid job, and then to the assembly meeting. After that, he would study:

Every waking hour was supposed to be gainfully occupied, making money if possible. It was said that work keeps you from committing sin. But there was also an increasing element of fear – fear of being publicly ridiculed, fear of being 'shut up' or thrown out of fellowship, fear of being shouted at in the meeting.

For me personally, the System of 1965 was a turning point in my life. I started thinking about leaving the Brethren, and realised I would have to stand up to these bullies in the future.

Charles left a year or two later.

'Sophie', an Australian woman, who was a girl at the time, remembers the System as one of a number of traumas in her young life. She would fill out her time sheet assiduously, running to the train station in the morning so she could do two minutes of extra homework:

> Mine was extremely impressive. I used every minute. You had to write how long you were praying for and what you read in the Bible, and if I went and swept the floor or something – every single minute, so you wouldn't have one idle minute ... I think I became really hyper, I couldn't sleep, I was so wound up all the time.[7]

Each week she would submit the sheet to her mother, whom she still assumes sent it on to John Hales in Sydney. Her mother remembers receiving the assiduously completed sheets, but says, 'I don't think we ever had time to look at them.'[8]

'The time sheets were a real pig,' says another former member. 'We had to account for every minute of every day.'[9]

Late in 1965, the System came crashing down around the ears of the brash and ambitious brothers from Sydney. James Taylor Junior suddenly seemed to wake up to what was happening in the antipodes, and to listen to the disquiet of his flock about life under the Hales System. Particular concern was expressed at a series of meetings in October in Barbados. Taylor turned on his Sydney leaders and meted out the ultimate punishment: excommunication. John and W. Bruce were both 'withdrawn from' for the sin of setting up a rival to the assembly, and for bringing commerce into the meeting.

"The meanness – treating the brethren as if they were the dust. The devil was in that, to humiliate the brethren ... God does not forget how His people are treated,' Taylor told the faithful after the punishment in 1965.[10]

'It came from a system, a central system with a dictator at the head of it. Now it is out. We threw it out. No more of it! We will get back to the local assembly's direct relation with Christ.'

In typically lurid (if slightly opaque) language, Taylor even equated the instigators of the System with the rise of the 'man of sin', whom Brethren believe will attempt to rule the earth with the power of the devil:

> The man of sin is a natural man, and he will be a man of great powers; he will have tremendous influence of power over men. That is what the antichrist will be ... any pushing forward of natural ability in the assembly, is just what the man of sin is ... The brethren have been frightened through this thing. The fear was the fear of man.

Taylor also pointed out that people with comparatively few financial means were able to accomplish great things, officially cutting the link between wealth and Godliness that the Hales brothers had tried to establish.

In some areas, the System became known as the 'Australian influence'. In a letter written in January 1966, just months after the Hales's excommunication, James Symington (an American farmer and the man who was later to succeed Taylor as Man of God) called it an 'organization which was thrust upon us', saying, 'I see no benefit at all'.[11] In another letter the following month, Symington advised a Brethren member to send a bill to those who wasted his time with financial advice they did not ask for, and even to sue for damages.[12]

John Hales immediately set about trying to show repentance, to set things right, and to ensure his re-admittance to his faith. In the process, both he and brother W. Bruce sent contrite, handwritten letters, dated 18 November 1965, to Brian Deck, a brother in Motueka, New Zealand. John Hales's letter is the most revealing document about what life was like during the System days, and more so because it comes from the hand of the man who perpetrated it. It is worth quoting in full:

> I have sinned against you and your wife and household and the saints and the assembly in Motueka at the meetings in May. My course has not been in the Spirit but in the flesh and there has been much transgression, but the things that weigh on me are these.
>
> The way in which the status and exercises of the assembly in Motueka were set aside and not given any place to. Much that was offensive in speaking and unbecoming was allowed in the meetings. I think in particular of the way I spoke to one brother concerning his contribution to the special collection. This was wholly anti-Christian and grievously injurious to the brother.
>
> There were references to two other brothers concerning their private income, one for being small and one for being large. Besides a direct transgression against the brothers, it brought in the spirit of the world and commerce and worldly advantage and the ridiculing of a saint of God.
>
> I am ashamed of the way I spoke to your wife at the family table. I was expressing my judgment which I now see to have derived from the flesh and not of the Spirit. I'd transgressed most grievously.
>
> I transgressed against you too in having part in commercial meetings in your house at the time of the meetings. It is clear too that the interference in your business matters was a transgression on my part. I am appalled as I think of the kind of things I have allowed in the assembly and among the saints in contrast to the spirit of the men who have laboured and lived among you and live yet.
>
> I am horrified at the dishonour to the Lord and to His assembly as the kind of alien spiritual conduct this has been so active in the holy things of God. I am grieved at the pain and suffering I have

inflicted on the saints. I am under discipline for my course but I desire to convey something to you to put right in some way the awful wrong I have done.

About a year later, John Hales was restored to the Brethren. But the fall of W. Bruce was harder; his time in exile, longer. The man who had once been at the epicentre of the group and the great Australian hope for world domination, was, by 1980, driving a taxi in Sydney, his dreams of becoming the Man of God dashed.

Just over 21 years later, in 1987, brother John Hales was finally able to live the dream: he became the sect's supreme leader, the Man of God. But, during his 15 years as leader, neither he nor his brother made any overt attempt to reintroduce the System which had so damaged their first push for influence. There was one exception to this. One relic of his beliefs did survive, which Hales demonstrated when he began setting up the Brethren private-school system.

In modern times, Hales's son and successor as leader, Bruce D. Hales, spends considerable time and energy during his own preaching, working to clear his father's name of its various historical stains. But he has done much more than that – he has breathed new life into aspects of his father's mid-1960s project. And the schools have become the central feature of this new System.

There has been no move to introduce timesheets, nor any overt pressure for Brethren businessmen to provide financial details to any other member. But Hales has started training a new generation of Brethren accountants through the sect's own registered training organisations, and businesses are encouraged to use them, though it is not compulsory. And he has also reinvigorated the Business Seminars.

Starting in 2005, these seminars, like most of the business-oriented activity Hales initiated, had as one of their stated objectives to 'provide an additional source of funding for the school education program'.[13] They were the brainchild of Victorian leader John

Gadsden. Gadsden is the son of Alan, John Hales' right-hand man, and Bruce Hales brought him back to the Brethren after a long and financially successful stint out of fellowship.

The seminars were run by Melbourne-based company called Pro Vision Marketing, the trading name of the trustee for one of the Brethren education management trusts. Platforms were set up in the warehouses of Brethren businessmen, and a number of heavy hitters were seated above the throng of hundreds, or perhaps thousands, of devotees, who had paid $500 per head to hear the three-hour talk. Books were produced of transcripts of what was said, and participants were charged $150 for each.

One of these transcripts, of a series of seminars in Australia in early 2005, leaked out. It showed Hales unashamedly linking his seminar with the 1960s System. The 'mission statement' printed in the front of the transcript booklet says that the program 'follows the pattern set on by beloved Mr John S. Hales in the early 1960s when he provided helpful advice and direction to the Brethren in their business activities'.

The advice, according to the mission statement, would 'represent sound and proven business methods which do not rely on this world's system of shady practices and principles of compromise, and electronic networking'.

To avoid the charge that the seminars were a 'rival to the assembly', Hales borrowed the words of his father: 'We need to be able to filter everything we say in these seminars through the word of God.' The 'word' chosen to cover it was from Paul's letter to the Romans, in which the Romans were exhorted to help Phoebe because 'she also has been a helper of many, and of myself'. This help, they explain to the listeners, was not spiritual; Phoebe would have been 'a practical helper, and maybe in Paul's business, or the household area'. It was, in the Brethren style, rather a tortured analogy, suggesting Hales' seminar was helping his constituents in the same (biblically endorsed) way.

Hales's dead father was even present, in the form of a taped voice dug up from a seminar almost exactly 40 years earlier, before his excommunication, during which he was making some remarks about business organisation, sales, and marketing.

Hales made a number of references to his father during the 2005 seminars. At one point in a Hobart seminar in January, he said it was a 'good exercise in self-discipline' to measure your time: 'I know it was introduced fairly widely in the sixties ... I know some years ago ... I used to try and plan my day down to every half hour.'

He also referred his father's approach to ethical business.

' "Firstly, integrity with the government departments",' Hales quoted his father, referring specifically to the tax department:

Integrity was the first point, purpose, and principle of your business. Secondly was, 'Do the best you can for your client'. Thirdly was, 'If we make some money on the way through, then that is incidental'. Well, I have admitted from time to time that I occasionally might have put [number] three up to one. I wouldn't admit anything further than that.

In fact, Hales explicitly regards integrity in dealing with the tax department as a matter of individual conscience. In one of the periodic documents that the Brethren release to explain and justify themselves, they posed a frequently asked question: 'If someone is gifted funds regularly and it becomes their main income, isn't this taxable income?' The answer is: 'Individuals' taxation matters are their responsibility. It is their responsibility to seek their own independent professional taxation advice and to abide by it.'[14]

In fact, the chief beneficiary of tax-free gifts as income is the world leader of the Brethren at any time, who earns a significant, and unquantifiable, amount of income from the white envelopes stuffed with cash that are donated at meetings around the world and brought to him by the travelling faithful. Wherever he goes to preach, cash gifts are also left on his seat in the assembly hall, in appreciation of the 'exercise' of guiding the flock.

Tax payments on these gifts is a sensitive issue in the Brethren. In 1977, the then Man of God, Jim Symington, faced an investigation from the feared US tax investigator, the Internal Revenue Service, over the millions he received in this way and partly spent on prime North Dakota farmland. Rather than stopping the payments, or paying tax on them, he advised his flock to vary the amounts they gave him, and their frequency, to suggest that they were gifts, and not payments for services. In a letter to the local leaders of the flock in 1977, he also suggested that, 'If one of the brethren from your locality is approached by the IRS in this matter, it would be wise to seek counsel before any questions are answered'.[15]

At Bruce Hales' Business Seminars of 2005, for the most part, the proceedings were entirely devoid of religious commentary. They provided plain-spoken advice on efficient business practice – how to measure gross profit, how to treat sales staff, how to most effectively market Brethren businesses when modern technology, barcodes, and access to the Yellow Pages was banned. Hales came across in the transcripts as an arrogant, business-savvy, occasionally funny, occasionally self-deprecatory character.

As an aside, telemarketing, the scourge of dinnertime with the family, is something that the Brethren have enthusiastically adopted since Bruce Hales's brother, Daniel, spruiked its merits during the 2005 Business Seminars. In the United States, the central school charitable fund appears to offer this service to its companies centrally, but in Australia it is still more ad hoc. Girls occupying their time between school and procreation are encouraged to become telemarketers, as are 'widows for the truth' – those in single limbo because of a husband who has left the sect. Daniel Hales called telemarketing a 'secret weapon for the Brethren' and suggested that nobody minded getting a call.

'They like people calling them – nobody minds being telemarketed', Daniel Hales told the faithful in Sydney in February 2005. 'I put on a sister who was afraid, and hadn't even answered a phone in the 50 years of her life. Now she makes about 10,000 calls a year and loves it.'

In the seminars, Hales also addressed the 'weaknesses' which, in 2005, were hurting Brethren businesses – their inability to advertise, or to use computers and mobile phones. At that time, Hales was still strongly preaching in his religious ministry that such equipment was defiling, a 'tool of the devil', an 'instrument of hell', and a fast track to excommunication, as well as a 'the greatest tool of disorganisation' that a business could ever encounter. So Gadsden told those assembled for a business seminar in Wagga in February 2005 that these handicaps were no more than 'perceived weaknesses', and they could be turned into strengths by clever, and morally upright, business practice.

But just six months later, by July 2005, it had become clear that business realities had overcome any of these religious scruples. Brethren businesses were already resorting to increasingly creative tactics to get around the church's ban. Some were housing computers and fax machines in the nearby offices of 'worldly' people, or borrowing their equipment. Others employed worldly people to perform the devilish functions for them. Brethren schools were massive owners and leasers of fax machines, which they would rent out, at above commercial rates, to local Exclusive Brethren businesses.

Another common way around the problem was for Brethren businessmen to lease a computer from a 'worldly' company. This indicated that they were interpreting the ban on computers as preventing them from *owning* the object, but not necessarily from *using* one they had leased.

For a rigidly controlling, financially jealous sect, this was untenable. Brethren funds were being paid at commercial rates to outsiders, and Brethren were exposing themselves, however vicariously, to access to the internet (the 'pipeline of filth'). Why should a Brethren company not do the leasing and, in the meantime, sanitise the computers and remove all potential for offensiveness from them? All it required was a little bit of movement on the part of the Lord.

In July 2005, just months after Hales and Gadsden were telling the Brethren that their business 'weaknesses' were actually strengths, the top Brethren, including Hales, sent a signed letter, with the word 'Confidential' stamped in bold across it, to businesses around the Brethren world. The letter announced that sect leaders themselves were setting up a new company, National Office Assist, to ease their flock into the worldly business of new technology:

> It has become increasingly apparent in recent times that there is the need for a quality and reliable accounting and bookkeeping service for many Brethren's businesses.
>
> National Office Assist will provide this service enabling Brethren's businesses to operate in a more efficient manner without needing to depend on worldly contractors for the outsourcing of their requirements.

The company would provide computers, training, and employment for 'some of our brethren ... without the need of owning computers or directly employing persons to operate computers' and 'without reliance on unsatisfactory worldly sub-contract services'.

National Office Assist would even offer other administrative services, including bookkeeping and accounting. Perhaps realising the reaction this might provoke among those who remembered with fear his father's System, Hales assured the flock that, 'Written assurance will be provided to ensure that Brethren's business information will be kept completely confidential.'

All equipment, the letter insisted, would be owned by National

Office Assist, and 'no authority is given for individual businesses to purchase their own computer equipment'. In the event, all NOA computers are cut-down versions, called 'Wordex' machines, which are loaded with basic word-processing, spreadsheet, and accounting programs, as well as email, but provide no access to the worldwide web.

National Office Assist is a $1 company whose shares are fully owned by one of the senior Sydney Brethren, John Anderson, who owns a medical-supplies company and is part of Bruce Hales' coterie of loyalists. He is also the chief executive of the Sydney Brethren school, MET. National Office Assist is part of a wider range of companies that includes NOA Group Pty Ltd and NOA Tax Pty Ltd, all registered at the same address and with senior Brethren as directors.

When the existence of National Office Assist was originally revealed, it looked like a new way to link, and even control, every Brethren business from a central point, to keep details of individual businesses, or even to enrich certain powerful individuals. But former Brethren say this has not happened. The coercion here is a little more subtle but, in the context of the Brethren, very powerful indeed.

At the time of writing, no Brethren business was permitted to own its own computer or fax machine; all were leased from National Office Assist. Finally recognising that computers are a crucial business (and, for that matter, educational) tool, the Brethren have allowed them, but they are still considered sinful and defiling. This means that if a member of the Brethren defies the central edicts and owns a computer in his own right (including in his home), he runs the risk of being withdrawn from. This convenient fact has allowed the business brains in Hales' operation to compel hundreds of ordinary churchgoers from around the world to lease their computers from a single, monopolistic Brethren company, channelling all the profits through entities associated with Hales and his loyalists.

But, according to the original letter, the company is not geared to profit the leaders individually. It was introduced to the Brethren as a business entity that would 'help to provide for the future financial needs of the testimony including schooling and other requirements'.

The setting up of National Office Assist signalled the start of the revolution in Brethren financial affairs. Its financial accounts are not publicly available, but it has clearly been a resounding success. We can guess at this because the Brethren soon started to replicate the model across a vast array of products, from fuel to logistics.

In May 2005, a special meeting of the Victorian school organisation Glenvale Education Inc. was held at John Gadsden's business premises in Thomastown, an industrial suburb north of Melbourne. The entity's seven members present voted to include in its constitution an authorisation to trade. Similar meetings were held by school governing bodies in every state of Australia.

It was a crucial step in the development of a whole new raft of Brethren enterprises that were set up to provide financial security to schools and other unnamed good causes. These enterprises conduct businesses that pay no tax because all their profits are directed to the charity, or school fund, with which they are associated. They increasingly tie Brethren businesses together in what resembles a huge and growing loyalty scheme. Brethren elders in each locality seek special deals with worldly companies, on the basis of their purchasing power, to obtain discounts on goods and services they themselves cannot supply, such as telecommunications, cars and stationery. In return for their custom, the company agrees to pay a percentage of turnover to the charitable or school fund.

Alternatively, where they can, the Brethren set up their own businesses to cater exclusively to their own.

All Brethren mobile phones, and many home phones, for example, are purchased by the Brethren through worldly telecommunications provider GoTalk. GoTalk treats the Exclusive Brethren as a business customer, and gives a generous rebate to the schools. Brethren are also exhorted to use worldly business Corporate Express for all their stationery needs, because it has agreed to give 25 cents for each dollar spent to a Brethren entity, One Fund, which makes quarterly disbursements to schools. There has been talk of a similar bulk-purchase agreement being negotiated with one of the supermarket chains.

One Fund is at the centre of this web of new business operations. 'One Fund' is the trading name of the One Fund Trust. Its directors are senior Brethren insiders, including National Office Assist's John Anderson, and Mark Mackenzie, a Sydney-based pump salesman and Hales footsoldier who did sterling political service for him by setting up the controversial company Willmac, which channelled $370,000 in political advertising towards the Howard government at the 2004 election.

They oversee a company that is the central trading entity of an array of charities, companies, trusts, and trading names, all set up to harness the purchasing power of about 15,000 Brethren and their well-heeled businesses, and to divert the money back to their schools.

The marketing effort of One Fund plays on the fears of Brethren people, exhorting them to 'Trade with people you can trust'. Among its trading activities is the production of a quarterly colour magazine called *Inform Advertiser*, which is distributed to Brethren households worldwide, and which spruiks Brethren businesses to other Brethren. In the December 2007 edition, the word 'Brethren' is so rarely mentioned that it seems like deliberate avoidance. There are, however, several telltale signs that the sect produced it. Among these are the advertisements for a wide variety of headscarves, including silk, elastic, and even crocheted examples, as well as hair clips and bows for those eschewing the full head covering.

There are also rather more ads for long skirts than you would find in a worldly magazine. A washing trolley, designed by students of the Brethren's Westmount School in Hamilton New Zealand, is pitched to 'husbands, working kids, parents whose wife/mother/daughter needs their workload lightened'.

And in the vehicle sales section, almost every item is either a people-mover (for the typically large Brethren family), or a light-industrial vehicle. A nine-bedroom house in Condobolin is advertised for sale. A block of land in Leeton is also advertised as an 'urgent sale' because a 'young brother wants to get married, but can't live on a no-bedroom block of land ... In case you haven't realised, I am very keen to sell ...' A news clipping service is advertised as, 'The weekly ... summary of international and Australian news that you need in 15 minutes. Save time, and keep defiling papers out!'

Another One Fund initiative is a book called *Inform* that includes photographs and information about all Australian Exclusive Brethren school campuses and their students' achievements. Advertisements in *Inform* are touted as '100 per cent tax deductible'.

One Fund does not simply run its own fundraising activities, however. It also operates business under other trading names, including Onefuel, Onefleet, and Logistics One. All are based on the same idea as National Office Assist: they centralise purchasing among a well-heeled and compliant customer base, reap tax-free profits, and distribute them to the schools. These companies are linked to each other and to the Brethren through a complex series of trusts, trading names, state-registered business names, and companies – entities such as Eastern Education Management and Southern Education Management, Comet Bridge, and the National Assistance Fund.

Onefuel started in 2006, and its executives negotiated with oil company Caltex to give Brethren businesses and individuals access to the company's Starcard payment system for petrol and gas. Onefuel promises that customers pay pump price for fuel, but Caltex puts a proportion of that amount towards fundraising for Brethren schools.

Logistics One, set up in 2007, is a buying scheme using international freight-forwarding companies 1st Fleet and TNT Express. The more business the Brethren generate, the higher the rebate to their schools.

One Fleet is a buying group that has negotiated special deals with car companies for Brethren transport needs. Buying cheap people-movers through Onefleet generates an administration fee that 'has widespread benefits to our whole community and is not directed to any particular State', the paperwork says. So much buying power does One Fleet potentially wield that Mercedes Benz Australia offered to import a special-edition 'tried and proven, vastly more powerful, V6 diesel' version of one of their people-movers 'that has not previously been brought into Australia', if there were enough expressions of interest through the company.

The Brethren schools around the country, through the 'Trustee for the On Track Tyres Trust', also run a series of businesses importing Maxxis tyres from Thailand and selling them through wholesale outlets in different states of Australia known as Tyremax and Sprinter Tyres.

And all of the money earned is tax-free. In 2007, the Federal Court of Australia ruled that charities were allowed to run businesses to earn money, without paying any tax, as long as the charitable purpose was the only motive for making a profit. It was a decision that overturned an original ruling by the Australian Tax Office. One Fund is a charity that runs businesses and, from the profits of those businesses, makes quarterly distributions to schools.

By using these methods, the Brethren are trying to take a tax-free cut of every dollar spent by their devotees on goods and services. They have even set up their own, for-profit private health fund, 'onemedifund', in Australia – a big step for a sect that used to consider all insurance a slight against God's ability to look after His saints. The fund started taking members in February 2007 and, by 30 June, had 171 members and revenue of $21,000 – a small start to something that is clearly designed to grow into a fund for all Australian members of the sect. When they were setting it up, the Brethren applied to the government to have onemedifund registered as a 'closed' fund – available only to members of the flock – but they were knocked back by the health insurance regulator, PHIAC, because it did not meet the requirements for a closed fund under Australian anti-discrimination law. onemedifund, as a result, is required by law to accept anybody who applies as a member.

But, unlike most Australian health funds, onemedifund is run to make a profit. The profits (if and when they begin to flow) will, according to its corporate structure, flow to a company called Acghaf, fully owned by Kevin Dunlop, a Brethren accountant and personal friend of Bruce Hales, who lives in the picturesque New South Wales town of Bowral. Dunlop's name crops up as a director or trustee in many new Brethren business entities, as well as others at the heart of the Brethren empire, including the UK-based disseminator of the Man of God's teachings, the Bible and Gospel Trust. It is unclear if Dunlop gets to keep the onemedifund profits or what mechanism exists to make sure he distributes them to others.

All of these Brethren funds and businesses are advertised on the basis that they are a good financial deal, both financially for individuals and also for the wider Brethren community. But there is a hint of Brethren-style coercion, too. The men in charge of the Onefuel scheme make it clear that they know exactly who has not yet signed up. A July 2006 letter addressed to those who have not responded to an earlier letter states baldly that 'approximately 54 per cent of the potential customers nationally are currently participating ... we need a higher percentage of participators'.

Inform Advertiser tells Brethren readers that they don't 'have to' advertise, 'but remember that it's good to become known as a giver – even if your business won't gain from it'. These statements say to average Brethren members that their donations and participation are being watched, and that, whatever his financial success, a man must also be generous in giving to Brethren causes if he wants to be well-thought of.

This is much more covert than the overt approach of the John Hales 'System' of the 1960s, but it shares some of the same DNA. Like his father, Hales junior is clearly still taking an interest in the commercial affairs of a new generation of Brethren businesses, and in the amounts they donate to the church. And, according to 'Janie', who recently left the sect, when rank-and-file Brethren members use these companies for their basic business and personal needs, the opportunities for centralised surveillance are greater than ever.

'If you've got an EB mobile phone on a GoTalk bill, and if the boss has the bill, it's still not really your phone to use as you want. In some ways [the control] is worse. They know even more about you.'

Theoretically, Brethren leaders could also monitor what is being written in emails sent through National Office Assist-owned Wordex machines.

Australia's opaque companies and charities disclosure regime means that we know very little about the operations and success of these new Brethren businesses. But similar companies that exist in other countries where the Exclusive Brethren live are more open to scrutiny.

UK schools raise funds using the same business model as in Australia and the US. Unlike in Australia, though, the annual accounts of British charities are freely available, and these give important information about how the system works.

Since about 2003, the individual Brethren schools in Britain have been run by local communities through registered charitable trusts. But a central charity, called the Focus Learning Trust, oversees these trusts. It develops the curriculum, and distributes government and private funds to the schools. The trust also runs a large business. In the UK it is called Unifocus Limited, and this company provided more than £4 million income to Focus Learning Trust on turnover of more than £27 million in the 2005–06 financial year (the last accounts available at the time of writing). Unifocus's accounts, rather obliquely, say that the company's principal activity was 'the sale of goods for the purpose of raising funds for its parent charity, Focus Learning Trust'.[16] It also rents out fax machines and other office equipment to schools.

Interestingly, the Focus Learning Trust accounts also show a large amount of money flowing from the tax-free business and charitable income generated in the United Kingdom to places in the world where there are, presumably, less-friendly funding regimes for non-government schools in general, or Brethren schools in particular. The Focus Learning Trust accounts shows distributions of £260,000 to 'educational charities' in Sweden, Switzerland, the Caribbean, Germany, France, Italy, Denmark, and Argentina.

There was no need to distribute funds to Australia, because the government funding is so generous. In fact, a guess at just how much the Australian schools manage to generate in income (more of this in Chapter 8) suggests it is very likely that the Brethren down under are net contributors to schools in other countries, particularly the United States.

The Australian Brethren never boast about this. But a former American member of the Brethren, Don Monday, said he knew of three loans to schools in his locality from brothers in Australia – one loan came from Bruce Hales, and another from Australian school leader John Anderson:

> I would've thought that there was probably money coming in from other countries into the United States because in general the United States would've been one of the poor [ones], partially because of a lack of big business, but partially because of the small amount of Brethren in the States. There would have been need of support, I would think, from outside.[17]

If any of this money had been generated by the various Brethren loyalty schemes in Australia, sending it offshore is not something they would be likely to boast about. The Australian Brethren might be less enthusiastic about contributing if they know that some of their money is going to another country.

In the United States, the central school trust is called Sterling, and the business that raises funds for it is called Silver Bridge. Don Monday wrote in 2006 that Brethren companies were asked to lease their fax machines through Sterling, and that they were 'also "encouraged" to buy their office supplies, do their shipping, and buy their packaging supplies through Silver Bridge'.[18] Monday said the business model of having businesses use fax machines in the schools was part tax dodge and partly a way of funnelling large amounts of money into the schools. 'The company I worked for ... would have been charged $US650 a month for the use of the fax machine [and] we might have sent as many as five or six faxes a day.' Other companies hired the same machine at similar rates, he said. 'The man I specifically worked for said that it was a way that he could funnel money into the schools and get a tax credit for it.'[19]

Monday said that 'phone service, bookkeeping services, and telemarketing' were also offered as services by Sterling, and, by the time he left, mobile phones 'were being tried out in view of leasing them for business only'.

The accounts of the UK's Focus Learning Trust also point to an aspect of Exclusive Brethren financial life which, until now, has been difficult to quantify: the scale of interest-free loans from wealthy individuals to Brethren causes and individuals.

The Focus Learning Trust disclosed 'related party transactions' showing that seven of its trustees, directors of Unifocus, or their businesses made interest-free loans of £530,000 to the trust, in amounts ranging from £20,000 to £300,000, in one year. Almost all of the loans were for the purchase of property, and almost all were repaid from the earnings of the business within one 12-month period.

Well-off Brethren members are expected to contribute enormous sums to buy communal property such as schools and churches, or to leave those sums to the Brethren in their wills. But these figures also go a long way to explaining the secret of the success of Exclusive Brethren private companies and enterprises: the cost to individuals of raising money is effectively zero.

If a young 'worldly' person were to want to raise funds to buy a business, he or she would usually need to borrow from a bank at commercial interest rates. Even if the bank did agree to lend the money, it would usually not cover the full cost of the business or enterprise: the rest of the funds would need to come from other sources, either from savings built up over years, or equity investments, or loans from more than one lender.

In the Brethren, by contrast, money is lent, interest free, by relatives or other local leaders from their usually substantial cash reserves. A Brethren lender is capable of providing 100 per cent of the capital cost of a business. More often than not, the new business owner will have guaranteed customers and suppliers, too. The only catch is that Brethren don't like being either lenders or borrowers, and the pressure is on the young person to repay the loan quickly. This is much easier, of course, when the cost of capital is nil.

There is a catch, though, in lending money to churches and schools. In about 2003, Hales called special meetings of local flocks around the world and ordered local Brethren communities to sign over the titles of all the schools in every locality around the world to him, Bruce D. Hales, and whoever succeeded him as 'Minister of the Lord in the Recovery'. Previously, the school properties had been owned by the local trusts.

What this means is that, in the event that Hales or one of his successors is caught, as James Taylor Junior was, in an undeniable scandal, and the flock was to consider withdrawing from him, the church would be faced with the prospect of losing every asset it had communally bought and paid for. In effect, it makes Bruce D. Hales one of the biggest individual property-owners on the planet, with holdings estimated by one former Brethren member at $4 billion.

Although Hales gets no direct financial benefit from all this, it gives him tenure in a lucrative job that will last until his death or, as the Brethren see it, the imminent end of the world. Property is yet another of the binding forces in the Brethren.

In 2005, at around the time that these various Brethren business schemes were established, another plan emerged from Bruce Hales's Sydney headquarters that offered significant advantages to individual Brethren, and the possibility of much more money being made available for the schools. But it would require hundreds of Australian Exclusive Brethren-run businesses around the country to go through a radical restructuring. And it skated quite close to the law.

Until this time, Brethren businesses had mostly been run as family partnerships, owned by the husband and wife. But in 2004 Hales made a clever appointment. He lured corporate lawyer Phillip Wiseman away from his lucrative job as a partner in a national law firm, Blake Dawson Waldron, to work in Hales' Ermington headquarters for the Exclusive Brethren.

Wiseman is an expert in the law of trusts and, in 2002, before being hired by Hales, was candid about the fact that trusts can be an attractive way of structuring your affairs so that you pay the 30 per cent corporate tax-rate rather than the 48.5 per cent top individual rate: 'This gives many people 18.5 reasons to do something,' he said at the time.

Trusts can also distribute income to all members of a family (called income-splitting), which has the effect of reducing individual tax-burdens. Doing this has the happy benefit of increasing access, even for quite wealthy people, to welfare payments. Particularly favoured in the Brethren, where mothers often have many children, and do not work outside the home, is the Family Tax Benefit B, introduced by John Howard to support stay-at-home mums.

This is how it works. Trusts pay no tax as long as their profits are distributed in the same year they are earned; it is the beneficiaries who pay income tax on the money received. However, if a Brethren member makes the local school one of the beneficiaries of his family or trading trust, nobody pays tax on the money distributed to the school, because the school is a tax-free entity.

'It was unofficially pointed out that it was a good way to give more to the school without actually having less money left for yourself,' says one Brethren observer:[20]

> So, in a normal business, if your company has a profit of $100,000, after tax you might have, say, maybe $60,000 left. You need $30,000 to live on, and the other $30,000 goes to the school. But with a trust you can give $50,000 to the school without paying tax on it, then pay tax on the remaining $50,000 and have the $30,000 left that you live on. You don't lose a cent, but the school/charity gets an extra $20,000.

Of course, the loser of that $20,000 is the tax office.

When the beneficiaries of your trust are all the members of a family (and Exclusive Brethren families are large, with four or more children common), the tax burden falls further. A family with six adult children and two parents, for example, could split a profit of $100,000 eight ways, giving each a notional profit of $12,000, entitling them to pay no income tax whatsoever and to receive the maximum-available welfare payments, youth allowances, Family Tax benefits, and other Centrelink payments.

This provides the largest benefits for families with children who are over 18, because there are strict limits on how much a child under 18 can earn in income. Once a child has grown up, and is working for the family business, his or her salary, which is also paid from the family trust, is carefully calibrated to minimise tax and the salary cost to the company's books. The union will not complain because, under Brethren rules, union membership is prohibited.

But that is not the end of it. Under the old family partnership model, all of the profits of a business are taxed at individual marginal tax-rates of somewhere between 30 per cent and 45 per cent. Using sophisticated tax planning, succession planning, and retirement-income planning, the Brethren have been advised on how to cap their tax rate at 30 per cent, at most, for every cent they earn.

The strategy for the many wealthier members of the sect involves combining family trusts into family partnerships, and using companies, schools, churches, and individual family members as eligible recipients of taxable business profits. It also involves using self-managed family superannuation funds as the owners of the business land and buildings. The business then pays some of the profits, in the form of rent, into the superannuation fund, at a minimal tax rate of 15 per cent, to be withdrawn as the parents reach retirement age, potentially tax free.

All this allows very rich people to minimise tax, and also to claim social-security benefits.

Over the course of 2005 and 2006, the word went out to the Australian Brethren that if they wanted to increase their contributions to their schools while maintaining, or even improving, their own finances, they should seek immediate professional advice and restructure their businesses along these lines, introducing trusts into the equation. Dozens of businesses did so.

The structure allows a business with large profits to distribute property, profits, and beneficiaries around a large number of entities in order to cap their income-tax rate. The participants in this money-go-round can also renegotiate the terms of those relationships at any time to find the most tax-effective model, without triggering a capital-gains-tax liability. It is cutting-edge tax planning.

The Brethren might like to separate themselves from the world in all matters to avoid contamination but, when it comes to welfare, they have no problem taking money earned by other Australians and paid through the tax system. We would call it milking the taxpayer. As previously mentioned, they call it 'spoiling the Egyptians'. In the Bible, God gave the Israelites the spoils of Egypt as Moses led them out of slavery. The Brethren say it is a case of God diverting wealth from the wicked (worldly people who killed the Lord Jesus) to the righteous (the 'saints', or Exclusive Brethren). It gives a biblical gloss to a legal but morally questionable practice.

One former Brethren parent explains exactly how assiduous members of the sect were in his case in reaping welfare payments:

> They use the government for everything they possibly can. I've been dragged through the Child Support Agency, I've had Centrelink ring me to work out the exact date my child left my care. My wife was on child endowment [family tax benefits]. They get everything they possibly can.[21]

Another former Brethren member, Bruce Suggate, recalls what happened when his son was taken to the other side of the country in an attempt to keep him within the sect:

> He left on the Friday. On the Monday in my mailbox was a letter from Centrelink. I reckon they took him to Centrelink on the Wednesday before he left to get him to apply for the away-from-home rate of Youth Allowance.[22]

For the first few years of Bruce Hales's regime, members of the Exclusive Brethren were expected to attend numerous school fundraising nights each year and to give donations of tens of thousands of dollars from their after-tax income. But under his new system of family and trading trusts, the Brethren have been able to radically boost the tax-exempt funds flowing into the schools without the need for inefficient and time-consuming fundraisers.

Under the Australian government's model for funding private

schools, there is no disincentive at all for schools to raise millions of dollars; it does not affect their public funding. And the Brethren have carefully engineered the structure of their schools to enable them to harvest the most generous possible federal government grants. (For more about this, see Chapter 8.)

But there was one potential hitch in the Brethren trust-restructuring plan: the Australian Tax Office ruled in June 2005 that if a parent does a deal with a private school to give the school a large tax-free donation and, in return, the school makes an agreement that links the donation 'directly or indirectly' to a reduction in that person's fees, it is illegal. The tax office considers such an arrangement to have been set up specifically to avoid tax in return for the benefit of a private education.

The Brethren were concerned enough about this ruling to seek high-powered legal advice about whether their system constituted tax evasion, and whether the Tax Commissioner could challenge them on it. The lawyer who provided the advice considered the Brethren system to be in the clear because it was not a specific arrangement set up to benefit one particular child or family. It might benefit the sect as a whole through the almost entirely tax-free education of its children, but this was diffuse enough not to be considered an individual arrangement, the lawyer said.

What this means for Brethren parents generally is that the schools need to demand just $1800 to $2000 in after-tax income for fees – among the lowest for any private school in the country – with big concessions for large families and those few unable to afford the cost.

From the schools' point of view, the new funding arrangements are lucrative, but they are uneven across the country. Schools attended by the children of the city-based Brethren elite have much more access to capital than average.

So the Brethren have set up another entity, which has also been granted charitable status, called the National Assistance Fund. This entity takes and redistributes the money from richer schools and sends it to the rest. It is unclear how this fund dovetails with One Fund, and whether it sends the money to the Brethren in other countries who are struggling with less-generous government school-funding models – though we do know that the British equivalent entity does this.

The new business structures within the Brethren are complex, lucrative, and entirely legal. But how do they fit with the strictures of John Hales, who said that 'integrity (with the tax office) was the first point, purpose and principle of your business'?

Answering a frequently asked question on their website about members of the Brethren structuring their business as charities, or providing 'significant funds to the church through their own charitable trust' to avoid tax, the sect leaders say: 'Brethren are encouraged to conduct their affairs in a simple, law abiding and honest fashion. No tax havens are used and no tax evasion is condoned.'[23]

The arrangements put in place over recent years may not be illegal, but on no fair analysis could they be considered simple. The key beneficiaries of all this financial engineering, according to the documents available, are the Brethren schools – although Australia's patchy disclosure regime makes this impossible to verify.

The Brethren are able to set up such a funding structure because they have a unique ability to ensure the compliance and discretion of their members. Who but the wealthiest philanthropist in general society would donate so lavishly to schools? Who else would agree to restructure their business in order to benefit a school if there was not a direct, corresponding, individual reduction in fees?

This tight-knit community does what is expected of it and what is asked of it, which benefits its loyalists in a way that the general community cannot hope to match, and punishes those who fall out of the system in equal measure. In some ways, it is an example of how society could work if all of us were dealing with people 'you can trust'.

When it comes to charities generally, the Brethren use their existence as a church to claim tax-free status for as many activities as they can. For example, a charity helps fund the extensive overseas travel that all Brethren members undertake to attend regular worldwide meetings. The Hughes Travel Trust, which acts as the Brethren travel agent, is registered as a charity in the UK and in Australia.

British charities commission documents show that the UK operation (which also covers Europe), earned and spent more than £3.7 million, tax free, in 2005, mostly through its own business activities. The aims of this charity are said to be the 'relief of poverty and sickness and the advancement of religion amongst Christian believers known as the Brethren, and the provision of subsidised travel for those Brethren in necessitous circumstances'. It does this by seeking 'to obtain the most economic and acceptable fares from the proven air and surface carriers'. It would be interesting to find out if it also funds Bruce Hales's $3000–$5000 per hour expenses for the use of a private jet to fly to meetings.

The trustees of Brethren charities also rely on the increasingly rare practice of street preaching to justify their charitable status. 'Included in these objectives are attending open air preachings of the word of God,' they say, suggesting that this is of 'public benefit'.[24] However, while some Brethren, particularly older ones, continue to preach on the streets, the practice has all but stopped among younger Brethren in many localities.

The Brethren now realise that they are under increasing scrutiny by the media, and the general public is taking a greater interest in their unusual ways. They also now no longer have John Howard, their protector, as prime minister in Australia. They can be expected to be scrupulously careful that they do nothing illegal, even if they need the best legal advice that their ample funds can buy to ensure that they remain on the right side of the law. Through these schemes, the desire of Bruce Hales to both enrich his community and keep its children totally separate from the world are entwined. It is the modern version of the 1960s 'System' invented by his father.

The Exclusive Brethren's biblical hero is the apostle Paul. In John Nelson Darby's translation of his letter to the Philippians, Paul writes: 'Do all things without murmurings and reasonings, that ye may be harmless and simple, irreproachable children of God in the midst of a crooked and perverted generation among whom ye appear as lights in [the] world.'[25] It is worth asking the question of today's Exclusive Brethren: would Paul approve of the modern commercial 'System'?

CHAPTER FIVE

The Alderton Family

The ding-dong of the doorbell came at 5.30 one Saturday morning in February 1980, as unexpected as it was frightening. And, just like the knocks on the door that were happening in the totalitarian regimes of eastern Europe at the time, it presaged something terrible.

'I had the scarf on, my hair down my back, ready to go to the church,' recalls Alison Alderton, who is now a woman of 85, full of sorrow and regret. 'It was two brothers. They said: "Mr Symington has come into things at Bathurst. Bob's to be withdrawn from, Alison's to be shut up. Gavin and Grace are to leave home." Just like that. It was unbelievable.'[1]

In those few words, the world and family of Bob and Alison Alderton fell apart. Bob was the leader of the Exclusive Brethren community in Bathurst. He was a wealthy, well-respected businessman and elder, with five daughters and a son, who lived in the magnificent Bishop's Court house on the south of the town, under the gaze of Mount Panorama. He had devoted his life and his ambitions to making his way up the Brethren ladder into a position of authority. By 1980, in the service of the Brethren doctrine of separation, he and Alison had already ruthlessly cut off two daughters, who were out of the sect and out of touch with their parents.

Then, suddenly, on the whim of world leader James Symington, their other four children were to be lost to them. The two youngest children, Gavin and Grace, who were still living at home, were given an hour to pack. Alison was also looking after her own mother, Granny Stewart, who lived with them. But she, too, was forced to move out.

But the most heart-wrenching loss was their youngest child, Grace: 'You know, the baby at the end of a family is a tremendous thrill. She was a real gift from God to us, and she was a total joy to us. And she was only 15,' Alison says. 'I'm sure you can't understand how such a thing could happen.'

Alison was withdrawn from because she was married to Bob. For Bob, his sin had been to attend a meeting some 16 years earlier, in 1964, and ask a question. This was such an extraordinary episode in the capricious rule of American 'Big' Jim Symington, the Brethren's then world leader, that it almost defies belief.

Symington had travelled to Australia in 1964 at the behest of his predecessor as Man of God, James Taylor Junior, to preach at meetings in Brisbane. But those familiar with the internal politics of the time recall that the Australian leaders, John and W. Bruce Hales, were insulted at this turn of events: they believed that W. Bruce had God's nod to become the world leader when Taylor died. So the Hales brothers snubbed the Brisbane meeting and refused to show up, sending instead their most acerbic lieutenants, who gave the American a hard time.

Sixteen years later, in 1980, Symington was in full power, half-way through his 16-year reign, and his word was law. Clive McCorkell, a Queensland brother attempting to gain favour, agreed to go through the tapes of the otherwise long-forgotten meeting of 1964, and to identify all the speakers. McCorkell reported the names to Symington, who promptly excommunicated them all – 16 men. Bob Alderton was one of them.

It was just one act of cruelty among thousands, but its ramifications have echoed down the years, through generations of these families. This is the story of one of those families.

Alison Alderton lost four children that day: Christine, Gavin, Jeanette, and Grace all remain in the Brethren, and therefore will have nothing to do with their mother. Those four now have offspring of their own. Alison will die not knowing any of those 18 grandchildren, nor the great-grandchildren who she knows exist, but cannot name or count, who remain in the sect. Bob died in 1992, but he and Alison had time to become reacquainted with Priscilla and 'Sophie' (who does not wish her real name to be used), the two daughters who were out of the sect by 1980. But, to this day, Alison's relationships with those daughters remain difficult and fragile.

Old wounds and the absence of a large part of their family hangs over all of their lives. It makes their stories difficult for them to contemplate and relate, even now, decades later.

Before their excommunication, the Aldertons seemed like the perfect Brethren family. Bob had a highly successful business, manufacturing and exporting furniture. In March 1969 he was inspired by a teaching of James Taylor Junior at a three-day meeting in Sydney, when he encouraged ambitious young men from the city to spread their wings and set up their own new powerbases in country towns around New South Wales.

Bob moved to Bathurst. He bought the beautiful, historic former Anglican bishop's residence, and donated land and cash to convert the stables of the property into a 300-seat Brethren meeting hall. From his new rural powerbase, he began climbing the ladder 'universally', donating large amounts of money to the sect, and attending meetings around the world, where his charisma and intelligence were giving him some renown.

Alison, too, a Brethren 'blue blood', was totally committed to her husband's ambition. She came from a family of high achievers – intelligent people, surgeons, musicians, and even a lord mayor of Sydney – before her part of the clan moved into the exclusive branch of Brethrenism. Thwarted by the iron rules of the sect from having a career, she turned her talent into support for her husband's aspirations.

Alison made their house the focus of Brethren social life in the town. Her old recipe books have pencilled notes next to some dishes saying, 'Serves 42'. Her children were numerous, beautiful, and perfectly dressed, with garments often hand-made by Alison. She said she was determined to 'make them into little Brethren'.

But, within this apparent idyll, this Exclusive Brethren display home, lurked dangerous pressures and rifts. Getting ahead under the harsh Brethren regimes of the 1960s and 1980s meant tearing down your rivals while remaining irreproachably clean yourself. The pressure to conform was enormous, and fear, shame, and punishment dominated the Aldertons' family life. These powerful controlling emotions ruined any chance that mother and children would bond with each other – Alison was too intent on making her children fit the mould.

But as powerful as the control was among the Alderton family, it still could not suppress passion, doubt, and free will. Those ordinary emotions, in conflict with the Brethren's doctrine, split this family in two. It is not fair to talk in detail about the children of Alison and Bob who remain 'in' the sect, because I have not interviewed them, and cannot. Alison says they regard her, their mother, as 'a disgrace, a real disgrace to the family' because she has chosen to speak publicly about the pain of her life.

But Alison Alderton is too old to flinch from the past. She is petite and white-haired and, at first glance, tending towards frailty. But when she looks back on her life, her voice is unwavering, and she speaks with conviction: 'I think what they go on with is absolutely, grossly evil. And they do it in the name of Christ! ... This isn't Christianity. It's terrible to link the name of Christ with it.'

She has no more mercy for herself, and her dominating emotion is shame. She allowed herself to become the enforcer of the Brethren's doctrine in her own family, upon her own children:

> I wasn't a good mother to any of my children ... I just tried to make them into little Brethren. We were place-seeking, rotten ... as bad as the worst. Legal, hard, cold. There's nothing I can be proud of. I worked very hard, and it's been a lot of wind. I entertained, but it wasn't serving the Lord, it was serving a man, and a system, and to get a place for ourselves.

Bob and Alison were so desperate in their attempts to climb to a position of prominence that even ordinary feelings of family fealty and love were not permitted to stand in their way.

Sophie spent the first 40 years of her life struggling with her upbringing in the Brethren. 'It's part of who I am,' she says now, 'but I don't want to focus on it. Now I'm in a really positive space in my life ... Every time I go back to thinking about the Brethren, it's just incredible pain, and anger.'[2]

The second eldest of the Alderton girls, Sophie, was passionate and tempestuous, but yearned for her parents' love and approval. She tried devoutness in an attempt to capture their attention. She took notes in church, memorised chapters of the Bible, and read Brethren ministry. She made a book of quotes of the great leaders to impress her parents. During the System days (see Chapter 4), she assiduously filled in her time book to prove her worthiness.

But now, when she looks back on life in the Exclusive Brethren, she sees an accumulating series of humiliations and hardship, the steady removal of joy from her life. When she was a young child, in 1960, a new rule was instituted that all books except the Bible were to be banned. A rare joy for the children of the Alderton household was the collection of children's picture books. But Brethren edicts demand instant responses, so the family burned them.

'It was when I was seven, and I remember we had a bonfire ...

we had to take all our beloved books out and set a match to them in the backyard,' Sophie said.

In this atmosphere, normal feelings such as grief were seen as dangerously subversive. In 1962, Alison was more than seven months pregnant, and Sophie, then aged 10 and starved of other softness in her life, was desperate for the baby to be born so she could hold it, coddle it, mother it. But the baby died in the womb, strangled by the umbilical cord. On the day she felt the baby stop kicking, Alison had dinner guests to prepare for, but she kept cooking and setting up. She organised for another Brethren family to help serve the dinner and, when Bob got home from work and the baby still had not kicked, they went into Crown Street hospital in Sydney. There it was confirmed that the baby was dead.

When Bob and Alison returned and announced this to the assembled family and guests, Sophie threw herself to the floor, bursting into tears, devastated by the loss. To Bob and Alison, she was questioning God's will.

> I was told to go immediately, not to my room, but to this other room, this dark, furnished area, and pray for forgiveness for questioning God. And I was told, 'Maybe it's because of you this baby's died, because of this fit, this immediate manifestation of the devil'; and I was told, 'Don't come out until you will never cry again about it. You were absolutely wrong to cry'.
>
> And I remember going to this room and it was night and the light was off and I was put in there. And I was trying to stop crying because crying was so evil, but I couldn't stop myself, and I was completely torn. And then thinking, well, maybe I *have* caused it to die. Because I can't stop crying. And I was trying to stop myself. Eventually I calmed down and didn't dare cry any more.

When the next baby, Grace, arrived two years later, she became the child that Sophie wanted to mother. Sophie held her constantly and taught her to read, well before she went to school, by reading the only books they were allowed: the Bible and the Brethren hymn book: 'She was so powerful for me,' Sophie said.

Sophie tried desperately to do what was expected of her. But in 1969, when she was 16, she slipped up when she was on a trip staying with cousins in Tasmania. In the adolescent belief that she was passionately in love with a particular Brethren boy, she climbed out of the bedroom window and went to him. They kissed and, she recalls, indulged in a little innocent fondling.

Back at home, she wanted to write to this boy, but knew she could not do so under the gaze of her parents, who checked their daughters' mail. So she booked herself a post office box. When the letter confirming the booking was sent from the post office to her parents' house, they opened it and read it, and became convinced that something 'wicked' was afoot.

'My father, who had never once picked me up from school in my life, turned up at the tech, dragged me out, and he was just so grave, I thought mum must have died or something,' Sophie recalls. She had no idea how they had found out what she had done, and sincerely believed it had been revealed to them by the harsh God she so feared. By the time she and her father arrived home, she had confessed her 'sins'. Waiting for her there was another 'priest', ready to continue the inquisition.

'I was taken under the house to a dark kind of a room with no windows, and these priests interrogated me: "Did he put his hand here? Did he do that? Did he do this?" A whole lot of things I hadn't even realised people did, because I was pretty innocent.'

That night, her father flew to Hobart – a big deal in 1969 – and joined the Tasmanian priests to give the young man a similar grilling, checking for lies, variations in the story. Sophie says she was 'shut up' for 10 long days. Sophie was initially locked in the billiards room under the house with no visitors except the 'priests', who came regularly to check her repentance and to go over the lurid details once again. She was later moved to the 'sunroom', which was also slightly removed from the main house. Food was left outside her door and she was escorted to the toilet three times a day, past a line-up of her horrified sisters, watching from a distance.

Sophie vividly recalls the terror of those days:

> The priests kept saying I haven't been granted the gift of repentance. And I was just pacing up and down and literally beating my breast, believing I was going to hell, which is what we were always told. And I really thought that God had revealed to them that I had committed this sin. And these men were licking their lips at this young girl. You know, 'Did he put his finger here?' – just disgusting, really. And my father was there. He was one of them. And my mother didn't even speak to me.
>
> I genuinely believed I was going to hell. You go to the meeting every night and it's all about the fire and brimstone of hell and the gnashing of teeth. You know, all this vivid imagery of hell, and I just felt that there was absolutely no hope: 'That's all I've got to look forward to unless God can grant me the gift of repentance'.
>
> And these priests kept saying that God had chosen not to grant me repentance, and it's a gift and he chooses it, and he hasn't given it to me. And I guess I was in just complete terror, like, psychological ... I just felt absolute terror. And I really believed it. It was so, so abusive. And I had no other frame of reference.
>
> I said to my mother only recently, 'What did you think when I was locked up? Did you worry about how I was?' Because I was really feeling suicidal – that was the first time in my life, certainly not the last ... And I said, 'Did you think about me, and how I was feeling?'

Alison says that, at the time, she was thinking only of herself and how her daughter's behaviour would damage their position:

I only knew what I heard from Bob, and I just thought she was a licentious, bad little girl. But I never spoke to her about it, and I went along with what was being done ... She was a girl who fell into a mistake and needed her mother to guide her. And I completely failed her. She needed her mother's love and support, and I failed her.

Priscilla, Sophie's younger sister, remembers the feeling in the house at the time:

I was disgusted. They were perves, all those Brethren men ... My feeling is the energy more than anything else; this dark, dark energy, and my sister's devastation. She was devastated. The tears! She was desperate. Absolutely desperate.³

Priscilla assumed, wrongly, that the young couple had had sex: 'Of course! You couldn't make that much fuss and just have snogged, for God's sake!

Eventually, Sophie was forgiven and returned to the society of the Brethren, but not before they had canvassed two other options: that she marry the boy she hardly knew; or that she be withdrawn from, 'leaving me out on the streets and going to hell'. But the forgiveness they gave was not real: in the eyes of her family and fellow Brethren, the incident left her 'stained by sin':

It labelled me – the way I saw myself, the way the priests treated me, the way the family shunned me – it was something we couldn't mention, it was so shameful. We just never talked about it. But when I married the following year, my father said to my future husband, she's a nice-enough girl, but never trust her.

Priscilla, 'Sophie's' younger sister, was the third eldest of the Alderton girls, and was always different from the others. She never showed any signs of compliance. She rebelled. She did not bond with her mother as a child and, 50 years later, their relationship remains tricky, 'needing care and vigilance', Priscilla said, though both are making stout attempts to repair it.

Priscilla is short and muscular, curly haired, broad shouldered, strong: 'Physically, I take after my father,' she says, as she asserts her physical presence in the room, subdues her two energetic Labradors, and curls her legs under her on the couch, ready to confront her history.

At the age of five, Priscilla realised that her experience of God was quite different from that of her parents. As she grew up, these spiritual feelings found a mentor in a 'worldly' man, her parents' gardener, Mr Cam:

> His idea of God was not to tread on ants, and to respect nature and to understand nature. I used to walk around with him the way my dogs follow me. And he'd show me things and teach me things about nature and animals. My mother had a large, blue willow mug for him that she kept for him alone, she never touched it, and neither did we, except to wash it and put it away, slightly apart from the other cups. There was a sense that you didn't touch anything that he touched. It was very strong.

Priscilla is a talented musician. Teaching music is her profession and, as a child, the piano was the centre of her private world. Her sense of God was associated with music, and freedom, 'and very much to do with me singing'. She recalled standing on the 20-metre verandah of the family home and feeling she could float ecstatically away. What her family called God when they went to church had nothing to do with this.

'So I sat back and thought, possibly from the age of eight, that the Brethren were bad for my mind,' she said.

Three years later, by the age of 11, she had made the decision that she would leave the sect. A strong part of this realisation was a fantasy that she would have a baby. She could imagine this baby – a girl – in her future life, and nothing was more real to her. There was no father. They would be poor. Their life would be tragic and heroic. And this baby was most definitely not going to be brought up in the Exclusive Brethren.

'I think that she was some aspect of my consciousness that I was going to bring up. I think she represented hope, which I was going to look after and nurture and mother. She was going to be *so* mothered, because I wasn't mothered the way I imagined mothering.'

The fantasy baby, as well as music, acted as talismans against the intrusions of the Brethren into Priscilla's inner life. When she needed to escape the tedium and physical discomfort of hours spent in church, she would retreat into her inner world and work out a song, or make up musical compositions until the intervals, harmonies, and voicing were just as she wanted them, then commit them to memory and play them, note perfect, when she made it home.

Throughout her adolescence, as she remained firm in her certainty that she would escape, Priscilla lied. In order to seem to meet the expectations of her family and her sect, she was forced constantly to pretend.

'I led a completely double life. It saved hours of family arguments to simply not tell my parents what I was doing. But I had to remember things all the time. I had to remember not to say things ... I felt anxious the whole time ... it's just that they couldn't stop me from being myself.'

But they tried. She recalls as a younger child the regular 'torture' of being locked up in a darkened room for what seemed to her like hours in the evenings, hiding behind couches 'waiting for Dad to come home to smack me'. The infractions were simply that she was being herself, Priscilla said, or disobedience of some edict or other. As a teenager, her sins became more mature – seeing her boyfriend, going to the movies, or being spotted by some 'goody two-shoes spy' being friendly with a 'worldly'.

'And my father would come home and he'd go crazy. He'd shut the bedroom door and I'd be in their bedroom and he'd interrogate me and quote the Bible to me. And he'd send himself crazy, most likely because I was not forthcoming with information or repentance.'

Despite the punishments, Priscilla said she adored her father, and was constantly trying to get close to him. She felt that the strictures of the Brethren were always standing in the way. But she loved travelling with him to the country, saying his 'country self was very different to his city, and Brethren self ... he seemed to relax and be more "normal" then'.

Back at home, Priscilla recalls making such a fuss about being punished one day while Bob was overseas on a three-month business trip, that Alison offered her an option: she could have one of her sisters take the punishment in her stead. Priscilla accepted the offer, and Christine, the eldest and most compliant of the sisters, was 'thoroughly slapped' in front of the family for Priscilla's transgressions. 'Such an image,' says Priscilla, haunted by it.

Priscilla's will, though, made it much harder for the Brethren to persecute her. She, like Sophie, had kissed a boy – a Brethren boyfriend, whom she started seeing when she was fourteen. Her parents knew about her liaisons because they had deputised a girl from another Brethren family to follow her and spy on the couple – a trick the Brethren sometimes use against those who appear to be moving beyond the limits of their control.

As a result of these investigations, Priscilla faced grillings in the family car from Bob – occasionally being asked whether her boyfriend had 'touched a breast, undone a button'. It was 'vile' said Priscilla; but, unlike Sophie, her older sister, she was never dragged into a darkened downstairs room, locked up, and interrogated for it. 'There was something about me that wasn't as vulnerable to that kind of behaviour because I wasn't trying to be good, and so I wasn't in conflict over my behaviour,' she said.

Priscilla remembers being constantly exhausted during her adolescence, not concentrating at school and nearly falling asleep because of the hours spent travelling to and from the night-time meetings, sometimes until 1.00 am. She recalls being pulled out of school to attend funerals on Wednesdays: 'funerals of people I only knew to look at, and whose dead bodies I was made to look at'.

But what she remembers most is tension – unbearable, relentless tension, particularly generated by Alison. It remains, she says, 'the thing I am most allergic to'. She recalls seeing her boyfriend in the regular large meetings in the Sydney suburb of Ashfield, 'and my mother would do everything she could to stop me looking at him; she would try to glare at him too, to stop him looking at me'.

Priscilla gained access to her inner world through music. In her teens, she played 'heaps of Beethoven sonatas' because they were 'great carriers of anger, full of *sturm und drang*'. But her father, feeling the music was 'idolatrous', used to physically drag her away from the piano, to 'deny ... my access to my private world'.

When Priscilla was entered into a local eisteddfod, Bob forced her to pull out by threatening to 'come and preach the word of the Lord on the stage. My father was embarrassing enough; he quite possibly would have done it,' she said. 'They wanted to break me; it was their whole aim. My mother used this expression all the time. It was so that I would come to know the Lord and depend on the Lord; and for me the most terrifying thing was to ever give them the power to break me.'

Some of these incidents are attributable to the Brethren's attitude to life, some to poor parenting, and some simply to the parenting styles of the time. But another incident was pure Brethren. When Priscilla was about 15, she found herself unable to reconcile herself to a new ruling that hats worn by the women must be replaced by scarves. As a result of this rebellion, one of the sect's few dentists (who later fell into serious disrepute professionally) gave her Valium – the drug of choice in those days for Brethren failing to cope.

'It's not that I was attached to hats in any way, shape or form, but I just couldn't believe that you had to "click" make a change, just because someone suddenly decided. I think the millinery was getting too eye-catching,' Priscilla said. She held out long after the scarf ruling, refusing to change, and insisting on wearing a hat.

Five months after her 17th birthday, in 1971, Priscilla left the sect. She moved in with a married ex-Brethren relative, but he tried to sexually assault her. Then she found a flat with two women who turned out to be psychiatric patients, before she moved in with the family of a school friend. There she continued the studies the Brethren had made her stop. Of this family, she said they 'brought me up, taught me about how the real world works, treated me like their own child, trained me in the many things of which I was ignorant'.

Priscilla said that her immediate response to being out of the Brethren was to tell the truth: 'Saying things straight was my way of feeling free of the Brethren, and the need to lie.' But her escape was not complete. Several times she was followed and found by the Brethren 'priests'. Three times they started off trying to talk her into returning, and ended up making overt attempts to sexually accost her. Another ex-Brethren man later spiked her drink and did rape her, she said.

'I'm sure I was a young, spunky girl in the Brethren who was protected by the family and then, all of a sudden I wasn't. It's that simple.'

But, after five months out, Priscilla had one burning regret: she had not managed to say goodbye to her two little sisters, Jeanette and Grace: 'I felt incomplete.' So she went back. Immediately on her return, she was led into the servants' quarters and 'shut up', with a sheet hung across the hallway to separate her from the rest of the house. She got the full treatment: 'The grilling and the curtain and everything. It was just revolting. Talk about alienating – it's hard to describe how it is to be treated in the same house as if you're untouchable.'

A roster of senior brothers came to talk to her all day to extract her confessions, with a particular emphasis on her sexual behaviour during her period 'out'. 'It was gross, and foul in the extreme,' Priscilla said.

When, eventually, Priscilla said enough for them to let her back into the house, she rejoined her sisters. 'I remember doing my little sisters' hair and talking to them and just crying and crying and crying and telling them that I loved them and I would love them for the rest of my life, that I would always love them, and it had nothing to do with them that I left. And the next day I left again.'

Priscilla's final departure shocked the family. One of the sisters described it much later, in a rare moment of amnesty, as the worst day of her life. For her part, Alison could not believe that one of her daughters would do something so shaming as to leave.

'I used to look at other people who'd lost a child and think what failures they were. And then it happened to me,' Alison said. She moved immediately to cut Priscilla off. Within three years of leaving, Priscilla had married a man who shared the painful experience of growing up in the Brethren. At 20 she was pregnant with her long-anticipated daughter, and suffering complications:

I'd ring up my mother and say, 'I've been told by the doctors to ask you is there high blood pressure in the family', and Alison would say, 'You must get right with the Lord'.[4] And I used to ring and beg and plead for all sorts of things, and often for money too, and they would say, 'You would be better off with the Lord than away from his people.'

They withdrew from me so completely that it was as if I was dead. Even these days, when I ring my mum she says things like, 'Oh, you've come back to life' or 'You've surfaced!', and often sounds surprised to hear from me, even if it's a week since I last rang.

Bob and Alison did give her some money, including a car, and $15,000 to buy her out of their will, Priscilla said. But there was no comfort, nor contact, nor love. Somehow, though, she survived those tough years. And 37 years later, she has only one regret: that she had lied about her intentions throughout her youth, and hid who she really was.

'My main regret is not leaving, but not being much more outrageous,' she said, waving her arms dramatically. 'I should have just been myself, completely myself, and let them deal with it ... Every soul who is a soul has the right to thrive and exist as a soul. I'm not a bad person and if I'd just been myself it would have created complete pandemonium. If I'd done it without hiding it, it would have changed everything.'

Sophie, the sister who had spent her childhood trying to find love and acceptance by following Brethren teachings, found herself on the wrong side of Brethren law three years later than Priscilla, for entirely different reasons. She was 22, married, and living in the country in the centre of New South Wales. Her husband was as young as she was, and, an orphan, just as damaged. They had two sons: a two-and-a-half-year-old and a seven-month-old baby.

Desperate and emotionally stunted, Sophie had an affair, for a week, with another Brethren man. Overcome by remorse, she confessed it during the same week. Both were excommunicated, and her husband was 'shut up' for being married to an adulterer.

'So here's my husband, who'd lost both his parents by the age of 12, and he was shut up because he was married to me. There was no compassion for him. Imagine the trauma for him,' Sophie said.

Despite the affair, Sophie and her husband made an attempt to stay together, but the shame and anger was unbearable, and there was no such thing as counselling, 'only judgment'. Their younger child, who was very disturbed by the family trauma, screamed constantly.

'We were fighting the whole time and screaming, and the whole house was just the kids screaming, me crying,' Sophie said. The marriage eventually broke down irrevocably, and she temporarily lost access to her children:

> When all this was happening, and I had no car and no phone, I walked to a public phone and I rang my parents and they said it was God's judgment, and hung up. I just felt that they actually wanted me to die because it would have rid them of the shame. And I just walked home and took a whole lot of Valium and drank sherry. And this went on for weeks.
>
> I went to the chemist and said I needed to buy strychnine. They said, 'What for?' I said, 'To kill rats on the farm'. They said I needed to get a permit from the Pastures Protection Board and then come back and they'd supply it. Well, if they'd handed it over then, I would have taken it. I had no emotional resources within myself. I had nothing, really, not one connection in the whole world, in the Brethren or without, I didn't know anyone.

The one exception was her sister Priscilla. They had made some tentative contact while Sophie was still in the Brethren; when Sophie was withdrawn from, the pair again looked to each other, although each was struggling with her own demons in her own way. In those hard years, it was some family connection at least.

Sophie's husband stayed out of the sect. Eventually, they reached an accommodation over access to her sons, but she was only able to bring up one of them:

> My boys grew up apart from each other. They knew they had grandparents, aunties and an uncle, because we had photos of them as children. But they had no idea where they were. They

didn't know how many cousins they had. There was no sense of connection to family. We felt very alone. And to me that's my biggest regret. It really affects the next generation.[5]

For eight years after she was withdrawn from, Sophie tried to contact her parents, 'but they'd just slam the phone down':

> Or I'd send them letters and they'd return them to sender, they wouldn't even open them. And I'd visit them occasionally to see if they were still alive, and they would slam the door in my face. If it was school holidays and the children were with me, they'd sit in the car shaking, because they were terrified of their grandparents, and I'd be crying.

Alison remembers this period well, as both girls who were 'out' tried to contact her: 'We'd just say, "We can't talk to you". I feel absolutely ashamed about that. It's so wicked. It makes you cold and hard and godless.'

A few years later, though, in 1980, the wheel turned, and Bob and Alison themselves found out what it was like on the wrong side of the Brethren's iron rules – out of fellowship, and lost to their four children who were still 'in'. After the axe fell, Bob and Alison resolved to work to comply with the punishment and to try to get back in. According to Alison, they accepted that 'God's got something to say to us'.

'Well, I didn't doubt that. I really was a Christian in my heart and I didn't doubt that our carryings-on weren't right ... I thought I was wrong. I knew we were wrong.'

In fact, despite being so thoroughly brainwashed by this sect, Alison had, long before she came under assembly discipline, harboured nagging doubts about some of the things she had seen happening around her.

'Lots of times terrible things happened in the Brethren. People were put out quite unrighteously, unjustly, unfairly, and I used to give Bob a hard time in bed: "How can we be right? How can this be right?"'

Even earlier than this, between 1960 and 1966, she said she had been 'secretly in deep depression' and had fantasised about leaving her home, or dying:

> And even Bob didn't know this; he was taken up with Brethren, he wasn't conscious of my side of it. But I was almost suicidal. I did want to clear out from home; I did want to get away from it all. I had dreams that perhaps I could be withdrawn from and live in the garage and just come up and look after the children. But then I thought of committing suicide in different ways, and I thought of clearing out and living in a country town and taking on a new name.

But she suppressed these feelings and carried on performing the tasks of the implacable domestic force behind the ambitious man – until they themselves were cut out of fellowship. As nothing like the emergence of the Brisbane tapes had ever happened in the Brethren before, Bob confidently predicted they would be back in fellowship in two weeks. Alison's punishment was to be 'shut up' – nominally still inside the sect, though unable to participate in worship, to socialise, or to see anyone to speak to, except for 'priests'. Bob was excommunicated. The peculiarities of this punishment meant that they were forced to stay separate from each other and their family, so that Bob did not contaminate her chances of being restored to the assembly.

Bob was dispatched to a room downstairs in their three-storey house. Alison continued to keep house, cooking for him and delivering his dinner on a tray. They would speak occasionally over business necessities, but they did not share a bed or a table. He would communicate with her by writing little notes – 'Thank you very much, very nice' – left on the meal tray. Alison collected these notes and mounted them in a school exercise book. She also began to keep a diary of her feelings.

The priests would visit sporadically, but the good news of their reinstatement did not come, and still did not come. The months passed. Since their house was next to the church (built on land they had donated), Alison could watch from her window as her beloved Gavin and Grace walked to the daily services. She could see them, separated from them by glass and dogma, but was not allowed to have anything to do with them.

Alison cannot cry any more about these events. She wants to, but the tears do not come. When her children were first taken from her, though, it was different: 'I used to cry and cry about Grace. Yes, I used to cry. It used to physically hurt me. Really, tore my heart, physically. Gavin and the others too, but Grace, she was still the child in the nest.'

(Grace has since written a letter to Alison – the only letter she has ever written to her – in which she insists it was wrong of her mother to view events this way: 'I wasn't stolen from you. You and Dad sent me with your blessing to be with the Brethren,' she wrote.[6])

Alison and Bob realised that, for her to have a chance to 'get back', he would need to move out of the family home. So he bought a new house and, after making them wait, Symington gave his permission for Bob to move and Alison to be 'released', as long as they signed a separation agreement, prepared by the Brethren.

The end of Alison's torment was near. It was to come at the administrative meeting of the Brethren on a Tuesday night – called, ironically, the 'care meeting'. One of the local priests, Mr S, said that she should come to his family's house to eat that night before the meeting. She did. The meeting took place, and Alison was restored to fellowship. That night, Gavin and Grace, tearfully, came home to her. But still it was not over:

A young man in Bathurst, wanting to climb up, rang Mr Symington and said, 'Mr S ate with her before she was released.'

So here was I; I had Gavin and Grace at home, they'd been home two-and-a-half weeks. And I was sitting at the table writing a letter, and I looked out the window, and here were two brothers coming – it was a different two brothers because Mr S was withdrawn from now – and they said, 'Mr Symington has come into some matters in Bathurst, and Alison's to be shut up again, and Gavin and Grace to leave home again.' Well, you couldn't believe what that was like.

The children left that day. Alison, on her own, without Bob or her children, felt like a 'leper, unclean, unfit for fellowship'. She had been shut up for 'not being handled properly'. So she waited and waited for the priests to come and handle her properly.

'But they didn't come and didn't come, and I nearly was out of my mind. Every sound I would think it might be the brothers coming,' she said:

> Well, I have post-traumatic amnesia, and I've still got it, because I don't know what happened. All I knew was that I woke up in one of the brothers' houses with an incredible headache. How I got there I don't know. They must have come and seen me after about three months, and, however they found me, they felt I was not fit to be left at home. So one of the brothers had taken me out of the house ... and that's always been a blank.
>
> Well, the Brethren looked after me very kindly, but separately – wouldn't eat with me, wouldn't have anything to do with me.

During this period, Alison's story made it to the pages of Symington's ministry. Speaking in America, the Man of God reflected on the facts of her case and said that the brothers should have left her 'until she was hysterical'. Apparently, her treatment to this point had not been tough enough for his liking.

After some time at the house of her fellow Brethren, Alison returned home briefly to collect some things. While she was there, Sophie's ex-husband came to the house with her two little grandsons.

'And he said the children want to kiss their granny. Well, look, I was 100 per cent Brethren, but I wasn't so un-Christian that I would refuse to kiss those two little boys. And I kissed them. I didn't let them in the house, but I kissed them.'

Her fatal mistake was to tell her Brethren hosts about the visit from her grandsons. That night they dispatched her home, saying she was 'ever so much better'. The following night, she was withdrawn from.

'It was because I'd kissed those little boys – I'd broken down separation. And they said, "You're none of our business now, you're to go and see Bob."'

Six months had elapsed since the first ring on the doorbell, shutting her up, and now she was excommunicated entirely, on an equal footing with the disgraced Bob. He moved back in with Alison. Still, though, she and Bob did not repudiate this cult they had been brought up in – such was the power of fear and doctrine, and the lure of family. They set themselves to wait until they were restored.

For two-and-a-half more long years, until February 1983, they lived in disgrace, maintaining separation from the outside world. They were not permitted to talk to any of their family who were 'in' the Brethren, and they refused to speak to Priscilla or Sophie, because they were 'out'. They ignored their neighbours and the friends they had once entertained so lavishly, and waited with each other as their sole comfort for the sporadic visits from the Brethren 'priests', who themselves admitted they had no idea why the couple was still out of fellowship.

That they waited so long seems astounding to people who have not suffered the level of indoctrination imposed on Bob and

Alison. But another victim of Symington, a former Brethren leader in Australia, Ron Fawkes, relates a similar story about his shock excommunication in 1984:

> I was physically, emotionally, mentally totally devastated because it was so unexpected. I lived like a hermit virtually for seven years. I begged to be reconciled because at that stage I knew nothing different, it was my life. And I loved my wife and children. I ached for them, I begged for them.[7]

In the long evenings of their period in limbo, Bob and Alison read the Bible and the ministry of Jim Symington, trying to find solace in their religion.

Bob loved gardening and, since for three years he had believed he would be back in fellowship 'next week', he maintained a fertile vegetable patch so he could present his children with fresh produce when he was able once again to see them. But harvests came and went, with nobody else to feed. 'We used to get a box from the greengrocer and take them down to the park and put them out with a notice on them saying "Home grown, help yourself",' Alison said.

Finally, when Grace turned 18 and was about to be married, Symington relented, and Bob and Alison were to be restored in time for the wedding day. Then something extraordinary happened. On the verge of obtaining what they had so ardently hoped for, they had a revelation:

> It was the eleventh of February 1983, at 7.30 at night, and we had been out for three years. I was knitting, and Bob was sitting reading Mr Symington's ministry. And he put the book down and he just made a few remarks – I can't remember what they were – and I put my knitting down and I said, 'Bob, you don't agree with Mr Symington.'

And he said his heart was in his mouth because I might get up and say, 'I'm going to have to leave you'. But he just quietly said, 'No, I don't, because of this and this.' And I just said, 'That's right.' And the whole pack of cards collapsed. We just knelt down and said, 'Lord, open our eyes.' And we said we can never go back there.

In that moment, they saw the truth about the sect they had been involved in. But they knew their decision meant they would lose four of their children, probably forever.

'My father said, before he died, and cried his heart out as he said it, that the very worst thing he did was to leave Gracie behind in the Brethren,' Priscilla said.

The years after 1983 were a gradual unfurling into the world for Bob and Alison. The first thing they did was to try to explain their odd behaviour to their worldly neighbours. The neighbours wept, and said they had known all along. Then they made contact with their two daughters who were 'out', Priscilla and Sophie, beginning the long and imperfect process of trying to repair some of the damage they had done to those relationships. Bob also started contacting all the people he could think of whom he had 'handled' during his years as a leader of the Brethren, to apologise to them for any brutality, and to seek their forgiveness.

By leaving, they gained access to two lost daughters, and a life free of fear and pressure. But what they lost was enormous: 'I lost my mother, my two brothers and sister, all living, and my four children,' Alison said. Alison's mother lived for 11 years after she was taken from her care, but Alison never spoke to Granny Stewart again. She saw her just once, from a distance. After her mother's death, Alison received a brief note informing her of the fact, and telling her the number of the plot at the cemetery where she was buried.

'The Brethren break up families – all those relationships are broken,' she said.

Like many former Brethren, Alison and Bob remained fervent, active Christians. It was only after they left that they felt they were able to properly live by Christian beliefs. They realised that, in the Brethren they had 'served a man, not the Lord', Alison said.

Well into her eighties, as an act of repentance and faith, Alison would travel to Sydney's Central Station to give out religious tracts on the country platform. But she is still trying to convince herself that her many sins are forgiven:

> I believe the scripture that if we confess our sins He will cleanse us from all unrighteousness. I think it's an insult to the Lord Jesus, who's taken the punishment for my sins, not to see that it's all forgiven. It is hard to take this in, though, because I know what I've done.

In their post-Brethren life, Alison and Bob became prominent 'opposers' of the sect, taking any opportunity to speak up against it. Bob compiled a damning list of Symington's teaching, along with biblical quotations, and then posted it to many of the Brethren to try to point out how far their ministry had diverged from the Bible. In the early 1990s, Alison and Bob sent letters to the Brethren in Bathurst to try to open their eyes to the reality of what they were worshipping. The reply from their son, Gavin, and two other elders, warned them to stop trying to 'influence people's minds against the Brethren and against the Lord'.

The reply was as hurtful as the Brethren could make it:

> To take only one example to illustrate your want of uprightness you accuse the brethren of breaking up marriages. Your own family is a witness of the opposite. The four children with us remain happily married to this day and the two with you have broken marriages.

The letter demanded that the couple withdraw all accusations against the Brethren and promise not to repeat them. If not, they would 'take such action to prevent a repetition' – an implied threat of legal action. No such action was forthcoming

For 20 years, Alison continued trying to contact her 'in' children, writing to them often and receiving the usual dismissals. But suddenly, during Bruce Hales's Review in 2003, the Aldertons' case was 'put right' and apologies issued. Alison was approached to return to the fold, and her loved ones finally visited her:

> So, after 23 years, I saw Grace, at 38, for the first time since she was 15. These children who I hadn't seen for 23 years all came visiting me – and the ones from Perth came over to see me. I had visits all year. And it was so painful. There was just tears, and begging me to come back, and, them saying, 'You've gone away from what's right, and we love you and we want you back.' They'd take turns. The room would be full of people, and they'd bring their children. And I'd be sitting there and they'd each take a turn to sort of kneel beside me, look into my eyes and beg me to come back. It was terrible. I was glad when they gave me up as a bad job!

Was she ever tempted to return? 'Never. It was never a consideration. Look, you couldn't go back into that darkness. I'd have to turn my back on the Lord Jesus, and I could not exist without Him.'

Priscilla also felt the consequences of the Review of 2003: 'It felt like the Great Wall of China opened for about three hours and closed again,' Priscilla said. She has seen each of her sisters again, once. She felt 'total love and connectedness' with them. But she was also alarmed by how meek they seemed. The men she found 'horrible' for their 'assumption of authority and superiority, without the benefit of substance, culture, education or grace'. Priscilla thinks there has been one single further contact since – a call from Christine to ask her not to contact Jeanette again, 'as it upset her too much'.

Sophie has seen Grace, Gavin, and Jeanette since the Review. But, for her, these visits only stirred up old feelings that she had been consigning to the past since 1993. In that year, she flew to Perth to visit Grace, the sister she had felt so passionately protective of, but whom she had not seen for 17 years, since Grace was eleven. Grace recognised her, said, 'You know I can't talk to you', then slammed the door in her face:

> And I started driving back to the city, and then I completely broke down and got hopelessly lost ... I stayed in the hotel room for 48 hours without leaving. And by the time I got out of that room I had accepted my situation. I didn't even try to call my other two sisters, both living in Perth, both living in the Brethren. I just made peace with it.

When Grace visited Sophie in 2007, for the first and only time, she apologised for slamming the door on her sister 14 years earlier. But Sophie dates the beginning of her 'acceptance and personal growth' from that time in 1993, 'when I accepted that Grace didn't want to see me':

> I don't feel like a victim any more. I feel that I've got a very meaningful and fulfilling life. I've got a really good marriage, I've got two sons doing very well, a fulfilling career. I've worked overseas, built schools and hospitals in China ... I work with refugees and I can identify with people who are struggling, who have lost everything, because I've been there.

Sophie remains angry, though, at the strong public support the Exclusive Brethren attracted from the government of John Howard. Just weeks before the 2007 Australian election, she squeezed through the crowd at the Granny Smith festival in his electorate to confront him.

'I grabbed his hand in both of mine and said, "Mr Howard, I'm Sophie, and I'm an ex-Exclusive Brethren, and I feel utterly and totally betrayed by you. There are thousands of us who have lost our families." And he just kept saying, "I'm sorry, I'm sorry," and was shaking his head like Noddy. He heard, though. I just felt he heard. At least I got the message through.'

All the Alderton women fear that by telling their stories, their family members still within the Brethren will be ostracised or damaged in their position. Priscilla said that, just as Christine was punished for her transgression when they were children, 'the Brethren will do it again; make her have the smack because of me'.

In 2006, Alison told a truncated version of her tale in Melbourne's *Age* newspaper.[8] According to Priscilla, this 'created tidal waves, tsunamis' within the sect. Whenever any of them is contacted by family members, they are begged not to 'speak against' the Brethren publicly. In February 2008, Grace wrote a letter to Alison, saying she regretted that her mother had been 'so badly poisoned against the Brethren, whom I love', and wishing that she had not 'got away from what you saw was true in Mr Hales'.

'Mum, please, even if it's only for my sake, *stop* attacking the Brethren and trying to influence others against them. We are aware that you have continued to do this and it causes us so much pain,' Grace wrote. And then came a line that Alison interpreted as an implied threat: 'Please don't try to turn me against my *own* convictions or it may affect my being able to care for you when you need it.'

This threat became much more explicit in mid-2008 when Alison fell ill and spent time in hospital. One of her Brethren daughters, Jeanette, found out and visited her, and then presented her with a proposition: if Alison signed a document promising she would never speak publicly against the Brethren again, she would be readmitted to access with her family before she died. If she refused, she would continue to be ostracised. Alison refused: 'He that practises the truth comes to the light,' she told them.

'It's obvious,' said Priscilla, 'that my brother and sisters are being shamed within the context of the Brethren because of their mother. It's obvious in their behaviour and conversation.'

But it is not enough to stop the Alderton women from speaking out. They want the Exclusive Brethren to know that the sect cannot absolve itself of the wrongs it has done just by apologising for them. While each of them have, in their personal lives, grown strong and independent, they believe the sect is still inflicting damage on people close to them – the members of their family who are not permitted to have a normal relationship with them. By maintaining the doctrine of separation, that damage is amplified down the years.

'Their apologies are absolutely meaningless,' Sophie said:

> We've all grown up just longing for family. I don't understand what this review is about, but without giving family back, how can there be healing? The rest is just psychological torment – you get one visit, have a couple of hours together, and then they go away, and you never see them again.
>
> The thing that would bring meaning would be for to me to have access to my sisters and brother in a normal way. An apology without any action is meaningless, and the only action that's meaningful is being a sister to my sisters and my brother.

CHAPTER SIX

Albury

In January 2006, W. Bruce Hales, the elderly uncle of the Man of God, descended upon the New South Wales border town of Albury and delivered a memorable spray to the assembled faithful.

Albury is a picturesque and thriving country town, built at the intersection of two great trade routes, the Murray River and the Hume Highway. Its Exclusive Brethren community is prosperously engaged in small and medium-sized industrial businesses.

In his sermon, W. Bruce accused his brethren of the worst of sins, likening their community to 'Sodom and Gomorrah'. Accusing them of laxness and corruption, he quoted a passage from the book of Isaiah about a 'sinful nation, a people laden with iniquity, a seed of evildoers, children that corrupt themselves'.

'We've gone on with social activities, we've made the fellowship into a worldly club. We've concealed evil, and concealed it, and concealed it, and if we keep doing it, beloved, we'll lose His presence. We'll lose the presence of God!'

W. Bruce Hales was one of the Brethren aristocracy – son-in-law to one world leader, brother to a second, and uncle to a third – coming from the world headquarters in Sydney to this small community of Brethren members, and letting fly. Even allowing for

W. Bruce's habitual bluntness, the local Brethren observers were dumbfounded: 'Ashen faces; shocked into silence,' recalls one who was present at the Tuesday-night meeting.

'Oh, I'm sorry to have to speak like this,' W. Bruce went on, 'but it's time to change, beloved, it's time to change, change drastically. Put away all the sham, the hypocrisy, the appearances, the love of appearances.' He said the 'priesthood has failed', and the 'Lord has turned against us'. His solution was to urge the town's elders to 'get the sword out', to become ruthless in punishments.

'One of the most sorrowful things you find is such a lax attitude to the sin against God's presence, that they'll actually defend their children ... you're depriving your children of God's mercy and forgiveness by hiding and diminishing the judgment of sin.'

W. Bruce died not long after this harangue; but a year later, one of the senior serving leaders of the Albury Brethren, Chris Shore, remained somewhat mystified by it: 'I couldn't claim to be able to explain everything he said, and what he was referring to there,' he said. 'What he had been told prior to coming to Albury, well, he'd never spoken to me.'[1]

But a close look at the history of the Albury Brethren reveals that W. Bruce had a point, at least in one respect: this community has felt more pain and suffering than any small society should have to bear. It was in Albury that two young girls were sexually molested by the man they had been sent to live with after their mother lost the ability to look after them, and then they were ostracised for reporting the assaults to police. Here, a confused man, who had lost three father-figures to the doctrine of separation, threatened to bomb the court where the sexual assault case was being heard. Here, the mentally ill Kenneth Rogers committed suicide in 2004 on the doorstep of the warehouse owned by one of the sect's local leaders, after his hopes of being reunited with his long-estranged family were dashed. Here, one man's entire family was spirited away from him one day while he was at work. And it was here, too, that a renowned Brethren surgeon died at the age of 82 while living in exile in his wife's garage, his food left daily at the door.

The Brethren acknowledge that Albury is a 'troublesome' locality. The conventional explanation is that it has to do with the continuing tension between two rival sets of families who first settled there in 1970 – one set from Melbourne, the other from Sydney. But, from the outside, the cause seems deeper. The events here suggest that, however much the doctrine of separation seems to be softening within the Brethren, the core doctrine is alive and well. Albury has been, and remains, a living case-study of what happens when a religious group tries to police the boundaries of its faith and to maintain strict separation from sin by relying on judgmentalism and heavy-handed regulation. What W. Bruce recommended as its cure is, in fact, the cause of the problem.

Vernon Sealey was a pioneer in the emerging art of maxillofacial surgery in the 1950s and 1960s, and beyond. He was described by fellow specialists as 'a legend'.[2] This form of surgery is an exacting discipline; it grew from dentistry, and evolved hand in glove with plastic surgery as a way to treat injuries to the face seen in soldiers, sailors, and airmen during the first and second world wars.

Partly thanks to the work of Vernon Sealey, maxillofacial surgery is now considered a stand-alone medical specialty. Dr Sealey had a 'very, very highly regarded surgical career' in Melbourne, according to a fellow surgeon, John Hennessy. But, in 1970, he heard a call from God. Sealey was a leading member of the Exclusive Brethren and, just as the sect was imploding due to the erratic tutelage of James Taylor Junior, he decided to move his flock from Melbourne to the New South Wales border town of Albury and begin a new Brethren locality there, in hitherto Godless land.

Hennessy, who took over Sealey's Albury surgical practice in 1978, recalls an impeccably groomed man, his black hair swept back from his forehead, who was interested in the latest surgical techniques until well after his retirement. He performed operations across the board, from simply oral surgery to the reconstruction of faces that had been severely damaged as a result of major road trauma, interpersonal violence, and gunshots. John Hennessy said he was 'working at the sophisticated end of the spectrum in a pretty small hospital'.

'He said he came here to set up his church, and then his intention was to retire; but he felt he had such unique skills in this community that he should offer them.'

It's true that Dr Sealey was considered slightly odd by his medical colleagues because of his habit of preaching the Gospel on street corners. True to Brethren philosophy, he would talk and sit with his colleagues, but would not eat or drink with them. 'His religion was such that going anywhere beyond a professional relationship was impossible,' Hennessy said. Professionally, however, he was 'communicative, warm, educational and enthusiastic', and, after his retirement, Sealey made monthly visits to Hennessy's surgery until he was well into his seventies, observing operations and asking questions.

'Then he just vanished,' Hennessy recalls. 'The phone calls stopped, visits stopped, everything stopped. I met his son, Graeme, in town one day and he said, "No, he's passed away some time ago, peacefully at home".'

But this was not strictly true. Dr Vernon Sealey, the co-founder of the Albury Brethren, had felt the lash of the faith to which he had devoted his life. He died a neglected old man, nursing a broken leg, having spent his last three years living in the brown suburban garage at the back of his wife's house, cut off from any contact with his family, and eating the food that she left for him at the door.

Dr Sealey died on 26 May 1992, aged 82. He was serving his second stint of excommunication from the Brethren. He had first been 'withdrawn from' in 1976, and was 'out' for six years, his sin having been to question the infallibility of the Man of God of the day, Jim Symington. During that period he worked in other people's gardens, mowing lawns and fixing up their vegetable patches. He told Hennessy that his church had told him he was not able to participate any longer and that he was doing 'penance'.

'"I have to be humble like Jesus and work in the garden", he used to say,' Hennessy recalls. 'I thought it was a disgrace. I'm a Christian, and these indiscretions wouldn't even raise an eyebrow in my church.'

While he was 'out', Sealey learned to cook, embarked on a fitness regime, and connected with the world by buying his first television set. But in 1982 he gave it all up again when he was allowed back in to the sect to witness the wedding of his granddaughter to Warren McAlpin, a young man from a good Brethren family. The condition was that Sealey had to sign all his assets into his wife's name. This made him entirely dependent on the slight charity of his family when it came to his second bout of excommunication in 1989, again for questioning what he saw as the Brethren's habit of placing a man above the Lord. Aged 79 and with no assets to his name, Dr Sealey had nowhere to live but the garage of his wife's house.

By this time, McAlpin had himself left the Brethren, and often secretly visited Dr Sealey in the garage at night while the Brethren were attending their meetings. McAlpin recalls that Dr Sealey spoke about the fact that just about every family he knew was suffering because of the doctrine of separation, and was visibly upset to hear that McAlpin's family had been broken up.

'He also expressed concern about John Hales's name needing to be mentioned by Brethren generally at the Lord's Supper [communion], believing that the place of Christ should have remained above that of man. I was later to find out that this issue was one of the main reasons that the Brethren had withdrawn from him,' McAlpin said.[3]

After three years living in the garage, Sealey's health deteriorated and he died. 'I thought it was outrageous and disgusting,' Hennessy said. 'With all the attention and care he had given the community and his church, that was a time in life that maximum care should have been returned to him, with grace and gratitude.'

But the indignities visited on this eminent surgeon did not end when he died. His funeral was held at the small local hall, rather than the main hall in the town, and his coffin was kept closed rather than open, as is the Brethren custom. And according to two witnesses at the graveside, Sealey's son Graeme oversaw a ceremony in which the coffin was buried the wrong way around, with Dr Sealey's feet pointing towards the headstone.

This version of events is vehemently denied by Graeme Sealey, who says the story is 'malicious and untrue'. He says that the world leader of the day, John Hales, was consulted over the manner of Dr Sealey's burial and had told him to, 'Just proceed normally' – which was what happened.

Either way, the facts of Dr Sealey's excommunication and his sad end have now been reviewed by the Albury Brethren under the guidance of the latest world leader, Bruce Hales. One of the current Albury leaders, Chris Shore, now agrees that the surgeon should not have been withdrawn from, at least on the second occasion. 'It wouldn't stand. From time to time, things are looked at – did we really do things fairly and right? And things have had to be adjusted ... I wouldn't take the ground of being perfect,' Shore admits.[4]

The forgiving of Dr Sealey was conducted during Bruce Hales's 'Review', a widespread reconsideration of old assembly judgments. It would be cold comfort to the doctor, who was 12 years dead when he was absolved of his 'sins', but perhaps it salves the consciences of those, including his own son, who helped enforce a judgment they now concede was wrong.

But even if you are alive, and the judgment meted out to you is reviewed, it makes no difference to your life. Warren McAlpin's case has been reconsidered by the Albury Brethren, and acknowledged to be wrong, but his two sons grew up almost entirely without him, with only a couple of fleeting visits during the Review of

2003. McAlpin was a fourth-generation Brethren member from a high-profile family. But in 1989, at the age of 28, after watching and enduring much sadness in the sect, he said he was shown the light about God by one of his staff members, Martin Cross, a well-known football identity in the Albury–Wodonga area, and his son-in-law, Tony Thomson.

Cross and Thomson, both Christians, but never members of the Brethren, immediately felt the punishment of the sect for their mentoring of McAlpin and showing what he now calls 'true Christianity' towards him. As a result of McAlpin's conversion away from the sect, Thomson was sacked from his long-standing Brethren employment with one of the Albury leaders, Graeme Sealey, within 24 hours.

Then, after McAlpin made known to the Brethren that he did not wish to continue with the sect, John Hales, the then world leader, sent a secret message through the Albury leadership to McAlpin's wife. Hales said, through another local leader, Darryl Suggate, 'We have ways and means to get you free from your husband.' After receiving this message, Mr McAlpin visited the leaders and told them angrily that they would not break up his family. He told them to tell Hales 'that his message came from the pits of hell'. McAlpin was summarily withdrawn from for 'speaking against the Man of God'.

The following day, he had a visit from two local leaders, Allan Hocking and Darryl Suggate. They informed him of the decision to withdraw from him and why. They also asked to speak to his wife. McAlpin made the mistake of allowing his wife to talk to the two 'priests', and they informed her that she had now to separate within the house from her husband. McAlpin continued to live with his wife in this way as he tried to convince her and their sons to leave the sect with him. But, one day while he was at work, the Brethren came and cleaned out his home, and moved his wife and children to a secret location. Another Brethren man parked outside McAlpin's workplace and kept watch to make sure that he did not head homewards.

He later learnt that his wife had been told by the Albury elders that if she left the Brethren with him, 'God will take one of your children' – in other words, he would die. This clinched her decision to stay with the Brethren, McAlpin said.

But just as the judgments on Vernon Sealey and Warren McAlpin were being overturned, another scandal was breaking out in Albury that would divide the Brethren community in two. It would result in two men being jailed, three families damaged, and multiple children denied contact with their fathers. It would also lead to an accusation that the sect's world leader had tried to cover up the sexual abuse of two young girls.

Lindsay Jensen was a senior and wealthy Brethren businessman and a trustee of the sect's local private school. He was well liked, but was not considered a sect elder, partly because he had the reputation of being lustful towards the women of the flock. In the words of Brethren spokesman Tony McCorkell, he was regarded as 'a bit loose-moralled'.[5]

Despite this, in 2002, a dreadful series of events led to two vulnerable young girls being sent to live in his house. The story began in 1999 when the girls' father left the family home, unable any longer to hide the fact that he was homosexual.[6] In Brethren demonology, this is *the* most terrible sin, the subject of distaste and revulsion – being, as Bruce Hales put it, 'unnatural against the anatomy'.[7] Brethren medical doctor Mark Craddock, one of Hales' personal physicians, later described the father as having a 'sordid history of infidelity involving a long-term alternative relationship', and also being 'a loser by any decent person's standards'.[8]

Despite the distaste with which the Brethren regarded him, this man had managed, after great effort, to maintain some access to his children, with fortnightly visits being organised at the home of the children's grandparents. Other Brethren were present at these four-hour visits, the father says, and it 'certainly was a hostile environment'.

But in March 2002 the girls' mother suffered a terrible accident, in which both her thigh bones were broken, putting her in a wheelchair and rendering her incapable of looking after her children. Even though the father was still in Albury, he was not considered by the Brethren to be a candidate to care for the children. Instead, they were sent to a local family, the Jensens. Two months later, in May, the elder of the two girls, who was 12, just turning 13, told her grandfather that her host had sexually abused her.

But the Brethren immediately dismissed the complaint because, according to the official version, the girl had a 'tendency to make up stories', and Jensen denied it. To complicate the situation, the girls' mother, despite her invalid state, had also had an affair with Jensen.

In two separate trials in 2005 and 2006, Jensen was convicted on eight charges of sexual assault of the two sisters, including one count of sexual intercourse without consent, and sentenced to five years' jail, with a non-parole period of three years. The sentencing judge, Gay Murrell, commented that the relationship between victim and abuser was 'was brought about because of membership of the church'.

But getting to the point where the justice system was able to do its work was a long, tortuous, and psychologically scarring experience for the girls and their mother, who needed to thread their way through a Brethren community and hierarchy that was determined to prevent the story coming out. (It must be emphasised in this account that Jensen continues to maintain his innocence; his wife and family are standing by him.)

When the older girl first reported the crime, so deep was the disbelief of her that Jensen's wife was allowed to interview her, with Jensen himself entering the room towards the end of the session. They extracted from the girl an admission that she had lied, and that her naughtiness and sinfulness were to blame for her false allegations. And there the situation rested for a full year, even though the father, who was still in contact with his daughters, noticed 'by their change of behaviour that something was wrong'.

In May 2003, 15 months after the first report, the situation took another dramatic turn: the younger sister, who was nine, made an entirely separate complaint of sexual abuse against Jensen. At this point, the girls' mother began to want to act. Horrified at what her daughters were saying, she wanted to seek counselling for them both. But, according to the father, this is when 'the cover-up happened in earnest'. The girls' mother was warned by her fellow Brethren that this would mean exposing the sect to the worldly authorities. In Brethren theology, the assembly is the final court, and there is a strong taboo against reporting fellow sect members to police.

This delayed the mother seeking help for another month; but, in June 2003, she went to see a grief counsellor, who apparently reported the allegations to the NSW Department of Community Services, though this fact was not known to the Brethren.

By this time, the story had begun to get currency on the Brethren grapevine. Another local man, Bruce Suggate, who was later to play his own dramatic role in events, recalls it was '*the* topic of conversation'. In this small and almost totally enclosed society, whose members have nothing much to do for entertainment, the gossip mill churns more viciously than usual. The local leaders felt they needed to do something. Chris Shore said he thought it was the 'kindest thing' to do to send two women, his wife and the wife of another local leader, to interview the girls. In July 2003, the two women conducted three interviews with the girls over a number of hours.

The father described it as a grilling. 'They questioned and cross-questioned them very closely for hours, to the point that when the police became involved they were dismayed because of the contamination of the evidence,' said the father. 'The younger one found it highly intimidating and very, very distressing, because she knew that the basic assumption or impression was that it was likely she was making it up.'

Shore disagrees. 'Well, it wasn't [a grilling]. That's not fair. That doesn't represent the situation at all ... I think there were two visits; and each visit may have taken an hour,' he said.

Shore now acknowledges that 'we were totally in the deep end'. He did not refer the matter to the police because 'I didn't even know that was the way to proceed – we'd never heard of these child sex news cases before. Never ever.'

When Shore was asked when Mr Hales was made aware of the allegations, he was uncertain: 'I don't know what to say on that one; it was our responsibility, not Bruce Hales's ... What might be said in passing is another matter.' Did Shore go to him for instructions? 'To be fair, if you're going to do that, you've got to give him the whole case, and we never did that.'

But, according to Jensen's wife, 'Bruce Hales was fully advised of the situation immediately that events took place.'[9] The victims' father agrees that the Man of God knew from the start. Under New South Wales law, a person who is aware of a sexual assault on reasonable grounds may be under an obligation to report it to the authorities. No report was made at this stage.

In fact, among the leadership and , in the wider Brethren society, the ranks were closing around Jensen, and excluding the victims and their mother. The vast majority of the community believed Jensen's version of events, which was, and remains, that he was innocent of all allegations. Jensen was, after all, popular, rich, and male. Those making complaints against him were mere girls and a woman who had been abandoned by a man who turned out to be homosexual: people who carried no weight whatsoever in the Brethren view of the world. According to the girls' father, 'They were jeered at outside church, the kids were surrounded and shouted at, while Jensen carried on his life with impunity.'

The mother later told her ex-husband that other Brethren women had said that speaking to police was 'the spirit of murder'. One told her, 'It would be better for a millstone to be hung around your neck and for you to be cast into the depths of the sea rather than go to the police.' This version of events is disputed by the Brethren, who say this conversation did not relate to speaking to the police, but to another subject. On the father's account, though, the full weight of the mother's strictly controlled upbringing was being applied by her community to prevent her from taking the issue to the authorities. Meanwhile, the grapevine accusing his girls 'went around the world', the father said. 'These two testy little girls, making up stories.'

This situation went on for a month until, in August 2003, Jensen went to the school that the older girl attended to go to a meeting of trustees. The older girl confronted him, and the mother came and took her home. Now, 15 months after the first allegation was raised, a non-Brethren person, the schoolteacher, acted, reporting the allegation to the Department of Community Services. The Brethren elders also responded to the girls' strong reaction at the school, and Jensen was asked to hand in his resignation as a trustee.

'We tried to round him up and pull him into line. We didn't just back off and say, "You're a good boy". He wasn't, and we told him so,' Shore said.

According to the official Brethren version of events, it was only at this point that Bruce Hales was informed. They say he immediately ordered them to seek legal advice, which was to report the suspicions to authorities, but that this had already been done by the school. Two days later, Jensen was further disciplined by being put in a 'shut up' or 'confined' position, meaning he was unable to attend meetings of the Brethren or interact with other members, including his family. But he was not 'withdrawn from'.

Even now, according to McCorkell, the majority of the local Brethren stayed firmly on the side of Jensen: 'There is a whole heap of bitching and moaning and fighting and carrying on in the Albury church, and Jensen's wife is running around saying to people, 'He's been excommunicated and he hasn't even been arrested yet, this is outrageous, this is slanderous.' And half the church are going, 'We like Jensen, and he's a nice bloke.'

This situation continued for four months until the end of 2003 when, in December, the church hierarchy weakened and received Jensen back into fellowship. It was done, according to the official Brethren version of events, because 'of no substantial witness' of the events. Shore acknowledges the error, saying, 'In hindsight, other steps may have been taken had the church known what to do, but the church had no experience in dealing with these types of situations.'

This act of readmitting Jensen to fellowship finally made the girls and their mother so angry that they ignored the strictures of their entire upbringing, and went to the police to make a formal complaint. It is difficult to imagine the courage this would take. They were risking, as they saw it, being estranged from everything they believed in, including their God.

According to the father, the only thing, even now, that convinced the mother to take the case to the police was that 'the Director of Public Prosecutions would be the one prosecuting Jensen, not her or her daughters'. But the move made their lives within the Brethren even more unbearable:

> She was basically shunned from the community to the point where she couldn't go to church herself, even though she was an avid follower ... they twisted my ex-wife's mind to make her think it was a sin to speak against another person, even though he had molested children. She dealt with major guilt that she had allowed police to get involved.

In March the following year, 2004, Jensen was arrested and released on bail. The police also placed an apprehended violence order against him, restricting him from contacting the two girls or their mother. At this point, Jensen was once again 'shut up' – no Brethren person is permitted to attend the assembly when they are under an order of the worldly courts. But he was not 'withdrawn from', which to some sent a clear signal that the church hierarchy still believed he had not really done anything wrong.

In fact, in the background, Bruce Hales was still supporting Jensen. His wife remembers clearly a message being passed from Hales, through the Albury elders, to her husband: 'If it was me,' Hales was reported as saying, 'and I hadn't done it, I would hire the best the lawyers and fight it.'

The arrest only served to step up the campaign of vilification against the victims. The girls were jeered at, excluded, and made fun of. People taunted them as 'Lindsay lovers'. The mother's house was repeatedly egged, eggs were left under the doormat and smashed on the windows, and the car was scratched, the father says. A small faction of the town's Brethren community supported the mother – and Chris Shore was part of that group – but they were clearly outnumbered by those who supported Jensen. Bruce Suggate clearly remembers that the girls were widely considered to be liars who had made the whole thing up.

The mother's mental health, already fragile, deteriorated further until, in early 2005, she had a full physical and nervous breakdown, and ended up in a psychiatric institution. The children's father came from his home in Sydney for an access visit, at the end of which the girls would not leave him. In remarkable circumstances for any Brethren family, his ex-wife asked him to stay with her, so he moved back into the family home to care for the children.

He remained there, sleeping in a separate room from his ex-wife, for more than two months. After he moved out, his continuing involvement with his ex-wife and children was regular and intimate over a total of nine months. He took his wife to her psychiatric appointments, to visit doctors for her legs, and was involved in her daily life in a caring capacity, at her request, while living in a different house. His deep knowledge of events comes from what he saw, and what his ex-wife told him, during this period.

But the father's move back in was not taken lightly by the local Brethren. While he was at the house, one of the girls' uncles broke into a filing cabinet in the house and took a passport as part of an attempt to send one of them to live with relatives in the United States. The Brethren acknowledge that this happened, but say that the sect itself is not to blame: 'We regard this as a family issue and do not agree with what happened,' according to one document.[10]

The Brethren also launched a court case to take one of the girls away from their parents and give guardianship to another Brethren family – a move that the Brethren say was 'in the best interests of the daughter' and because she did not want to live with her father. This case was later withdrawn.

In October 2005, more than three years after his offences first came to light, Jensen went to court in Albury to be tried on the charges against the elder of the sisters. He was found guilty. Late the following year, in a hearing in Sydney, he was found guilty of the charges regarding the other sister. In 2007, he was sentenced, in two seperate hearings, to a total of five years' imprisonment.

After the guilty verdict in the first trial, the pendulum finally swung against Jensen in the Brethren's eyes. In January 2006, he was withdrawn from, and the sect that had supported him and his family suddenly began to ostracise him. The sect's support, belatedly, swung behind the children's mother, and every effort was expended to keep her and her daughters in the sect, and together as a family unit. She was moved away from Albury, and Hales personally tried to convince her daughters to stay with her and the Brethren, and not their father. The law firm that had launched a case in mid-2005 to remove one of the children from her mother and father was, just 18 months later, in late 2006, sending out legal letters on the mother's behalf.

The mother, with the help of the Sydney Brethren elite, has since put the position that the Brethren and Hales have always acted properly; it was just individuals, including Jensen and her ex-husband, who were the villains of the piece.[11]

For the Jensen family, these events were also catastrophic. His wife and children, whom the sect had supported up until that point, were withdrawn from and shunned, just as their husband and father was being taken from them, and their need for the support of the only community they had known was at its most profound. Jensen's wife says that her husband is 'very restful that one day the truth will come to light, and at present he leaves it in the hands of his God'. Jail, she says, has put her husband's 'relationship with his God on a much more personal level than ever before'.

But the ripples caused by this case did not stop with these two families: they were to have tragic consequences further afield, too. In October 2005, as Lindsay Jensen was facing court in Albury, Bruce Suggate was a mess. Clinically depressed, he'd had a nervous breakdown 18 months earlier. He was taking anti-depressant medication, and was drinking too much. He was under pressure at work and, six months earlier, had admitted to being unfaithful to his wife, for which he had been put under assembly discipline and, later, forgiven.

Suggate was born into the Exclusive Brethren, but he was not a highly regarded man. In fact, he was at or near the bottom rung – an employee, not a businessman, with no theological talent, whose family had long been considered disreputable and had sat in the back row of the assembly for decades. His psychiatrist was to describe him later as being 'a somewhat simple man of average IQ'. Suggate had never been much good at school, nor at the meetings where he said he was 'bored shitless' and would 'just go to sleep'.[12]

But in 2005 the Jensen saga was galvanising the whole Albury Brethren community. And on 24 October, at the Albury District Court, the trial of this leading man of the community was due to begin.

The case incensed Bruce Suggate. It was wrong, according to the precepts that had been drummed into him from childhood, for one member of the Brethren to pursue criminal charges against another. So at 8.15 am on the day the court was to convene, Suggate went to a public phone booth near the Coles Supermarket in suburban Lavington, about 3 kilometres north of the Albury court. He rang the police station, which abuts the courtroom, and told a constable there that, 'There is a court hearing today at the Albury Court for the matter of Jensen and X ... It is a three-day sitting and there will be a suicide bomber in court also.' And then he hung up. The call prompted an immediate response. The court was evacuated and searched. Additional security was added, and everybody entering the court was frisked and checked with metal detectors.

No bomb was found, and the trial proceeded. So, at 1.10 pm that afternoon, Suggate rang the police again and said there was a bomb going off at 9.00 pm at the victims' home, giving the address and making mention of the 'bitch that's sitting at court at the moment'. The following day, he rang 000 and threatened again to bomb the court. The next day, he reported a brawl at the victims' address, which the police attended, only to find it was another hoax. Then followed another bomb threat on the home of the victims, and a threat against one of their Brethren supporters, Chris Shore. In the following days, Suggate made more bomb threats, as well as reporting two shootings and a fire.

In all, according to a police statement, he made 11 threats of violence in a three-week period, all against the child victims and their mother, or their supporters. 'I felt it was wrong to be amongst the Brethren and doing what she was doing and taking Lindsay to court. I felt because of my upbringing that it was a terrible thing to do,' Suggate explained later.[13]

When he was finally arrested, on 15 December 2005, Suggate initially denied the charges. But, faced with overwhelming evidence, he eventually pleaded guilty. He told police he had been drunk, depressed, and 'driven by the devil' when he made the threats. Suggate was sentenced to four months' jail. It was an experience that would change his life. 'I never dreamed of going to jail,' Suggate said a year after his release:

> I thought I was untouchable. I always thought the Brethren were untouchable people – no-one can touch us because we're going to go to heaven, everyone else is going to go to hell. We are a chosen race of kingly priests, and we are the best people. We're the only saved ones. And you can't send me to jail! I won't go to jail! It was the biggest shell-shock ever!

Suggate says when the sentence was read, 'The bottom dropped out of me ... But it was a life-saving experience.' After 40 years of living the Brethren lifestyle, it was in prison that Bruce Suggate had his first real religious experience. 'It was God. God meant me to go to jail to think positive. And I spent hours alone in jail, looking back on my past, and I was let out of a cardboard box!'

The box Bruce describes was the stress and pressure imposed by religion, family, work, and the accretion of a lifetime of emotional scars – and also of never being up to scratch. 'You dreaded that you wouldn't go to heaven because you were a bastard. Because you couldn't keep up with it. I wasn't up to the standard, I couldn't keep meeting all their goals.' In Suggate's life, the 'devil' that he believed was driving him was less an external force than a complex brew of personal tragedies enforced on his family by the Brethren and their uncompromising ways over 40 years.

Suggate was the youngest of five children in a family whose parents moved, along with Vernon Sealey's group, from Melbourne to help build the new Brethren settlement in Albury in 1970. He was four. Bruce's father, Eric, was an alcoholic (Bruce says it runs in the family). When Bruce was 11, Eric was withdrawn for his alcoholism. Bruce never saw his father alive again – the Exclusive Brethren's rules of separation prevented it. Bruce remembers little of his father beyond his drinking, his woodworking, the fact that they used to eat ice-cream together, and that they collected beer bottles for cash. Suggate says his father 'used to yell and swear' when he was drunk, but 'he didn't used to hit'. Beyond that, there is nothing.

When Bruce's father was withdrawn from, his mother was required to follow. But Bruce's older brother, the ambitious Darryl, swiftly fixed the situation by helping organise his parents' official separation. This meant that his mother would return to the Brethren, and the children would stay within the sect, but that their father would be locked out forever. In the brief period when both parents were outside the sect, though, the five children were sent to live with a local man, John McAlpin. Bruce became very attached to McAlpin, and came to view him as a father figure. But, soon afterwards, he too was excommunicated for having breached a rule about not advertising one's business: he had promoted his range-hood business in a series of national pamphlets.

So young Bruce fell to viewing his older brother Dennis like a father. But, eight years after that, in 1989, Dennis, too, was removed from his life. 'Dennis went to a Slim Dusty concert. He went swimming in the river. That's what got him withdrawn from,' Bruce says. 'But they were trying to nail him for a long time. He was too genuine; he was too normal. He did what he wanted. He enjoyed life. And he was my father – I treated him like a dad.'

Bruce Suggate lost three father-figures to the doctrine of separation, and it affects him to this day. There were other losses – among them, Vernon Sealey, who had operated on Bruce's mother after she had a car accident and mangled her jaw. Bruce regarded Sealey as a spiritual guide, and he gave the boy the attention he craved: 'He helped me; gave me work at his house for pocket money, helped me on a religious basis. He was a comfort to me. Anyone I could have blown off steam with just disappeared,' Bruce said.

At 22, Bruce Suggate married a young Brethren woman from Whangarei in New Zealand, and brought her to live with him in Albury. According to Bruce, she had not been allowed to see the town beforehand and wept for days after her arrival, saying that she had made the biggest mistake of her life. They had three children in quick succession.

Bruce did see his father one more time. It was in 1995, when Eric Suggate died. Bruce and his brothers Darryl and Trevor were sent with a local leader, Ron Jensen, to pick up his father's body at his small, one-bedroom unit. 'We saw him in his bed, still. My dad. And he had his Bible open beside his bed,' Bruce said, tears welling in his eyes. Bruce watched the other men search the room for his father's will, and then Trevor sent him outside, saying, 'Get out, you'll never forget the noise his body makes when they move it.'

'The next thing I saw when they took Dad away in the car, we had to pick up the mattress and put it outside for the dump truck to pick it up. And I'll never forget it. The mattress. You know what I mean? Poor Dad. You poor soul.'

At his father's funeral, Bruce's brother Dennis Suggate, six years out of the Brethren, put his arm around his little brother's shoulder to comfort him. Chris Shore, determined to maintain separation even now, peeled it off again. Shore denies doing this: 'I can't think why. It would be a very emotional time,' he said.

Back at work, Bruce said he 'cried and cried and cried for the next few days'. But there was no escape – his enmeshment in the sect was typically complete. For 18 years from 1986, Bruce worked for a Brethren company, his brother Darryl's garden-shed manufacturing business, Durabuilt Products. All his friends were Brethren, and his spare time was taken up in church meetings that he neither enjoyed nor understood. Asked by a psychiatrist, later, who were the people most interested in his life he replied, 'church friends'.

But Bruce found it increasingly difficult to live with the contradiction that the church to which his life was devoted was responsible for removing from him the people he loved most. He started doing odd and destructive things at work, trying to undermine his brother's business by sending reports to the tax office and workplace safety authorities. Bruce's rivalry with his young nephews, who were coming to an age where they were taking more responsibility in the business, mounted until they were in open conflict. He was also attacking any other person he felt was against him, and trying to undermine them. Suggate made a nuisance of himself to anybody he saw standing in his way. According to Bruce, he was acting this way because the stress on him was becoming unbearable. 'Everything just built up and up and up, and my brain just gave out,' Suggate says.

On 29 April 2004, at 6.00 am, he woke up feeling as though his head was 'cut down the middle'. It was a nervous breakdown and the start of a major depressive illness that was to put him out of action for months. Bruce and his wife stopped going to meetings as they dealt with his illness and the feelings they could not begin to express openly within the Brethren, but their children kept attending.

On one Thursday night in March 2005, their younger son, who was 11, threw a water bomb at Darryl's car as he left the meeting hall. Darryl's local leadership was, at the time, suffering, and he had become a target of harassment by some of the local youngsters. Another of Bruce's brothers, Trevor, a prominent businessman in Albury, allegedly lashed back at Bruce's son.

Bruce did not witness the events, but was told by other Brethren who were at the meeting hall that night that Trevor had lifted the boy up by the neck and had thrown him head first to the pavement. Whatever the truth of this, Bruce said he could see the red marks on his son's neck. The boy was brought home and, 'shaken and white', fell screaming to the floor in the lounge room. Bruce called the police, who came to the house, where a large number of Brethren had also gathered. Bruce spent the night with his son at the doctors, but immediately there was pressure put on him by his fellow Brethren not to press charges.

Bruce persevered for a while with his allegations, and the police gathered evidence; but, eventually, he was convinced by two of the most senior Albury Brethren to sign a letter promising to withdraw the charges: 'I was forced to [sign it]. I had to! I was told to sign it. What if I hadn't? [I'd have been] withdrawn from, because I had a charge against my brother!'

The effect of the assault on the boy, according to Bruce, was to make him a 'totally different' kid: 'He went into his shell. Since then he always shut his bedroom door, locked himself into his bedroom.'

By the time the Jensen issue had become the main talking point among the Brethren in Albury, Suggate was 'stressed to the limit'. His wife and Jensen's wife were talking to each other regularly, so Bruce was full of the story that Jensen was innocent and that the little girls were wilful liars, 'chronically dishonest'.

And so, thinking nothing more than that he had to disrupt the court proceedings for the mother 'and make her crack,' he embarked on a course of action that was to put him in jail. In early May 2006, Suggate was sent on the long journey to Junee prison to begin his four-month sentence. Just days later, as he languished, confused and frightened in prison, two local Brethren leaders came to see him. They told him he had been withdrawn from at the Saturday morning 'care meeting', and that the following day they would bring papers for him to sign that would formally separate him from his wife.

Without his anti-depression medication, and without having time to read through them, he was told by a prison guard that he had to sign the papers, because people were waiting for them. The papers purported to remove his rights to his home, his wife, his children, and his belongings. He signed. 'What else could I do? I was as weak as a kitten, I was mental up top. I'd had no medication for six days, and all I had on my mind was my wife and three children.'

Suggate was later sent to complete his sentence at Kirkconnell prison in Yetholme, New South Wales. During his time there, his only visitors were senior Exclusive Brethren – his family did not come.

In late August 2006, Suggate was released. He was picked up by two senior members of the sect, Chris and Simon Shore; and, despite pleading to be allowed to go home, he was installed in an isolated house. Then began three weeks of 'priestly visits' from the sect elders. After that, they left him unattended for 23 days, returning only to say they had been too busy to see him.

Suggate felt abandoned. He pined for his family. He was desperate to be accepted back by the Brethren, to the only life he'd ever known, and to move back into his house with his wife and children. He wrote to Bruce Hales three times begging to be readmitted, even asking if he could go to the meeting in nearby Wangaratta.

Suggate said that his psychiatrist, Dr Graham Burrows, had agreed with him that the worst thing that could have happened to him emotionally was to not be able to return to his wife and three children after his period in prison. But to Chris Shore, any return at that point was impossible under the Brethren's rules, since Suggate was under a court-imposed good-behaviour bond. He says that the offer of a house, with meals, was generous. Most importantly, he said that the separation was Bruce's wife's idea: 'She would have cheerfully divorced him. She had grounds, scriptural grounds, to divorce him,' Shore says. Bruce's wife later wrote herself: 'I had no confidence or trust in him at all. I definitely didn't want him back, and still don't.'

Shore and Suggate's wife are referring to the fact that Bruce had been unfaithful to her – the only grounds for divorce recognised by the Brethren. This charge makes Bruce furious: 'I admitted to that, and was publicly forgiven for it in the assembly, and my wife accepted me back. Now they are bringing it up again all these years later.'

Despite their differences, between September and December 2006, Bruce and his wife met twice, at the insistence of world leader

Bruce Hales, in the house he had been provided with. She agreed to have him back, but only if he had changed. Bruce said later that this meant he would need to have been 'broken, smashed, completely compliant ... But in jail, I'd moved on too far,' he said.

But, as this emotionally fragile man went out and found a number of physical jobs to try to occupy himself, the indignities continued to be piled onto his head. On several occasions at night, he saw some Brethren members following him. In December 2006, Suggate discovered by seeing it in the newspaper that the house he owned with his wife had been advertised for sale. He was able to stop the sale. Then somebody played a hoax on him – calling him into a job interview that did not exist. It was the final straw. He considered suicide, but then resolved that he had finished with the sect he had been brought up in. On 27 March 2007, he realised that he could never go back.

As Bruce's parole period was finishing, his brother Darryl took him back to court again to obtain apprehended violence orders to prevent him from approaching members of his family. With Bruce's record, he had no chance of defending the orders, and was forced to consent to staying 200 metres away from any member of his family, including his own mother, and to stay away from any Brethren church or school in New South Wales.

Finally, in late May 2007, he got a break: his younger son, then 16, came to live with him. According to Bruce, since the alleged assault on him, the boy had 'always struggled at school, and you could never get him out of his shell. But the first time I saw him [after getting out of jail], he said, "Dad, I've come to it that you don't need to be in a religion to know God. You can have your own links with God and when you die you'll go to heaven".'

But within hours of moving in with Bruce, the pressure began from the Brethren to get the boy 'back'. The phone started ringing, with Brethren friends seeking his company. Reluctantly, just 28 hours after his son had arrived to live with him, Bruce agreed to let him go on a day-tour of Melbourne, a three-hour drive away, with another young Brethren man. But this was no shopping trip: it was actually a tour of New South Wales, including an alcohol-fuelled fishing trip – the 'buck's weekend' of his companion, the son of another broken Albury family, who was about to get married. Bruce's son was away for five days, during which time Bruce had no idea where he was.

A few days after his return, while Bruce was at work, his son was moved out of his father's unit by other Brethren, including Bruce's older son. Bruce got there in time and demanded to see his younger son. That afternoon, the boy came to the unit.

'Poor kid – he was shaking, eyes quivering, mouth,' Bruce recalls. 'As he was leaving I said, "I'll pray for you." Kissed him. He didn't kiss me, he was quite petrified.'

Later, the boy was taken to another buck's night and then, at 3.00 am, was driven to Melbourne, put on a plane, and sent to Perth. At the time of writing, Bruce said he thought his son had been moved three times, so that he could not get in contact with him. 'Eight nights he had with me,' Bruce said. 'He was kidnapped from me, because I was told nothing when he left.'

'This is Bruce, unfortunately; part of his weakness is to be untruthful,' says Chris Shore:

> He told his boy that the Brethren didn't want to help him, didn't want him back, and I think [his son] felt sorry for him, felt sucked in ... And I think when [he] sussed it out and found it not to be the truth at all, I think he realised his father was just bulldusting him. And I think [the boy] had had enough.

As for moving to Perth:

> It certainly wasn't our suggestion, or mine anyway. It was [the boy's] suggestion as my understanding. He wanted to go to Perth

... to get away ... No one is pressured about anything. You can make suggestions and hint a few things, but ...

Bruce Suggate is totally out of the Brethren now. He has no contact with his wife and three children, and is shunned by members of the sect generally. This man, who has been damaged terribly by the strictures of the sect, and has inflicted awful damage himself on others, including the victims of sexual assault, says he has now found a real God who gives him succour, not judgment.

'I am more with God than ever before in my last 42 years, and my faith is very strong. One door shuts and another opens. Going to jail taught me to value human life and to care for and consider people more,' he said. However, he still finds it very hard to go to church 'because I had it shoved down my throat, seven days a week, for 40 years'.

Suggate is also trying to change his life. He wrote 78 letters from jail, apologising to all the victims of his crimes and other transgressions against people in the sect. He is seeing a psychiatrist, and he has embarked on further education in the aged-care industry.

But, because of the doctrine of separation, he must do all this alone, without the support of any of his family, or anybody in the community he grew up in. It is a monumental struggle for an emotionally fragile man.

In compiling the sorry recent history of the Exclusive Brethren in Albury, I have collected half-a-dozen statements, conducted many interviews with people from both sides of the fence, and viewed police statements, psychiatric reports, and court records.

From this story emerges a common thread. Whenever the people who have been shunned or feel betrayed by the Exclusive Brethren speak, they paint a picture of an oppressive organisation that had influence in every part of their lives, which manipulated, coerced, and directed them. Asked what he feels like, now that he is out of the Brethren, Bruce Suggate answers simply: 'No dread.'

But when the Brethren are asked about the same events, they paint a quite different picture: here, individuals act entirely of their own will, without interference from the sect, which simply plays a supporting role. The mother of the sexually abused girls simply decided that she would not report their stories to police; Bruce Suggate's son left home and went to Perth of his own free will; Bruce himself simply resolved to issue bomb threats against the court because he was mad, or bad. The tangled history of the Albury Brethren suggests that the real story is not that straightforward.

Part III
Politics

CHAPTER SEVEN

Persuasion

'Beloved Brethren,' the letter opened, 'The current situation regarding Government in Australia has never been more critical.' It was September 2004, a month before the election in which John Howard faced Mark Latham in the fight of his political life to that point. And, with this hyperbolic flourish, Bruce D. Hales, the Exclusive Brethren's Elect Vessel, was firing the starter's gun on his church's first official foray into electoral politics.

What Hales did was momentous in the history of his sect. He broke 175 years of tradition by officially endorsing the involvement of its members in election campaigning for the first time. It was a move that had startling consequences – not only for the Brethren, but for John Howard himself. 'Never has such a letter ever been amongst the Brethren, never,' said Ron Fawkes, a former Australian leader of the sect, who has been 'out' since he was withdrawn from in 1984.

'At the very highest level, it's giving a direction for the Brethren to get involved in the political sphere.'[1]

The letter was signed by Hales and seven other prominent Australian Brethren leaders, and it propelled the faithful around the country, and around the world, into immediate political action.

In Australia, they set up a holding company; raised hundreds of thousands of dollars; designed, printed, and distributed leaflets; bought newspaper advertisements; made phone calls to lobby and canvass; organised people to attend and disrupt a public meeting; and ordered their young men onto the streets to drop leaflets in letterboxes, all in support of John Howard, and in full-blooded opposition to the Left, particularly the Greens. Just what a departure this is for the Brethren is illustrated by the beliefs of their first leader, John Nelson Darby, who laid out the rules for interacting with government.

'We do not mix in politics; we are not of the world: we do not vote,' Darby wrote to the editor of French Catholic journal *Francais* in 1878. 'We submit to the established authorities, whatever they may be, *insofar as they command nothing expressly contrary to the will of Christ* (my italics).'[2]

Government, in the Brethren world view, is appointed and upheld by God, and therefore to participate in the process by which it is chosen is to become entangled in the 'world system' that Darby so despised. But the last phrase quoted is important, and points to a more nuanced approach to contact with government than is generally understood.

Since the 1940s in Australia, and quite unnoticed by the general public and the media, this sect has been watching out for laws and regulations that are, according to them, 'contrary to the will of Christ'. When they see such laws, Brethren members approach politicians directly, seek meetings, and ask for – and sometimes get – special treatment. The toehold that the Brethren have found and exploited in this lobbying has been their argument that they are guided by genuine religious 'conscience'. When they put this argument, they found that politicians, worried about transgressing religious freedom, were inclined to listen very carefully.

Former treasurer Peter Costello reflected the power of the argument when asked to explain why he had consented to meet the

Exclusive Brethren. He said it was not a crime to do so: 'In fact, the crime would be if a member of parliament refused to meet anybody on the basis of their religious convictions.'³

Transgressing against religious freedom is, understandably, a powerful taboo for politicians – not least because the religious lobby generally has seen a resurgence in power in Australia in recent years. But the question of how much attention the secular law should pay to religious sensibilities is a vexed one in all liberal polities that are keen to maintain the division between church and state.

Over many years of quiet, behind-the-scenes work, the Exclusive Brethren, representing just 15,000 people in Australia, have enjoyed success far beyond their numerical strength. They have gained open-door access to the highest ministerial offices in the land. Those whom they have lobbied confirm that most of their efforts have been spent on the so-called moral issues: abortion, stem-cell experimentation and euthanasia, and the Exclusive Brethren's hot-button issue of homosexuality – they particularly abhor the idea that gay relationships might be formally recognised in some way.

But when you have as many rules and regulations as the Brethren have, all of which are allegedly dictated by God, it is relatively easy to find an issue of conscience on which to peg a special request. Since early in the twentieth century, the members of this sect have taken advantage of conscientious-objection clauses to the otherwise compulsory act of voting in elections, and they have also claimed a conscientious objection to bearing arms in military service. But, quite often, the operation of the spiritual 'conscience' of the Exclusive Brethren also has a beneficial effect on their finances.

Such is the case with industrial relations, which, in the 1940s, first brought the Brethren into regular contact with politicians around the world. The sect's lobbying on this subject established relationships that they have used on many other issues over the years, and shows how such special deals are first won and then subjected to 'bracket creep' as time, and lobbying, wears on.

In the mid-1940s, the Elect Vessel of the day, James Taylor Senior, decided that the Brethren could not be 'in fellowship' with any outside organisation, and that therefore members could not join a trade union. A small businessman himself (in the rag trade), Taylor developed a strong aversion to unions, and he preached in the assembly against their influence. In the Brethren, of course, the prejudices of one powerful individual quickly become a matter of conscience for the entire group. The order went out that Brethren members had to immediately disassociate themselves from any union, and also from any guild or association of employers, such as chambers of commerce.

In Australia in the 1940s, this was a problem for Brethren firms. Union-preference clauses in state and Commonwealth legislation made membership of unions compulsory for most employees, particularly those working under an industrial award. Here was a law that was clearly, in Brethren minds, 'contrary to the will of Christ'. So church elders began a campaign of lobbying, at the level of state governments, to exempt their businesses, on the ground of conscience, from union-preference clauses.

The lobbyists' first success was in Queensland, in 1948, where they convinced a Labor premier, Ned Hanlon, to make them exempt. Hanlon was a former union official who recanted his former beliefs as he grew older and, as premier, sent in the police to suppress union demonstrations during the 1948 Queensland railway strike. He allowed Brethren people to object on conscientious grounds to being union members. New South Wales came under pressure from the sect next and, in 1951, followed Queensland with their own exemption. In 1956, conscientious objection for the Brethren became part of the Commonwealth Conciliation and Arbitration Act, after which it flowed to the statute books of all other states except Victoria.

The Brethren representations to governments, federal and state, continued throughout the 1960s and 1970s, and were almost exclusively made to discuss some aspect of industrial relations law. Ron Fawkes remembers visiting Malcolm Fraser in the 1970s to lobby on the industrial relations issue. But in 1974 something happened that would change the Brethren's relationship with politics forever: the election of a promising young Liberal MP, the local member in the seat of Bennelong, where many of the Brethren high-fliers lived. His name was John Howard.

From quite early on, according to Bob Hales, a distant cousin of Bruce Hales, the Brethren identified Howard 'basically as their hero'.[4]

'I know [Bruce Hales' father] John Hales backed him from the 1970s, when he was treasurer. He was seen as the ideal candidate for prime ministership long before he was anywhere near that position.'

Howard came to parliament with an established reputation as an advocate for the 'new Right'. He was economically dry, an exponent of small government, fiscal conservatism, and workplace deregulation. Howard was also an avowed Christian, which commended him strongly to the Brethren. According to Fawkes, this 'suited the Brethren down to the ground, and that's why they championed him'.[5] The politician and the Brethren leaders had a mutual antipathy to trade unions, and a determination to minimise their influence in Australian life. They had a similar background and outlook in other ways, too, including their north-western Sydney upbringing, and a small-business mindset (Howard's father ran a petrol station).

John Hales's Meadowbank home, Bruce Hales's Ermington business headquarters and his West Ryde home, and the Brethren school headquarters are all in Bennelong, which is a constituency of small businesses, and light-industrial and commercial enterprises. Howard and Bruce Hales both attended Canterbury Boys' High school, though they were not contemporaries, with Hales junior the younger by about 15 years.

The circumstances of the first meetings between Howard and John Hales are lost in the mists of time. But one former Brethren member, once a confidante of John Hales, said that they had 'worked on him at a local level' because they 'wanted him onside in view of getting their ideas recognised'.[6]

In 1989, Howard met John Hales's son, the current world leader, Bruce D. Hales, for the first time. The Exclusive Brethren's chief parliamentary lobbyist, Warwick John, explained that, 'In days past, Mr Hales would greet and shake hands with Mr Howard in Eastwood Square [a shopping centre in Bennelong]'.[7] Bruce Hales clearly regarded his relationship with the prime minister very highly. He was in the habit of exalting Howard to his flock as 'a born economic manager' with 'Christian values': 'As we told him the other day, he has the economy by the throat'.[8]

On Howard's part, he was no doubt attracted by the apparently clean-cut, conservative, and God-fearing image of these constituents who were so keen to meet and flatter him. But even senior staff members who were close to Howard in Canberra are somewhat perplexed about why Howard had formed such a close relationship with the Brethren; ultimately, this will probably remain a mystery. When Howard was asked about it, he always described the Brethren as constituents, and a former Canberra staff member said he did not sit in on the meetings when the Brethren came to visit for that reason.

One former staffer suggested that Howard met the Brethren 'because they had interests out that way [in Bennelong] and they had said things that appeared to be very supportive of him'. Another said, 'Because they were in his electorate, and of a small-business constituency, Howard had a relationship with them.' A third said, 'It was an electorate-related thing. I was aware of the odd appointment being made to meet these people, but it was a matter essentially administered at the electorate level.'[9]

But one senior Liberal Party apparatchik told me: 'You don't meet with all constituents; it's just not true. Even if an organisation has lots of supporters, they might meet with a member of parliament, but meeting with the prime minister is quite different ... It would seem most unlikely that the PM would be engaging with them and meeting them if they weren't offering something.'[10] Specifically what they were offering remains undisclosed.

One of the issues on which Howard and the Brethren firmly agree is industrial relations policy. When it came to industrial relations, and other issues of 'conscience', the election of John Howard as prime minister in 1996 represented the best news the Brethren had ever had from the political sphere. By that time, thanks to the ascendency of the new Right in Australian politics, a strong move had been afoot for over a decade to rid employers of the union 'closed shop'.

This movement for 'freedom of association' provisions in legislation found its expression in the same year that the Howard government was elected, when federal Liberal minister Peter Reith introduced his 1996 industrial relations legislation. In Reith's Act, the cast-iron freedom *not* to join a union was enshrined in federal law for the first time.

Theoretically, this development should have rendered irrelevant the conscientious-objection clauses won by the Brethren in the 1940s and 1950s. Being under no compulsion to join a union, surely their members could simply exercise their legal right not to? Or so Reith and his legislative drafters believed when they drew up the new Workplace Relations Act: they dropped the Brethren conscientious-objection clause at the drafting stage.

But the Brethren disagreed. They began a furious lobbying effort to keep their special exemption. Democrats Senator Andrew Murray, who was negotiating the fine detail with Reith, recalls that, during the final stages of the negotiations, the minister rang him 'to say he was being heavily lobbied by them, and (effectively) wanted to be rid of the lobbyists':

> [Reith] saw it as a minor 'nuisance', saw no reason not to continue past practice for this small religious group if it meant so much to them, and asked whether I and the Democrats would object to their previous status being continued. I replied no. I saw it as a small unimportant side issue amidst the broader controversy and big policy issues of the Bill.[11]

But in one of the Howard government's next cracks at workplace reform in 2001, the Brethren, completely undetected by the general public, won a new clause that was a significant advance on their past position: they convinced the government to allow them, if they employed fewer than 20 staff, to prevent a union official from even *visiting* their workplace to talk to the employees. The only catch was that their employees had to agree.

Three years later, the new minister, Kevin Andrews, was working under Howard's close supervision to craft WorkChoices, the final attempt to kill off the union movement. At this point, the Brethren's special deal became complete. WorkChoices imposed strict conditions on union entry to any workplace, but it became absolute for Brethren employers: they could deny entry to a union representative, no matter what the issue, whether or not their employees agreed. Having the Brethren consult their employees about the issue was judged by the government to be unduly onerous for them.

From a governance point of view, this exemption makes no sense. If their employees are members of the Brethren, the exclusion is unnecessary (since they are prevented by their religion from joining a union). But if someone is employed by a Brethren firm, and is not a church member (and Bruce Hales tells us there are 4000 such employees in Australia),[12] why should he or she be denied access to a union simply because of their boss's religion?

Fawkes said that the Brethren's seeking of anti-union provisions were 'totally self-interest; much more self-interest than conscience'.[13] It does not appear to be a question of pay: Fawkes recalled that

Brethren businesses, on the whole, paid above the award in his day, and copies of the transcripts of Bruce Hales's business seminars show him exhorting his members to pay their employees well.

But the provision does prevent employees from organising for any other reason – to advocate for a better lunchroom, or greater health and safety provisions, or to complain about ill treatment or discrimination. In New Zealand, a Brethren-owned medical-supplies company banned their multicultural staff from speaking any language other than English, even in the lunchroom, and then used their exemption certificate to prevent a union coming in hear the staff complaints.[14]

'They just hate the unions for some reason,' said Fawkes. 'I think it was just the mindset of the whole thing.'

Industrial relations has been one big success story for the Brethren, but their lobbying has gone much further and delivered other successes. In the realm of education, in the 1990s, the Brethren negotiated special deals with at least two state governments to allow their children cheap access to state-funded distance-education schools. The issue of conscience they relied on here was their aversion to their children associating with worldly children and being taught a curriculum that was 'defiling'. Their ability to obtain top-notch financial assistance for their own private schools has also been nothing less than miraculous (see next chapter).

In Ireland, the Brethren have controversially negotiated special provisions in pension legislation that exempt them from buying annuities, on the conscience ground that insurers and actuaries should not be calculating their probable date of death because only God can do this.[15] So financially attractive is the exemption they negotiated with the government that accountants for non-Brethren business people have started using it to their own clients' advantage.

But the Brethren's special claims of religious conscience have not always delivered the outcome they desired. In 1997, the sect sought from then finance minister John Fahey a tax exemption for the vehicles of their elders. They argued that their cars should be exempt on the same grounds as those driven by clergy in other faiths. But they withdrew the application when it was pointed out that their beliefs included one that clergy were 'dispensationally a sin against the Holy Spirit' – in other words, priests were against God's plan for the world.

In 1999, the Victorian government refused to grant the Brethren an exemption from paying electronic tolls on CityLink, a privatised extended freeway. A delegation of Brethren members had gone to the statutory government authority that was overseeing the road's construction to argue that they could not carry electronic tolling tags in their cars because they emitted radio waves, which are inherently devilish. They also argued that they should be exempted from any other method of being charged for travelling on the road. The bureaucrats refused their requests, and then headed off any attempt of the delegation to see the minister personally. The Brethren were forced to pay the tolls.

Like all lobbyists, the Brethren seek to form relationships with suggestible politicians and then to influence them. And, under Howard's benign gaze, this small religious sect found great success in its attempts to gain access to Liberal and National Party politicians. The breadth of the political network established in the coalition parties by the Brethren was laid bare when it was revealed that 11 Exclusive Brethren members had obtained special lobbyists' passes to get an almost permanent presence in Parliament House, and that they had been sponsored by no fewer than 13 different Howard government MPs, affirming that they were of good repute.[16] Of those 11 passes, six were still valid at the end of 2007. The parliamentary records do not easily allow a comparison of how many passes are issued for individual organisations, but it would be surprising if any other organisation in the country had more than six lobbyists to represent the interests of as few as 15,000 people.

The passholders did not identify themselves as members of

the 'Exclusive Brethren' on their applications – they were recorded in the parliamentary records as members of the 'Christian Lobby Group'. This tactic potentially masked the true identity of the Brethren contingent on Capital Hill, and it was also confusing, since three members of an entirely separate, more mainstream group, the Australian Christian Lobby, used the same name. These lobbyist passes allow their Brethren holders unfettered access to every office in the Australian legislature. The passes are intended for people who are in Parliament House for 30 or more days per year.

Among those giving the references to the lobbyists were the front rank of Howard's ministers – Alexander Downer, Brendan Nelson, Tony Abbott, and Tasmanian Senator Eric Abetz, who became a staunch public defender of the sect when they were under political fire. Warwick John, the leader of the Brethren's lobbying team, was sponsored by Michael Ferguson, a Tasmanian Christian fundamentalist who lost his seat of Bass at the 2007 election, and by former minister Danna Vale, John's local member. Vale's most memorable contribution to public debate was the lament that Australia was becoming a Muslim nation because the rest of us were 'aborting ourselves almost out of existence'.

Most of the politicians who have been the focus of the Brethren's lobbying efforts report that, like Howard, they were approached first at the electorate level by Brethren leaders who were also constituents. The leader in a particular location would seek out an MP – mostly a conservative Christian, of which there are a large number in parliament – and try to establish a link with him or her. The Brethren would assiduously use the networks thus formed to arrange meetings with other senior politicians, including ministers, to push their sectional interests on the grounds of conscience and religious freedom.

Howard's attorney-general, Philip Ruddock, said he had seen Brethren members attending party fundraisers, then lining up to meet the candidate or member afterwards, and attempting to organise more formal meetings.[17] In these meetings they are, by all reports, solicitous, charming, and intelligent.

Alan Cadman was a long-time Liberal backbencher and member for the Sydney seat of Mitchell. He said he had had contact with the Brethren first through their local leader in his electorate and then with others. He had been seeing them 'since Malcolm Fraser was the prime minister', and his dealings mainly regarded industrial relations. 'I questioned them as to whether they were seriously conscientious objectors. They are legitimate in that; they do hold the genuine beliefs that they observe, and they don't stray from them. I found them authentic and reliable,' Cadman said, adding that they were 'never tricky, or other than up-front in the way they dealt with me'.[18]

Jackie Kelly, the former Liberal member for the Sydney seat of Lindsay, was another ally of the Brethren in parliament. A conservative Christian herself, she said that Brethren representatives would often come to lobby her, mostly on moral issues, but once even on the subject of water.[19] Having done so, they would ask to be referred to another MP who might be useful. Kelly said it was 'quite nice that they were wanting to pray for us':

> They do have a very senior guy in Canberra, Warwick [John]. He's always there when you are voting ... It was well known in Canberra. Everyone in the parliament would say, 'The Brethren are here today – don't get thrown out!' They are very open in watching you, how you are behaving, conducting yourselves.

A senior Liberal tactician, who did not agree with the close relationships that some party members had with the Exclusive Brethren, said that members of parliament liked meeting them because 'they tended to reinforce their particular conservative views':

There are a hell of a lot of happy clappers in federal politics whose agenda is not necessarily a mainstream one. They are very hard to fight and resist for one reason; they are bloody well organised, and one of the basic rules of success in politics is organisation. These people are motivated to organise, and they're prepared to work longer and harder than their opponents.

Hales, more than any of his predecessors, pushed the need for making representations to government on subjects far beyond their historical preoccupations. In an undated piece of Bruce Hales testimony, he says:

> Government is here, as far as I can see, is only here for the saints [Brethren] ... A pointed appeal based on righteousness and a true testimony will affect men in government. I think the saints will have to continue at it until the rapture. At certain times we've let it go, and evil men have got in.[20]

Howard himself met delegations of Brethren members throughout his years in Canberra, including those as prime minister, until they became very familiar with each other. The Brethren repeatedly used this relationship to seek Howard out – sometimes for his help, sometimes to offer theirs to him. One letter, from Bruce Hales and others in 2000, pleads for Howard's intervention in a dispute with the New South Wales education department (see next chapter). The letter refers to the sect's 'contact with you over the years', and recalls the prime minister's 'sympathetic support in the past' – revealing that, by 2000, the relationship was already close and well established.

In 2002, when Bruce Hales came to power within the Brethren, the relationship appears to have stepped up another notch. It is unclear how regularly they met; but, in response to a freedom of information request, Howard's office reluctantly released five distinct pieces of correspondence from the Brethren to the then prime minister between 2003 and 2006, and one letter in response from Howard. The correspondence gives some idea of what went on in these meetings. It confirms that the senior Brethren felt so comfortable with the prime minister that they could flatter, cajole, and even gently admonish him as they traversed any number of issues over the years.

In May 2003, Howard was invited by George W. Bush to stay at his ranch on the eve of the American president's shipboard announcement of 'Mission Accomplished' in Iraq. To the Brethren, keen supporters of the Iraq war, this was a feat worthy of warm congratulations.

'It must be a great encouragement to The President and yourself that the Iraq regime has been overturned in such an expeditious way by the coalition forces,' they wrote in a letter addressed to the prime minister's Parliament House office. 'God has clearly supported and vindicated the initiative taken, and we are assured He will continue to do so as there is dependence on him for guidance.'[21]

After taking a swipe at the United Nation's 'inability to deal with such critical matters', the Brethren writers (whose names were blacked out on the documents for privacy reasons), signed off, saying they 'personally assure you of our undeviating prayerful support at every turn', and wished good health to Howard's 'wife and family'.

In September of that year, they took a different tone. The sect leaders were unhappy about then health minister Kay Patterson's Medicare package, then under development, and they wrote to express their concern. The authors said that Brethren representatives had been present at all but two of the public hearings of the parliamentary inquiry into the proposed legislation, and 'compiled information contained in approximately 160 of the published submissions'. They had also spoken with 'many people in the course of our daily business dealings', and concluded that the

Bill had 'provoked a very strong anti-government reaction'.[22]

'As you know we have fully supported your initiatives in many matters including Workplace Relations changes, the Iraq war and your strong support of the US President's stand against terrorism.'

The writers complained that their members who earned more than $50,000 per annum were 'obliged to pay the extra 1 per cent (Medicare) levy'. They were referring to the Medicare surcharge, which was added to the standard levy for people earning over $50,000 who were not members of private health funds. The Brethren had a conscientious objection to belonging to a private health fund (on the grounds that it would put them in fellowship with people outside the sect). They said that their members had been paying the surcharge 'without protest or request for relief ever since it was introduced and this would have cost the Brethren tens of millions of dollars over the past 16 years'. Then they proffered some political advice: 'We strongly believe that if you change Medicare in any shape or form before the next election, you will lose it ... If you consider it necessary to change Medicare we suggest you leave it till after the next election.'

One of their chief concerns, expressed in submissions to the parliamentary inquiry, was that, under Patterson's changes, disadvantaged people holding health care cards would be given priority access to bulk billing (no-fee medical treatment). These underprivileged people, they believed, would crowd out Brethren members seeking access to bulk-billed services. This was particularly unfair on them, they said, again because of their objection to private health-fund membership.

It must be said that the Brethren were not the only group complaining about Patterson's package, and there was significant disquiet about it within the government itself. Within three months of the Brethren's letter, Howard had replaced Kay Patterson as health minister, and had installed Tony Abbott to address the political problems in the portfolio. Abbott was given more generous funding to come up with a new, improved Medicare package, and part of this was to ditch the bulk-billing policy that the Brethren had objected to.

(The Brethren overcame their conscience objection to private health insurance shortly after these events, and set up their very own private health fund, onemedifund. They tried, but failed, to have the government regulator allow them to have it as a closed fund; so, if a worldly person applies to join it, they will be required to accept the application, and be 'in fellowship' with him or her. Onemedifund is also unusual in that it is run for profit.)

The following year, in May 2004, the Brethren's concern about Howard's electoral chances mounted further, with a worried letter addressed to him, saying that 'the media appears to be having a measure of success in their current campaign to destabilise your government'.[23] Their letter was a mixture of flattery and political advice. After telling Howard of their 'strongly held belief' that his 'policies and initiatives have clearly resulted in the current unparalleled prosperity that this country is enjoying', they suggested a way that he could continue to 'hold the initiative'.

'The attention of the public needs to be diverted from matters such as the Iraq war, the supposed ill treatment of Iraq prisoners and other contentious issues,' they wrote. Their suggested distraction was that Howard initiate the building of a water pipeline of the size of the Californian Water Project, which carried water hundreds of kilometres, and 'obviously makes the difference between desert and a flourishing metropolis':

> The magnitude, prosperity and economical advantage of such a project could be duplicated in Australia for the benefit of the entire country. Our suggestion is that this project could be readily funded using half the proceeds from the sale of Telstra, and the issue of government Water Bonds as an attractive investment opportunity.
>
> Each of the undersigned have had the pleasure of meeting you

over the past few years, and appreciate the immense courage you have shown in leading us through one of the most critical periods this country has known. Please be assured of our continual prayers for yourself, Mrs Howard and your family, that you all may be maintained in good health, and you will continue to lead Australia as under the hand of God, for the blessing of the people and the welfare of our nation.

It is interesting that, despite the Brethren's rule against investing in the stock market and other financial instruments, they were recommending a strategy to the prime minister based on market funding for an infrastructure project.

Until early 2004 there is no firm evidence that the Brethren offered Howard anything but regular get-togethers, moral support, prayers, and gratuitous advice. But, in September 2004, in time for the election in which Howard was seeking his fourth term, that all changed. In that election campaign, the Brethren kicked in $370,000 in advertisements, as well as boots on the ground, to support the prime minister and to attack his enemies, including the Greens.

In some ways, Mark Latham can be blamed for the advent of the Brethren as a political force. In September 2004, a month before the federal election that year, he was polling neck and neck with John Howard. Though Howard had pegged back his earlier deficit against Latham, and the public was starting to turn against the unpredictable Labor leader, it still seemed possible that Howard might be defeated.

To be strictly accurate, it was not the first time that the Brethren had worked on a campaign in Australia. In 1993, some adventurous spirits, led by Bruce Hales's brother, Stephen, had become active in the federal election campaign on behalf of John Hewson, though Hewson apparently had no knowledge of their involvement. According to Bob Hales, who worked on that campaign, it was run out of Stephen's factory, from where a group of activists coordinated advertisements in newspapers nationally. But he said it was more of a diversion for 'bored millionaires' than a well-thought-through strategy. In the end, all those who had participated in the 1993 campaign were forced to apologise for it by then world leader, John Hales.

But in 2004, the orders to participate came from the very top. Bruce Hales had become the leader on his father's death in 2002, and was witnessing his first federal election campaign as Man of God. With so much invested in Howard, the fear of losing him as prime minister to Latham was enough to jolt him into bucking 175 years of tradition and to order the involvement of his followers in Howard's re-election campaign.

Of particular concern to the Brethren was Latham's schools policy, which included a 'hit list' of 67 independent schools that were earmarked to lose funding. No Brethren schools were on that list, but the sect's own schools are among the most generously supported by federal funds in the country (see next chapter). The Brethren had a strong financial interest in keeping Howard's school-funding system, with all its sops for special-interest groups, just the way it was. Sect insiders say it was one of their main concerns about the Labor leader.

The September 2004 letter to the flock also makes it clear that Hales had noticed Latham's close friendship with former prime minister Gough Whitlam, his mentor and former employer:

> Many of you young people may not know of the awful years after Whitlam came to power when there was serious decline in moral standards resulting in bad laws, strikes and union strife, poor economic management, high unemployment, very high interest rates, difficult trading conditions and a country without a clear sense of direction.

By contrast, under the 'Christian men' in the government of

John Howard, 'national debt has been reduced, unemployment is down, interest rates are low and the Australian dollar is being reasonably sustained. We believe this will change dramatically if an alternative government is elected'.

The 'strengthening of our links with the US and UK are essential to the prosperity and stability of the nation and to protect us from the Asian threat', the eight signatories wrote. Howard, according to the letter, was facing a conspiracy by the opposition and the media to 'make him a liar based on falsehoods and distorted facts backed by large campaign funds from the trade union movement and support from radical minor parties'.

For anyone not steeped in the Brethren's arcane language, Hales's solution for these various catastrophes appeared somewhat anticlimactic: he exhorted his flock to 'be cast on our faces before God and be united in spirit and in prayer, so that He may come in for us in view of the present government being retained'. But to those in the Brethren, or who understand its unique speech patterns, the exhortation to be 'united in spirit' was nothing less than a call to arms.

And a call to arms it proved to be. Just six days after the letter was signed and distributed to assemblies worldwide, a Sydney pump salesman, Mark Mackenzie, spent $10 to register a new business, Willmac Enterprises Pty Ltd. This single-director company (Mackenzie was also the secretary and the sole shareholder) was, on paper, an unbelievably successful enterprise. In just three months of operating a business that was never really defined, purportedly from a derelict, abandoned suburban house in North Rocks in Sydney, it had made enough clear profit to spend $370,461 on electoral advertising to support Howard and castigate the Greens.

It was a massive spend, the fifth largest of any third-party donor in that campaign – more than the Australian Conservation Foundation and the Wilderness Society combined. The man at the centre of it, Mark Mackenzie, was a former employee of Stephen Hales, the brother of the Man of God and owner of the central Brethren pump franchise, All Pumps, who had engineered the 1993 John Hewson campaign.

An investigation by the ABC's *Four Corners* later revealed that most of the money that came into Willmac – $340,000 – was deposited by the Brethren's chief lobbyist, Warwick John, and most of that in large bundles of cash. The biggest single cash deposit was of $120,000.[24] John was neither an employee of Willmac nor a director. When he was asked about it later, he simply denied it: 'I can confirm that I have never deposited any money into Willmac Enterprises and to suggest otherwise is a complete fallacy'.[25]

Mackenzie's official line on Willmac was that the company 'made the money used from business earnings, not donations, but from income generated through business activity'.[26] It was a private company that was 'not owned or operated by the Exclusive Brethren', he said. If the money had been donated rather than raised by business transactions, the donors would have needed to be disclosed to the Australian Electoral Commission. No such disclosures were made, even by Warwick John.

Despite its phenomenal success, on paper, as a business, Willmac was closed about a year after the election. Whatever its structure, during just three weeks of the election campaign this little business bought pro-Howard advertisements across the country, which were booked and authorised by different members of the Brethren in different states. In the final three days of the election campaign, ads appeared from Bennelong to Perth to Brisbane.

Four Corners found that eleven ads published in local papers in South Australia were booked by the church's leader in that state, Warwick Joyce, but most were authorised by Doug Burgess, the principal of the Brethren school in Victoria. Mackenzie's company Willmac, based in New South Wales, paid for them. The advertisements and leaflets distributed in this coordinated blitz a few days before the federal election were all strongly pro-Howard and anti-

Green. They were resolutely anti-homosexual, and warned about the threat to the fabric of society if gay marriage were allowed. They had headings such as, 'We ARE Happy, John', 'The Green Delusion', and 'Why the Grass Won't Be Greener on the Other Side'.

There was more than just advertising, though. In 2004, Howard faced a challenge in his seat of Bennelong from Greens candidate Andrew Wilkie, a former intelligence analyst who had resigned in disgust at Australia's role in the Iraq war. Here was a candidate guaranteed to infuriate the Exclusive Brethren – he was a Green and against the Iraq war – and they made their displeasure known at a public meeting in the electorate, where Stephen Hales and a large group of others turned up and harassed Wilkie, who described them as 'very disruptive, very threatening, very aggressive'.[27] Young Brethren members also distributed leaflets against the Greens in the electorate.

There were also circumstantial links directly to the Liberal Party itself. When a concerned citizen of Adelaide, Bronte Trainor, rang her local paper, *The Advertiser*, to find out who had placed a full-page John Howard advertisement that was authorised by somebody at a school she had never heard of, the newspaper initially told her that the Liberal Party had placed it. The newspaper later retracted this version of the story. The *Ballarat Courier* newspaper in Victoria also identified the Liberal Party as the organisation that had placed two advertisements which had been authorised by Exclusive Brethren school principal Doug Burgess.

But no direct links between the Brethren and the Liberal Party organisation have been proven, and no Liberal politician has confessed to having had individual negotiations with them about what political help they might receive. However, if the experience of National Party candidate Robert Griffith is anything to go by, some candidates were being offered the full Brethren treatment.

Griffith was a fundamentalist Christian pastor from the New

South Wales town of Orange, with views the Brethren would have heartily agreed with. As the Howard government was pushing through its Marriage Amendment Bill in August 2004, which specifically denied legal recognition of same-sex marriages, Griffith burst into print on his website: 'The idea that same-sex partners could masquerade as real parents and be responsible for raising children was abhorrent to most people,' he wrote.[28] The comment earned Griffith a trip to the anti-discrimination tribunal in New South Wales, care of the energetic Sydney anti-discrimination activist Gary Burns, who argued that Griffith's comment incited hatred against homosexuals.

But the Brethren decided at around the same time that Griffith deserved their full support in his contest against the sitting member, independent MP Peter Andren. Andren was an opponent of the Iraq War and Howard's asylum-seeker policies, and he also campaigned for stronger electoral-funding disclosure laws. So, in September 2004, a delegation of Brethren members went to meet Griffith, and made him an offer he could not refuse. Griffith described this offer, under the title 'Secret Weapon from God', in a circular email to those he believed would support him:

> Please keep this news to yourself, just praise God and pray for more miracles like this one! The Plymouth Brethren have been convicted by God to get more involved on the political front. I have met with many of their key people in our region (and beyond). As a result of those meetings and lots of prayer, they have now given a commitment to support my campaign in a HUGE way. We are talking about a huge amount of money and personnel; four full electorate letter-box drops of targeted material ... printed at their expense. ?-page newspaper advertisements across the electorate every week, at their expense, and the list goes on! They have mobilised an army of 500 + people ready to walk the streets delivering material for my campaign.

This is a miracle! When this is over, the contribution from these brothers and sisters will be more than twice our current campaign budget! I just got off the phone with [the] Deputy Prime Minister, and John Anderson said that this was the most amazing news he had ever heard and that this was the miracle he had been praying for in Calare! The Brethren do not want to be public and too up front about this, so keep it to yourselves, but praise God from whom such miracles flow!![29]

This was the Brethren political promise in all its glory: big money, big advertising, big physical support. And if Griffith had become the member for Calare, he would have owed them a big favour. Unfortunately for Griffith, the existence of his 'secret weapon' leaked, and was reported in the local news.

It appears that the publication of their intentions deterred the Brethren, and little help was actually forthcoming. Griffith lodged a 'nil' return to the Australian Electoral Commission for donations to his campaign, and he lost big to Andren. The New South Wales National Party's return declares just one donation from Willmac to the Calare campaign, a modest $2315 for 'corflutes' – the posters on sticks that people plant in their front gardens. When I quizzed Griffith about what had happened in the end, he denied he was ever promised any concerted Brethren support, and he seemed to question the authenticity of the email itself. However, when I asked him exactly what he meant by this, he refused to elaborate and then hung up.[30]

The focus on secrecy in the Calare email highlights another feature of the Brethren's political tactics: minimal disclosure. When authorisation of advertising materials was required by law, individual Brethren members – sometimes obscure ones, sometimes using their middle names and false, or unused, addresses – were listed.

From that day to this, the sect's leaders have used 'plausible deniability' – the tactic invented by the CIA – to claim that only individuals had become involved in politics, not the church organisation itself. Despite the letter from Hales that started it all off; despite the senior Brethren personnel involved, and their level of coordination; and despite the high level of funding from mysterious sources, the Brethren maintain that every campaign has simply resulted from the unprompted actions of individual sect members, or groups of 'friends'.

'You've got to allow for spontaneity,' Bruce Hales's brother, Daniel, said later.[31]

Once Howard had been safely re-elected in Australia, and the Brethren's hand in it had gone undetected, the sect's election roadshow was off to the United States, where George W. Bush was facing his re-election campaign the following month, November 2004. Two weeks after election day in Australia, a group called the 'Thanksgiving 2004 Committee' was registered with the US Internal Revenue Service, four days after the deadline for reporting pre-election campaign expenditures.

During the campaign, the Thanksgiving committee raised and spent $636,522, with one single donor contributing $377,262. This donor was Bruce Hazell of London, England, a senior member of the Exclusive Brethren. This enormous sum of money seemed to have been funnelled through another company, Ratby Distributions, newly registered in London, whose purposes included making donations to political parties, and taking and defending legal actions. Bruce Hales had over Ratby 'absolute power of veto in all matters', according to its documents.[32] One of Ratby's directors was Philip McNaughton, a Sydney-based confidante of Hales, and the sect's occasional spokesman.

Thanks to the London money, the Thanksgiving 2004 committee took out a full-page advertisement in the *New York Times* on election day, under the headline, 'America Is In Safe Hands'. There was also an advertisement in the *Tampa Tribune* and a quarter-page ad in the *St Petersburg Times* endorsing Republican Mel Martinez for the US Senate. Martinez, a Cuban American, opposes abortion even in cases of rape and incest, and supports an amendment to the US Constitution to ban forever same-sex marriage.

These advertisements were signed by individuals who were all Brethren members, but who did not mention this fact anywhere. One member of the US organising group, Knoxville map-store owner Steve Truan, told the *St Petersburg Times* that he was 'working with a larger group', but he would not say who because, 'We like to fly beneath the radar'.[33]

A former American member of the Brethren, Don Monday, has said that behind all this advertising was the guiding hand of the Man of God, Bruce Hales. 'Everything that was passed down', all the correspondence produced to organise the fundraising and advertising activities, carried Hales's name, Monday said. In his version of the story, the interest in politics 'became a recurring topic' in the printed ministry emanating from the church in late 2004. A US–Canadian Election Commission was formed with both national and international committees, and local brothers from Monday's area were appointed to report to their local meetings about the workings of those committees.[34]

'These local contacts kept Brethren informed of political hot topics through newsletters and announcements at meetings. Special prayer meetings were scheduled, letter-writing and phone campaigns were organised, and contact names and addresses were distributed for donation purposes,' Monday said. 'Special trips of political interest were also planned.'

These activities were conducted in the Brethren meeting room, directly before or after a meeting, by means of information posted on the bulletin board in the foyer, by special mailings or hand-delivered letters, and by phone calls. Funds were raised in the same way, according to Monday. 'When there was money needed there would've been a plea go out for either personal donations or meeting room donations for any specific cause.' And yet the Brethren denied, and continue to deny, any organised church involvement in campaigning. The elders in the assembly where Monday used to attend say he is 'is an unreliable witness who has no credibility'.[35]

But Monday's story was backed up by another former American Brethren, Stelli Carmichael. She said she had become involved in telephone canvassing for the US mid-term elections as a direct result of a visit to the United States by Bruce Hales in October 2006.[36] She was provided with long lists of voters, and instructed to 'volunteer' to call them. Stelli's father, Bruce, a senior American Brethren member, responded to her comments in a statement, saying that his daughter had 'always been one to exaggerate things a bit out of proportion for a good story'. He confirmed that she had participated in campaigning, but only 'of her own accord'.[37]

After Bush's re-election, the campaign moved to Canada, where secrecy reached new heights. In 2005, the Canadian parliament was debating a motion to allow gay marriage, so the Brethren began an aggressive, anonymous, direct-mail campaign to tens of thousands of householders, urging them to contact their local member to tell them to vote against the legislation. The pamphlet said that, 'Marriage is about to be dumped in the garbage can of history'.[38] The sponsors were typically hard to spot, and were identified only by the title of their unregistered group, 'CCP' or 'Concerned Canadian Parents'. The only contact address was a post office box in a 7-11 store.

Don Monday said that the political activity around the Canadian Bill within the Brethren on both sides of the US–Canadian border had been frenetic. But when the press finally caught up with Ron Heggie, the Brethren man who had produced the pamphlets and placed the advertisements, he maintained the pretence that the sect itself was not involved: 'Those who think the Brethren are being unethical and deceptive don't understand their approach to the outside world,' he told the *Vancouver Sun*. 'It's not that we're hiding anything. It's just that we're not interested in grandstanding.'³⁹

In 2005, the controversy moved back to the antipodes, to the election for the national parliament in New Zealand. This is where the Exclusive Brethren's tactics began to unravel. As revealed by author Nicky Hager, the Brethren first advertised in his country in December 2004, in protest against that country's civil unions Bill to allow gay marriage.⁴⁰ But their campaign did not begin in earnest until eight months before the 2005 election, and it was done with the full, but secret, connivance of the National Party.

In April 2005, the Brethren spent $350,000 on advertisements that supported nuclear ships – a stand which the National Party and its leader, Don Brash, could not publicly support, but which would get people talking about the issue in a way that Brash hoped would advantage him. The emails reveal that Brash's staff were talking to the Brethren throughout this time, to work out how to respond to any sticky media questions about the ads.

On 8 June 2005, Brethren elder Ron Hickmott sent an email to New Zealand's then chief electoral officer to find out how he and his 'friends' could spend $1.2 million with the aim of producing 'extensive publications throughout the country with a theme showing and demonstrating mistrust in the current [Labour] Government and building trust in a [Don] Brash-led National Government'. New Zealand law at the time imposed strict caps on how much political parties could spend on advertising during election campaigns, and it also prevented third parties from circumventing the rules by doing the spending themselves. The Brethren wanted to find out exactly how close to the wind they could sail without having their ads come in under the National Party's funding cap.

As it turns out, they sailed very close indeed. In the two weeks leading up to the September election, the Brethren put out a blitz of pamphlets and advertisements. As in other countries, they were authorised by unknown people at sometimes false addresses. One was from a 'group' called 'New Zealand Advocates for Timely

Healthcare' which, Hager pointed out, 'does not appear to have any existence outside the pamphlet'.

The ads were very strongly pro-National, using words just like those the National Party was using, but stronger and blunter. Brash and his team were closely involved in consulting with the Brethren about the content and design of their material. In essence, Don Brash and his team conspired, during numerous meetings with the Brethren in 2005, for the sect to say the things he himself could not be seen to say publicly. But the Brethren agreed to ram home the points while Brash pretended to know nothing about it.

The Brethren, whose businesses rely heavily on telemarketing, also translated those existing systems into a phone-canvassing campaign on behalf of National. But in New Zealand, unlike elsewhere, the Brethren campaign was rumbled in advance of election day, because former members of the sect blew the whistle on the identity of those authorising the ads. Seven Brethren businessmen, the 'Secret Seven', were forced to step forward to lay claim to the campaign. In typical style, however, they denied that the sect itself was behind the campaign.

Interviewed in 2007 by *Four Corners*, one of the seven, Neville Simmonds, agreed that the campaign appeared organised, saying, 'we're quite organised sort of people'. But he maintained it was not organised from the top, saying only that 'between 25 and 50 of us ... persons I've had a friendship for many years' were involved.

Don Brash was much less able to dodge the issue. It became the biggest political scandal of the week before election day. After he had denied any knowledge of the campaign that he and his minders had spent months helping to cook up, he was forced, gradually, over the course of a few days, to admit that he had in fact known – a revelation that severely dented his cleanskin image with the populace.

Brash lost the election by a whisker. Pundits say that the controversy generated by the Brethren was largely to blame. And when Hager's book, *The Hollow Men*, was published late the following year, revealing the depth of Brash's complicity in the Brethren's activities, he was forced to quit the party's leadership. He was eventually forced to resign from parliament entirely when caught in another lie – he had said he had not even seen a crucial email regarding the Brethren which he had in fact seen, and forwarded with comments. Brash's successor as National leader, John Key, is still dogged by the issue, and is still claiming he knew nothing in advance about the Brethren campaign.

There are three codas to the New Zealand story. The first is that the government of Prime Minister Helen Clark used the Brethren experience to substantially tighten up the law surrounding electoral financing, at just the time that John Howard was loosening the law in Australia. The second is that the Brethren, though they believe that government is chosen by God, were still reluctant to accept their loss. They started a new campaign to tear down Clark, and one or more of the sect's members assigned private detectives to tail Clark and her husband, Peter Davis, digging around in rumours that he was gay. They then spread the story for release by the right-wing press. Never in New Zealand politics had such dirty political tactics been seen.

The third coda involves the Brethren's exposure in Australia. As the battle between this shadowy group and the Greens heated up in New Zealand in 2005, a Greens Party member in New Zealand sent 'The Green Delusion' pamphlet to Australian senator Bob Brown. This act became the key to retrospectively unmasking the Exclusive Brethren's activities in support of Howard in 2004. Brown's fellow Tasmanian senator Christine Milne immediately recognised that Green Delusion was the same pamphlet as the one that had been used against her in Tasmania in that election a year earlier.

'The layout was the same, the language was the same,' Milne said, though some small details were different.[41] Milne became curious, and began to hunt for answers. She began methodically collecting ads and pamphlets from the federal campaign in three states, and checking the names and addresses on them. It was these investigations that revealed the hand of members of the Exclusive Brethren behind much of the Australian material from 2004.

But as Milne's thoughts were coalescing in late 2005 and early 2006, the Brethren were embarking on a new campaign in Australia – in spite of the damage they had done themselves and the party they supported in New Zealand. In the Tasmanian state election in March 2006, a group of sect members organised a set of anti-Green advertisements and mass mail-outs, and even bought mobile trailers which a couple of members drove around the streets of Hobart wearing fright masks. It was from this campaign that apparent evidence of the direct links between the Exclusive Brethren and the campaign team of the Liberal Party in Australia have emerged.

In 2006, Damien Mantach was the hot-shot new Liberal Party state director who had high hopes of bringing his party back from the historic lows of its 2002 state election loss, and, perhaps, even giving it a chance at government. Mantach had been recruited to Tasmania from John Howard's federal election tactics machine in Parliament House, the Government Members' Secretariat. The secretariat, itself a secretive organisation, funded by taxpayer money but structured in a way that allowed it to avoid parliamentary scrutiny, had contributed to the Liberals' effective marginal-seats campaign in 2004. It is unclear whether Mantach ran across the Exclusive Brethren during his work at the secretariat, but he certainly had done so by the time of the 2006 state campaign in Tasmania.

The Brethren's advertisements in that campaign were typical of the type seen elsewhere: anti-Green and pro-conservative. One said that the Greens' policies to recognise the rights of transgender people would 'ruin families and societies'. Another said that full access to marriage laws for same-sex couples was a 'socially destructive change'. The ads were placed on the direction of a senior Brethren member, Graham Lewis, but three Tasmanian newspapers (the *Mercury*, the *Examiner*, and the *Advocate*) all sent the bills for them to the Liberal Party. The advertising departments of two of the papers said later they had billed the Liberals at the request of the Brethren's advertising agent, Chris Guesdon, a former Liberal Party operative who was also the Liberals' ad agent.

Mr Guesdon insists it was an administrative error – more accurately, three identical administrative errors – and he should have separated the accounts. The cost of the ads was ultimately paid by a company called TRADTAS, which was set up by three Exclusive Brethren members just 11 days before the poll; this was the same model used federally and in the United States.

It turned out that not only was the Liberal Party billed for the ads, but the party's Damien Mantach also helped design them. 'Did we discuss brochures and strategies as to how you might target the Green vote? Yeah, we did. Absolutely,' he told *The Australian* of his contact with the Brethren:

> Some of the advice I gave to the Brethren was pretty straight up and down, and that is: Green policies don't stack up and one of the best techniques is to highlight what their policies are and what those policies mean ... Did I say you should use this language or that language? No. We didn't get into that sort of detail. They were very concerned about the Greens' social policies.[42]

This information has come to light not because of Australia's electoral-disclosure regime, but because a transsexual activist, Martine Delaney, took action against the Liberal Party, Mr Guesdon, and the Exclusive Brethren in the Tasmanian Anti-Discrimination Commission on the grounds that the anti-Green advertisements incited hatred. Here, perhaps, was another example of what had happened in New Zealand – the conservative party outsourcing the most overtly offensive lines of their argument to the Brethren. This has not been proven, but the discrimination case was continuing at the time of writing.

As the Greens uncovered more evidence of irregularities and a lack of disclosure surrounding Brethren advertising, their leader, Bob Brown, introduced two different motions into federal parliament. The first, in August 2006, sought a Senate committee investigation into the Brethren's role in family breakdown and Australian politics, and also sought details of the sect's exemptions under the tax act, and the arrangements governing their schools. In arguing for the committee's inquiry, Milne said, 'I believe that in a democracy people have a right to transparency, and that is my objection to what is going on: there is no transparency.'[43]

The Liberal Party's response to the Greens' move for an inquiry was vigorous. Citing the religious-freedom argument, the Brethren's chief parliamentary defender, Tasmanian Liberal senator Eric Abetz, implied that Greens leader Bob Brown was akin to a Nazi:

> The Green motion that we are debating today is a steely, cold, calculated motion designed to intimidate, scapegoat and vilify a lawful religious minority – and their only sin is that they 'ventured into politics'. When the leader of a political party starts scapegoating religious minorities, the alarm bells of history should be ringing loud and clear.[44]

Labor also voted twice against the inquiry: not from any love of the Brethren, but in deference to the religious-freedom argument, and fearing that a campaign against a religious minority might do them wider damage among voters of many religious beliefs.

Also, in early 2006, the Australian Electoral Commission instituted an inquiry into Willmac's spending on the federal election – an inquiry that was to last 16 months.

As a result of all this scrutiny, the Brethren ran only a few newspaper ads when it came to the Victorian state election in November 2006, though they were expensive and prominent. It was a typical Brethren operation: the ads were booked with two Victorian newspapers by one man, Euan Lloyd Chirnside (using his less-preferred name, Euan); authorised by another, Ernest Morren (a not-very-well-known South African immigrant); and the address for the authorisation was the factory of a third man, Barry Joyce. The Brethren's involvement was reported in *The Age* on the same day that the ad appeared – it was, by then, becoming harder for them to fly beneath the radar.

But even after the Brethren's role in election campaigning had been uncovered, and the damage it had caused conservative causes in New Zealand and elsewhere had been revealed, John Howard continued his long habit of meeting with them. They met again on 18 September 2006 – the same day that, across the Tasman in New Zealand, Labor Prime Minister Helen Clark revealed that the Brethren had hired private detectives to dig dirt on her husband's private life, and spread rumours that he was gay. At that meeting in Howard's city office in Sydney, the Brethren promised to send him an academic paper by Monash University Professor Gary Bouma, which reports how low the sect's divorce rate is.

In a letter dated the following day, they enclosed that paper, and the sect leaders thanked the prime minister warmly for the meeting and also pursued their suggestion for a big water project, first raised in a meeting two years earlier. The Brethren correspondents suggested 'the financing of water projects ... using the large amounts of money lying dormant in super funds'.[45]

We get some idea of what Bruce Hales might have suggested to the prime minister at the September meeting when we look at what he told a meeting of his own flock at Kellyville in Sydney two months later, in November 2006. Here he argued, 'You can't blame God for the drought':

> God has provided enough rain for us, the governments haven't been doing what they should have been doing with it. Rain has been pouring off pretty much all edges of Australia for two hundred

years. Far, far, far more than we ever needed. Yet the sea is not full. Remarkable.

Howard penned a reply after the September meeting, thanking his interlocutors for the letter and Professor Bouma's paper, saying, 'I too enjoyed our recent discussions.' He also commiserated with the Brethren about Senator Bob Brown's attempts to initiate a Senate inquiry into their sect.[46] 'I am aware of the campaign against you by Senator Brown and others. You have plenty of company!' the prime minister wrote. On the subject of water, it is probably a coincidence that, just four months after this 2006 meeting, Howard announced a big-bang, $10 billion water infrastructure plan that involved taking over the administration of the Murray–Darling system from the states.

To put Bruce Hales' easy access to John Howard in context, the Reverend Dr Dean Drayton, former head of the Uniting Church, tried on four occasions to arrange meetings with the prime minister. Drayton tried both as president of his church nationally, and also as the representative of the National Council of Churches, which represents four million Christians. Each time he tried to meet, he was ignored or rebuffed. Once he was told that Mr Howard was 'too busy'. Dr Drayton was clearly not a Howard supporter, either politically or financially – he wanted to talk to Howard on subjects such as asylum-seekers and WorkChoices. Yet when Bruce Hales, representing only 15,000 Brethren in Australia, wanted to pass on his wonderment that the oceans had not yet overflowed, Howard made space in his diary. Unlike Drayton, the Exclusive Brethren had proven their political support for years.

But, by this time, the Exclusive Brethren were becoming a liability to any politician. Once their hand had been revealed behind the political activism across the globe, the media in Australia and New Zealand began becoming curious about this unusual group – and there is nothing as enticing to journalists as secrecy and evasion. Slowly, the story of the Brethren's lifestyle, its treatment of its members, and its regular access to politicians began to be revealed.

Transparency and scrutiny are what the Exclusive Brethren are most allergic to. They hate the media and journalists. In 1991, Bruce Hales' father, John, said of the media, 'We're hot, hot against these people ... They're the scourge of the Western world ... Don't let the brethren get caught by it.'[47]

So secretive are they that, despite three years of political action, the sect's ultimate leader, Bruce Hales, has not only refused all approaches to explain himself publicly, but he has even avoided being sighted or photographed. He travels in a private jet, is permanently escorted by bodyguards, and his terrestrial transport is a closed van which, when he is addressing meetings of his flock, drives him to and from the venue and then behind barriers within the locked compounds of his churches, to prevent him from being filmed or photographed.

The increasing media scrutiny prompted the Brethren to hire their first professional media spokesman, Tony McCorkell, in early 2007. Hales also hired Liberal-connected public relations firm Jackson Wells Morris to help them deal with what the firm called a 'hostile media'. They began training five or more senior sect members in the art of dealing with the media. The accessibility to the media of some Brethren members improved markedly after McCorkell's appointment and, on some issues, they became quite open for a time. Bruce Hales, though, has still never given an interview, and never explained his decision to catapult the sect into electoral politics.

In mid-2007, the Australian Electoral Commission turned its investigation of the sect over to the Australian Federal Police for investigation of the Willmac matters, to establish whether there had been any criminal behaviour. It's understood that the investigation centred around whether the Brethren had obstructed officers of the Commonwealth in their inquiries. (The police have laid no charges as a result of the investigation.) But, despite all of this, in August 2007, during the dying days of his administration, in the second-last session of federal parliament and with an election just months away, John Howard met once again with four senior Brethren members in his office in Parliament House. Among them were Bruce Hales, but also Mark Mackenzie, the sole director of Willmac – which was, at the time, under active police investigation – and Stephen Hales, who had been deeply involved every time the Brethren worked in an electoral campaign. The Brethren's own account of how the meeting came about describes an almost casual encounter.

'I was in Canberra and I greeted Mr Howard and enquired from him whether Mr Hales could meet him for a short discussion,' Warwick John wrote.[48] 'Mr Hales had agreed knowing the opportunities to meet Mr Howard these days were very scarce':

> There was no agenda for the meeting and nothing critical was discussed, only economic matters in general. Mr Howard is always interested in how small business is faring, and there was a brief discussion about TV shows concerning the Brethren. Mr Howard did not approve of the public vilification of the Brethren as a Christian church.

Quizzed later by journalists about this meeting, Howard continued his staunch defence of this sect, saying that the Brethren was:

> a legal, legitimate organisation ... they're Australian citizens ... and as prime minister I have met an enormous number of organisations. It's my job, and I find it quite astonishing that people think it's odd I have met representatives of a lawful organisation.[49]

By the time of the November 2007 federal election in Australia, the hand of the Exclusive Brethren was much less obvious. Their only overt activity was to attack Brown, in his home state, with a letter addressed 'To the citizens of Tasmania', which warned of the Greens leader's 'anti-development and immoral policies'. This time, though, they made an attempt at proper disclosure – the letter named 48 male and three female sect members, saying they were 'members of a Christian group commonly known as the Exclusive Brethren'. It was unfortunate that the address they used as a contact point was wrong, and the authorisers had to buy more space in a newspaper the following day to correct the error.

This is not necessarily to say that this was the Brethren's only political activity in that campaign. It is possible, in fact, that they flew even more effectively under the radar than ever, thanks to John Howard's new electoral-disclosure laws. A senior Liberal party source told me he had been approached by a group of earnest, conservatively dressed men in a city hotel building as the 2007 campaign got under way. They offered him a large, anonymous financial donation:

> They said, 'We are a private group.' I asked them if they voted – it was a testing question. They said they didn't. It was a very short discussion, and I made it very clear that I don't accept money from organisations if I don't know who they are and what they stand for. In my view, if you accept this money, you're arguably accepting some of their opinions. We're in the business of ideas, and so are the Exclusive Brethren. I regard many of the party's views and those of the Exclusive Brethren as inconsistent. What the party stands for should not be confused in the mind of the electorate by the acceptance of donations from fringe groups.[50]

In time for the last election, Howard had changed the electoral-funding laws so that any donation of less than $10,500 from any individual did not need to be disclosed. Theoretically, this meant that 100 Exclusive Brethren 'individuals' could each be moved, individually, to donate $10,499. This would mean almost $1.05 million of Brethren money could flow into a party's coffers without a single disclosure needing to be made. This is not to say that it did – just that it was possible.

Did a less principled or more desperate Liberal or National Party operative accept such an offer? We will never know, because Howard's electoral-donation regime means we will not be told.

When asked whether the issue of campaign funding was discussed at the Brethren's 8 August meeting in Howard's Canberra office, Warwick John said that 'no commitments or promises as to campaign support were discussed or agreed upon'.[51] The phrasing here allows significant wriggle room. He does not say, for example, if the issue of *donations* was discussed, nor whether the issue of campaigning was discussed *in general*, without any firm commitments made.

Asked by journalists whether the Exclusive Brethren had offered financial support at this last meeting, Howard's response was also heavily qualified, saying, 'They're things that you should talk to them, should talk to the Liberal Party organisation, about. I don't handle, in a direct sense, any fundraising matters related to the Liberal Party; they're handled by the organisation'.[52] The Liberal organisation has not answered any questions on this subject.

There is simply no other logical reason for Howard having agreed to the 8 August meeting. The presence of Stephen Hales and Mark Mackenzie makes it very likely that the topics discussed were the campaign and campaign funding, or donations.

Perhaps Howard was asking them to get active for him again, telling them how to contribute and stay 'beneath the radar'. Perhaps he was asking them to lay low. Perhaps he was simply seeking information from them about what they were planning. Either way, the meeting was meant to be a secret. That it was exposed publicly, and became yet another electoral liability for Howard, proved beyond doubt that, by the end of 2007, any help given by the Exclusive Brethren was no help at all.

Mark Textor runs the political-consultancy firm Crosby|Textor, which is used by conservative parties around the world for strategic advice. He knows what Australians think and how they can be manipulated, perhaps better than anybody else in the country. He says that the religious Right have an agenda 'that is not a mainstream one', and that the Brethren and their views are electorally 'radioactive':

> From a campaign perspective, the things they did on behalf of conservative parties often sounded so shrill in tone that they were not particularly effective ... their material was often cranky, and angry, particularly some of the material about Bob Brown. To me it was inappropriate at a time when voters are more likely to admire and respond to conviction politicians like Mr Brown, even under circumstances where they might not approve of all of their positions.
>
> The issues on which they chose to intervene in the campaign were rather narrow ones: their attitudes towards abortion in Australia, for instance, did not reflect in any time the sort of aspirations and views we ever picked up [in polling], nor what was acceptable as part of the political discourse.[53]

Since the demise of the Howard government in November 2007, perhaps the Brethren have simply lowered their sights when it comes to what they hope to achieve from political action. A month after polling day, the news emerged that the local chapter of the sect in Lithgow, in country New South Wales, had offered to fund Lithgow City Council's Supreme Court fight against a development application for a sex shop, the Flirt Adult Store. In the event, the appeal did not go ahead, and the store was allowed to open.

But the end of John Howard as prime minister has not meant the death of the links between the Brethren and elements of the

Liberal Party. When I called Danna Vale's office in February 2008 to ask about her endorsement of Warwick John, she failed to call back. But within 15 minutes of putting the question to her press officer, I received a phone call from the Exclusive Brethren's spokesman, who asked what I was intending to write about the Liberals and their relationship with the Brethren.

A few weeks later, in March, I called Howard's former electorate officer, now a New South Wales state MP, Anthony Roberts, and asked the same question. Roberts denied any knowledge whatsoever of the sect, saying he would have to Google them to find out. No more than 10 minutes later, the Brethren spokesman rang me to check again what I was writing about Howard and the Brethren. Roberts strenuously denied he had contacted any Brethren representative, saying he would not know how.

In New South Wales, one of the Liberal Party's most important religious right-wing factional powerbrokers is David Clarke who, along with Festival of Light MP Reverend Fred Nile, endorsed the applications of both Warwick John and David Stewart, the principal of the Brethren's New South Wales school, when they sought lobbyists' passes to state parliament house.

Brendan Nelson, briefly the federal Liberal leader after the 2007 election, and a former education minister, has also defended them. Nelson gave a reference for Brethren school chief executive John Anderson to obtain a lobbyist's pass to Parliament House. Nelson, through a spokesman, said that the Brethren were 'a legitimate organisation; they're entitled to a pass to Parliament House'.[54]

Kevin Rudd, the prime minister since late 2007, is, like Howard, a committed, church-going Christian, but he clearly has a more sceptical approach to the Exclusive Brethren than his predecessor. Rudd showed outright antipathy to the sect, even before he became opposition leader; but, in the lead-up to the election, he labelled them an 'extremist cult' that breaks up families.[55] He has consistently refused to meet them and, as opposition leader, before the

2007 election he signalled his intentions by asking the Australian Federal Police, the tax office, the money-laundering watchdog, Austrac, and the Australian Electoral Commission to investigate them. He also warned all Labor candidates not to accept any electoral donation from them, no matter how small, after one Brethren member apparently tried to entrap a candidate in the central-west of New South Wales by offering a $250 donation.

In February 2008, a group of 30 former Brethren members seized on these events to request of Rudd, the newly elected prime minister, an urgent investigation into various aspects of the Brethren's activities. They particularly wanted scrutiny into the taxpayer funding of Brethren schools; the Brethren's eligibility for the rate and tax exemptions available to mainstream churches; their political donations; the cost of Family Court proceedings they were involved in; the incidence of suicides, family breakdown, emotional abuse, pain, and family hardship caused by the doctrine of separation; and the alleged protection of child sexual abusers 'in cases often going back over 40 years'.[56]

Newly installed in government, and wary of confronting the politically difficult prospect of being seen to attack a particular religious minority, Rudd, through his chief of staff David Epstein, wrote back to the ex-Brethren. He maintained his general view of the sect, saying that he remained 'concerned' about various of their practices; but he rejected the ex-members' plea for an inquiry, citing religious freedom: 'The Government has not acceded to continuing requests for a wide-ranging inquiry into the Exclusive Brethren. The Government believes that such an inquiry could unreasonably interfere with the capacity of members of the Exclusive Brethren to practise their faith freely and openly.'[57]

Rudd's approach opens some very interesting questions about religious freedom in Australia, which I discuss briefly in the conclusion to this book.

Brethren sources say they are 'alert but not alarmed' at Rudd's election. They have survived for 175 years in a largely hostile world. They will maintain strong links with any sympathetic Liberal and National Party MPs that they can keep in touch with through opposition; and their lobbyists will work assiduously to woo outlying Rudd government members who are socially conservative and Christian.

Bruce Hales has told his flock that, 'I don't think we should ever let up making representation to government while we're here'.[58] They will argue tirelessly that all their activities are simply expressions of their religious freedom, and they will bide their time until they can once again exercise influence. Their best ally in politics may have gone, but the Exclusive Brethren are preparing, once again, to play the long game.

CHAPTER EIGHT

Schooling

A rowdy basketball game roamed over the outdoor court in front of the school as a dozen-or-more senior students in long, blue uniforms dodged, leaped, and shouted with teenage exuberance. As I skirted the edge of the court, three earnest, middle-aged men were waiting for me on the school steps. These were three of the Brethren's heaviest hitters, deputised by Bruce D. Hales to look after the sect's education program in his home state of New South Wales.

There stood David Stewart, the principal of the 16 campuses of MET, the New South Wales Exclusive Brethren school, and John Anderson, the owner of a medical-supplies business and the schools' chief executive. Pump salesman Stephen Hales, the older brother of the Man of God, leaned back on a rail, looking sceptically at the approaching journalist. They had dressed in neckties for the occasion – a sign that they were about to go into battle with the 'world'.

It was March 2007, and I had been invited to inspect the Australian headquarters of Brethren schooling, the MET Meadowbank campus, in the heart of Hales territory in the federal electorate of Bennelong. This was the first Australian Brethren school, built in 1992 in an old weatherboard house over the back fence from the family home of the former Man of God, John Hales. In this house the curriculum for all 16 New South Wales Exclusive campuses is produced, and the administration conducted. This was the address that Stephen Hales gave when he authorised pro-John Howard election pamphlets at the 2004 poll.

Since the Meadowbank campus was built, dozens of other Brethren private schools have opened their doors in Australia and around the world. It is the most important innovation in the regimes of John and Bruce Hales, the father and son who have led the sect since 1987. The purpose of the schools was, as Bruce Hales said in 2003, to deliver the young Brethren from worldly schools, 'an area of defilement and contamination'.[1]

The decision to move into schooling has made this robustly anti-intellectual group a small yet significant provider of education worldwide. It has also made them a massive recipient of tens of millions of dollars of government funding. It has become one of the most controversial things they have done. My invitation to inspect Meadowbank had come after I had written a number of news articles in *The Age* and *The Sydney Morning Herald* about the Brethren education system, particularly focusing on their unique and controversial funding model, which uses trading entities, such as a chain of tyre wholesale shops, to raise tax-free funds. The Brethren who had invited me on the tour wanted to explain to me how their funding system worked – to say that it was above board – but also to show me how normal an Exclusive Brethren school was.

And it *was* normal – just like any other school, only with smaller classes. Here was a game of basketball; here was eight-year-old Jarrod showing off his toy motorbike to his year three and year four composite class during show-and-tell. I met the teachers, who are all non-Brethren, relaxing in the staffroom at lunchtime, and also a group of 18 year-seven and year-eight students gathered in the computer lab, poring over their 'Wordex' machines, learning how to use Word and Excel. I was invited to take pictures.

'We're a firm believer in education. Because if you are not educated, you can't take in God's great moral thoughts,' David Stewart told me.[2]

In some ways, the Brethren schools are little different from the hundreds of other fundamentalist Christian schools around the country. They mostly teach the curriculum as laid out by the relevant state government or, where they are permitted to, a modified version that avoids the teaching of subjects they do not like, such as evolution and sex education. The parents are closely involved in the education of their children; and the community, in the case of the Brethren, through the trustees of the school, keep a very close eye on what is taught. They are less prescriptive in some ways than other Christian schools; although they expect demure behaviour from their teachers, they do not require them to sign statements attesting to their Christian faith.

For some Brethren children, the education is first class. State league tables show individual students putting in extremely good, state-topping performances, mostly in subjects such as business, maths, and food technology and, in the case of one girl in 2007, even in history and ancient history. But several things set Brethren schools apart from other low-fee Christian schools. No matter how good the academic results of their students, no matter what the interests and potential of their students, 0 per cent of Brethren students will go on to university. It is simply not allowed. Some will further their training with apprenticeships or technical qualifications, and the schools themselves are set up in Australia as registered training organisations to provide this service. But Brethren boys or girls wanting to broaden their minds beyond business and engineering by studying arts or science – indeed, any subject that requires university attendance – will be sadly thwarted.

For the girls, the situation is even more bleak. They cannot take a job that puts them in a position of authority over a man. The best that these bright girls can look forward to is a brief stint working in an office or as a telemarketer before they embark on marriage, complete with a large number of children and a life in which their only option is to be a homemaker. At best, they will become a silent partner in the business their husband runs.

The other thing that sets Brethren schools apart is the rigidity of their doctrine of separation. All religious schools are intended to educate children in the morals and values of their parents, away from the secular values of the public system. But most Christians ultimately want their children to then go out and make their mark in the world. Exclusive Brethren schools are different: they are a powerful instrument for keeping young children sequestered in their sect and protected from the world. Education is for the enrichment of the sect, not society at large; this was the whole point of establishing the schools in the first place.

Jacqui van der velde Gilbert, the curriculum coordinator at Meadowbank — a non-Brethren woman who helped set up the school — says that some non-Brethren children do attend Brethren schools in Australia. But she is reluctant to reveal details, and it's likely they number no more than a few and that they are mostly the children of staff members.

Separation is becoming even more comprehensive. On my visit to Meadowbank, I saw students from years three to year 12. The younger children were attending local government primary schools. There, even though they go home for lunch or eat at separate tables and do not participate in any social or fundraising activities, the children can at least meet and form friendships with their 'worldly' classmates until they are swept off to the nearest Brethren school. But MET, and all other Brethren schools, are in the process of expanding so they can educate even these children – everyone from five years old until graduation. Stewart confirmed in 2007 that the sect was 'desperately trying to find the facilities' to expand. Local councils and planning bodies worldwide are dealing with applications by the Exclusive Brethren to open new primary schools.

In private meetings of the Brethren, Man of God Bruce Hales is clear about the schools' purpose. Dr Roger Kirkpatrick, a Queensland-based medical doctor and Hales intimate, drew out the Man of God on the subject in a meeting in Berwick, Victoria, in July 2003: 'Deliverance from the educational system for developing minds would have a strong effect against the deterioration and the degradation of the race,' Dr Kirkpatrick declared.

'Yes ... I'm sure that's right,' Hales responded:

> We're not trying to deprive our young people of what's necessary, but I think the saints have got everything they need within their reach to provide everything that's needed for the education of the children ... so they can face up to the world, and find their way effectively through it, without coming under the power of it ... to deliver them from an area of defilement and contamination.[3]

In setting up an education system that perpetuates the notion of isolation, aloofness, and superiority, the Exclusive Brethren have had the explicit support and encouragement of mainly Liberal federal and state governments, and many millions of dollars of taxpayers' funds. And, as ever, one of their biggest supporters was former prime minister John Howard.

After leaving office, Howard spoke in unvarnished terms about his view of the world when he delivered the Irving Kristol lecture to the American Enterprise Institute in March 2008. And he put Christian organisations as the star at the centre of his social-policy firmament. 'A conservative edifice must always have at its centre the role of the family and what Americans call faith-based organisations in maintaining and strengthening social infrastructure,' he said:

> Maintaining a cultural bias in favour of families also means that governments should reinforce the role of parents in choosing what form of education their children receive ... The major growth sector

amongst independent schools has been in the low-fee independent Christian category. This is a direct result of more liberal funding arrangements initiated by my government. It is hard not to see this growth as other than a collective search by parents for a more values-based education experience for their children.

It is tempting to point out the contradiction between Howard's apparent support for the traditional family unit and his backing of a religious group that breaks families apart if they do not toe the theological line. But Howard, it appears, always bought the Brethren's line on this issue – that their authoritarian approach kept families together much more successfully than the wider society could manage, and that this was a good thing.

Setting up a new school in Australia requires constant, unremitting, and voluminous contact with government departments at both the state and federal levels. The state bureaucrats must register the school and inspect it, monitor the curriculum, and accredit the teachers. The state government also provides some funding. The federal government provides the bulk of the funding and a smaller amount of the regulation. As a result, as the Brethren have entered the educational sphere, they have found ample scope to do what they do so well: lobbying politicians for special treatment.

The Brethren push into education began in the late 1980s. Reflecting later on this period, Bruce Hales and his chief lobbyist, Warwick John, recalled 'that first education inquiry' in 1988, when Bruce's father, John Hales, was the Man of God, and the 'man in charge of [the inquiry] came down afterwards to speak to the sisters, young sisters, with their scarves on,' said Warwick John. 'Yes, we were there,' recalls Bruce Hales. 'And this man was affected by it [the sisters]. He was a good man, took up the brethren's case. That was really when the education thing started.'[4]

Though they do not spell out the details, this is very likely to be a reference to the Carrick Inquiry into education in New South

Wales, which laid the groundwork for the Liberal government of Nick Greiner to produce the *Education Reform Act 1990*. That Act, thanks to the lobbying of religious groups such as the Brethren, contained clauses allowing children to be exempted from attending certain classes, or school in general, on the grounds of 'conscience'. The Brethren heavily used these exemption certificates so that their children could avoid attending classes in sex education and evolution.

But this still was not enough for the sect and, in 1992, there was more of what David Stewart described as 'unexpected help' from politicians. This referred to a special deal granted to the Brethren by New South Wales Liberal schools minister Virginia Chadwick. She did two things for the Brethren: she helped them obtain permission from the federal Labor government to set up their own school campus in Meadowbank, and she also granted them almost unfettered access to the state-funded school of distance education. The state governments run distance schools to educate children who live in areas so remote that they cannot make it to a physical school.

But, under Chadwick, the Brethren, unlike any other group, was granted permission to use the New South Wales state distance-education system as their full-time school, whether or not their students were near a government school. The concession was momentous for the Brethren at the time: it meant that their children could continue to be educated at taxpayer expense without needing to be present in classrooms with other people's 'defiling' children.

Once they had achieved this breakthrough in New South Wales, the Brethren sought to have the model replicated in other states. Since 1990, the sect's elders in Victoria had been growing more alarmed at the direction that state education was taking, so they lobbied Labor premier Joan Kirner on the subject. Kirner agreed to direct school principals to take seriously the concerns of the Brethren regarding curriculum.

But, by 1992, the political scene was changing in the state of

Victoria, and new opportunities for Exclusive Brethren lobbying were about to open up. Voters were on the verge of ousting Kirner's tired, incompetent Labor government, and installing Liberal leader Jeff Kennett as premier. Sniffing the wind, four senior Victorian Brethren decided to importune the opposition education spokesman, Don Hayward, ahead of the election. They sent him a weighty, undated submission, whose purpose was to draw attention to the various ways in which the Brethren perceived the public education system was failing – a problem which they trusted 'will be the subject of review in the event of a change of Government in this state'.[5]

In summary, their submission argued that teaching had abandoned 'moral principles' in favour of 'sex and AIDS education', evolution, TVs in the classroom, computers, and 'defiling' literature full of 'fornication, adultery and sodomy ... blasphemy, violence, disregard for authority, filthy language'. They also could not tolerate the 'increasing and sometimes extreme emphasis on "independent" and "free and lateral" thinking'.

Their submission provided copies of pages from sex-education texts, and excerpts from the English syllabus. Reading materials that year included David Williamson's *The Removalists*, Tom Kenneally's *The Chant of Jimmy Blacksmith*, and a newspaper article entitled 'Prostitutes Teach VCE Students'. They apologised to Mr Hayward for the foul language, violence, and sex in 'such a volume of sample material which is obscene, degraded and abhorrent'. They also provided pages of testimonials from Brethren students about the alleged transgressions they had been forced to endure at the hands of teachers at state schools in subjects from science to physical education. 'It will be seen that serious violations of a child's right to moral integrity are being perpetrated,' they wrote.

The Brethren's bottom line was to beg of Hayward that their students be able to complete their year-11 and year-12 study by correspondence, using the distance-education school. In their submission they included an extract from the New South Wales law, enacted two years earlier by Hayward's interstate Liberal colleagues, which had opened the door to a very similar policy. Hayward, preparing himself for the real hope of ministerial office, then received a delegation of wealthy, well-groomed, and conservatively dressed men who were charming (in a slightly fawning way) and polite. They would have gently pressed their point by emphasising their unique religious history and their conscience, which in the areas of voting and industrial relations had already made them special cases in legislation.

The Brethren also sent a deputation to the education department in April 1992 to argue the same point. Their stated desire was that a future Liberal government 'amend the existing regulations relating to the enrolment of students in the School of Distance Education to allow the Brethren to enrol their children on the basis of conscience'.[6]

The document prepared for this meeting reveals more of the Brethren's concerns about life for their children in public school classrooms. They objected to 'analysis of alternative lifestyles' in the classroom, which was a 'direct thrust against the God given rights of parents'. They asserted that, 'blatant immorality is accommodated and condoned ... and so called "equality" is being taught based on the acceptance of the lowest moral denominators ... For example homosexuality is openly propounded as being "normal".' They feared that 'free and often unfettered class discussion is playing an increasingly greater part in education', and it 'comes up at any time in any lesson, from English to Home Economics and seriously compromises the committal of our children to moral integrity'. They stated that 'violence, drugs and promiscuity coupled with student and sadly teacher lawlessness are becoming more common'.

Six months later, in October 1992, the Kennett government was elected, and Don Hayward duly became education minister. Just over a year after that, he wrote to one member of these delegations, Euan Chirnside, saying, 'I am pleased to inform you that I have now approved of the Brethren enrolling Years 10, 11 and 12 students in the Distance Education Centre in 1994'.[7] What the Brethren had asked for, and what they had received, was exclusive status as the only special-interest group to have their very own category of enrolment in distance education. Documents also show that this was done on highly favourable financial terms. The special arrangement allowed them to pay only the difference between the cost of educating their students in a public school and the cost of distance education – about $100 per subject – which was much cheaper than either private school fees or home schooling.[8]

Having won that battle, the Brethren began the second part of their lobbying strategy – exploiting the thin edge of the wedge. Just 10 months after the initial approval, in August 1994, the Liberal parliamentary secretary for education, Stephen Elder, gave his approval, after lobbying, to extend the special deal to Brethren children in years 7 to 9, at a cost of just $850 per year.[9] And, two months later, the Brethren applied for a further concession to allow children from age five, known in Victoria as 'Prep', to also win special access to distance education.

In that submission, the three Brethren lobbyists argued that up to 30 per cent of primary-school class time was now taken up with 'unsuitable curriculum', including 'excursions, dancing, life education, swimming, camps, etc' – a problem they said was about to get much worse with the introduction of computers, videos, and satellite television.[10] The following month, the department approved this, their third application, at a cost of $1200 per student per year. In a period of just 12 months, the Brethren had won special educational status on grounds of conscience that allowed every Brethren student in the state concessional treatment that was available to no other group in Victoria.

The arrangement continued in Victoria for the next 10 years. But, over this time, it prompted an increasing amount of ill-feeling between the Brethren and the Victorian Department of Education because, having won these concessions, the Brethren kept pushing. Documents show them complaining about their fellow students, and criticising the dress and deportment of female distance-education teachers who took on-site seminars and who had the temerity to wear short skirts. They also made continuous complaints about the texts on the English literature curriculum.

'The distance-education centre was increasingly refusing to doctor its materials to suit their faith-based stuff,' one bureaucrat told me, on the condition of anonymity. 'They wouldn't even touch evolution, and some of the English books they complained about. A whole range of issues occurred, and the school, as part of a secular system, believed that people should be exposed to ideas and then come up with their own decisions.'[11]

By May 2000, we can guess that the state education department in New South Wales was experiencing similar problems, and the Carr Labor government told the Brethren that its free ride in distance education was about to end. This move was going to hit the Exclusive Brethren where it really hurt, in the hip pocket. At this point, a few Sydney-based Exclusive Brethren students were physically attending the Meadowbank school campus, and some were being educated by the Brethren's very own distance-education provider, MET Correspondence.

But the bulk of the Brethren's high school students in New South Wales – 250 of them – were relying on their special access to the state government distance school. In 2000, when the government announced it was about to withdraw the privilege, it meant that all 250 of those Brethren students were suddenly about to be transferred to the Brethren's own correspondence school at the cost of the sect – either that, or return to state education.

Documents obtained from the federal education department make it clear that the protests of the Brethren about this were falling on deaf Labor ears at the state level, so the lobbyists tried to get federal education ministers David Kemp and Amanda Vanstone to intervene – to no avail. So four MET school trustees, John Anderson, Stephen Hales, Warwick John, and Bruce D. Hales (the state distance education coordinator, two years before he became Man of God) went over the minister's head, and wrote to their long-time ally, John Howard, the prime minister, at his Gladesville electorate office.

'We feel that an urgent need has arisen necessitating a further approach to you in regard of a funding anomaly,' their letter opened.[12] After explaining the problem, and reminding Howard that they were in his electorate of Bennelong, they wrote that the change of policy was 'placing an inordinate and excessive demand on our resources and we believe that if the issues are considered impartially and indiscriminately funding will be provided without obstacle'.

What they wanted was the prime minister's intervention in the 'funding crisis', though they did not make a specific request:

> We are reluctant in any way to create a further burden for you with this correspondence knowing in some sense the immense pressures and workload that accompany your position. However, because of your sympathetic support in the past and the contact with you over the years, we felt compelled to bring this matter to your attention and seek your assistance.

They signed off:

> At this time we would like to assure you of our support and confirm that many heartfelt supplications are being made on your behalf and trust that you are encouraged to continue in your public moral stand and a dedicated family outlook and approach in increasingly difficult times.

Atop this letter was a revealing pair of handwritten notes,

added by bureaucrats as it found its way through the system. The first, written on the day that the letter was received at Howard's electorate office, warned the department, 'They are known to PM'. The second note directed the prime minister's department to 'pls prepare reply for PM's signature'. Six days later, probably at the prime minister's suggestion, three MET trustees wrote again, this time to federal education minister David Kemp, from whom they had already unsuccessfully sought help. Their letter explained that the 250 students could not return to government school classrooms because 'the reasons for their leaving nine years ago are now much intensified'.[13] They asked that he simply take the money the Commonwealth would otherwise have paid to New South Wales for those students and send it directly to the Meadowbank school so they could provide for the students. 'We look forward to meeting with you to consider this issue in the near future,' wrote Anderson, Stewart and Hales.

Three weeks later, on 22 June 2000, a reply was dispatched from the education department. In the context of the new funding model that was then being developed for private schools, Kemp had 'asked that the department consider ways in which recurrent funding may be made available' to the Brethren, the letter said.[14] It was, all things considered, excellent, prompt, and favourable service from the Commonwealth to those who were 'known to' the prime minister.

The deal they won out of the new government private-school funding system that Kemp was setting up was a financial windfall which perhaps even they did not expect. No evidence is available of what, if any, Brethren lobbying was directed towards the Howard government as it was formulating this policy, but the allocation allowed the sect to begin immediately phasing out their distance-education model, and to set up their own network of private schools.

Until 2001, Labor's model for funding private schools, the Education Resource Index, was based on a school's capacity to generate its own income. It calculated the need for government assistance on the basis of whether a school could raise enough money, through fees and fundraising, to provide adequately for its students. Kemp and Howard wanted to replace this with a model that measured the financial needs of families attending the schools, measured by the wealth profile of the suburbs they lived in. They called it the Socio-Economic Status (SES) model.

It sounds admirably equitable, and most educationists now agree it is a defensible model if it is applied correctly. But there were three extra features that Howard and Kemp added that massively advantaged private schools. The first was a big boost in the stream of money flowing to independent schools. The second was that Howard and his education minister wanted to remove any disincentive for schools to charge fees or otherwise raise funds of their own. Under their model, a school could raise unlimited money annually but still suffer no reduction in its government allocation. This has led to a situation where some private schools are able to accumulate large cash reserves and beautiful new buildings by hiking fees at the same time as their government funding booms.

But the third feature has advantaged only some schools, with the Brethren schools being one of the chief beneficiaries. It has made them better off by millions of dollars per year, with funding well in excess of what their SES entitlement would deliver them.

This is how it worked. In 1995, when the Brethren were still mainly in the business of providing distance education with a small number of students on the Meadowbank campus in Sydney, they applied to the Keating government for federal funding under Labor's forerunner, the ERI scheme. They were awarded what was known as category-12 status. The man who helped design and implement the scheme, Jim McMorrow, points out that category 12 was the most generous government supplementation it was possible to get, and was supposed to be reserved for 'the poorest schools in the lowest-income communities in the country ... and with largish average class sizes'.[15] In fact, it was Aboriginal schools and special schools for those with autism, or the hearing impaired, that were supposed to be the beneficiary of category-12 funding.

The Brethren's MET school in Meadowbank is, by contrast, in relatively affluent suburban Sydney, has small class sizes, and is financially supported by a community which boasts that it has no poverty. A Brethren document asserts that, 'A statistical survey of the Brethren over past decades would establish that they are found in the middle to upper levels of the socio-economic group. Any unemployment or poverty that may arise is not left unattended; it is fully provided for'.[16] It is unclear why the Brethren were placed in category 12; they say it was not a result of lobbying. McMorrow said that one of the weaknesses of the ERI funding model was that 'schools could manipulate it'.

Category 12 meant that the MET school was entitled to top-tier federal funding of 62.4 per cent of the full cost of educating a child in a government school. But when the figures under the Howard Government's new SES model were being calculated in 2000, the relative wealth of its families and the location of the school meant that MET was assessed as being eligible for much lower funding: just 42.5 per cent of the average government-school cost.

Howard, however, under pressure from religious and private-school lobby groups, agreed to make up the difference for any school that was worse off – to pay schools under whichever funding model delivered them more money. This amount was indexed in perpetuity. As a result of this deal, called 'funding maintenance', the MET school received the full 62.4 per cent – almost 50 per cent more cash per student from taxpayers than the government's own model said it was entitled to. Melrose Park, the South Australian school in the Brethren stable, was even better off – in the initial funding round it enjoyed a 51 per cent higher grant than it should have under SES.

On departmental figures in 2003, out of the 2652 non-government schools in Australia, the Howard government's system made the MET school the 40th-best-funded in the country. On average, Exclusive Brethren parents are among the richest in the country – they own their own houses and businesses, and they have a substantial financial-support network. Melrose Park in South Australia is only slightly lower in funding rankings than MET, at 44th on the list, and the Glenvale School in Victoria is 80th. (Glenvale gets its generous socio-economic status score because it is an oasis of Exclusive Brethren wealth in Pascoe Vale, an otherwise relatively disadvantaged area to Melbourne's north.) None of the six Brethren schools is outside the 33 per cent most generously funded schools in the entire country.[17]

The difference between what the MET school should have been paid (48.5 per cent of government school costs), and what they were paid (62.4 per cent) narrowed in the next funding round, starting in 2005, but it remained extremely favourable. As a result, in 2008, each of the 256 students at the MET school reaped $6584 per year in federal funds alone, with state funding on top of this.

The largesse of the 'funding maintained' category is not confined to the Exclusive Brethren – independent, non-Catholic as well as Catholic schools are also beneficiaries – but, even by the boasts of the Brethren themselves, they may well be its least-deserving recipient. Of the Brethren, it is particularly true to say, as eminent Melbourne university educationist Barry McGaw has said, that the funding of private schools means that 'a school pulls all the rich kids out of an area, and then reaps the extra government resources on the back of the poorer kids that are left behind'.[18]

But there is more. Over the same period, the Brethren have rapidly moved away from the distance-education model and have instead set up schools in cities and towns around the country. Under federal government funding rules, any new school that is set up must be assessed afresh for its SES status, and funded according to the new score. But the Brethren did not want to do this. They wanted to keep access to their super-special funding deal, even as they expanded outside the zone for which they reaped the funding. So they decided to grow by calling their new schools 'campuses' of the one central school, rather than new schools.

MET, for example, had built 16 'campuses' by 2008. One of them is in Lavington, near Albury, 600 kilometres from the school I visited, but its students are funded on the basis of a 1995 assessment of the needs of students hundreds of kilometres away in the western suburbs of Sydney. The Glenvale school in Victoria had 10 campuses, all assessed as if they were in the struggling northern suburbs of Melbourne, and the Agnew school in Queensland had eight.

In a departmental report to the Howard government on the school-funding policy in 2006, the Brethren were used as an example of the entrenched inequities of the system. The report, which was kept secret until after the Howard government's demise, said that the issue 'would need to be investigated further if funding maintenance continued' for the next four-year cycle.[19]

These facts combined mean that, with an estimated secondary-school student population in 2007 of just fewer than 2000 students, the sect's six school networks would receive 'spoils from the Egyptians' to the tune of almost $50 million in taxpayer recurrent funding in the next four-year school-funding round. Upon coming to office, the Rudd government decided to retain all aspects of the funding system for its first four years – honouring a promise made to silence the private-school lobby in advance of the 2007 election.

But that is still not the end of it. The Howard government also set up a system of federal capital grants to help non-government schools. The larger grants were assessed, by independent committees, on the basis of schools' needs and the capacity of their communities to raise capital funds. There was no way that the Exclusive Brethren would receive any such grant. But $154 million was also set aside for 'small grants' of less than $75,000 each. These applications received no financial scrutiny, and were effectively granted if the school could make a case for 'educational need'.

This is fertile ground for a group such as the Brethren. Some of their schools cottoned on to the program early: in 2005 and 2006, the first two years of the program, $313,600 was paid out to some of their campuses. But in 2007 they really let loose. The MET school alone reaped seven grants, for seven of its campuses in New South Wales. Most of the grants were just under the $75,000 limit that would have required financial scrutiny. The South Australian school, Melrose Park, received money for the upgrade of science facilities and other equipment. The Queensland school, Agnew, and the Glenvale school in Victoria, were given $138,000 in total to buy computers. These computers would have been supplied by the Exclusive Brethren company, National Office Assist. In other words, federal funds were handed to the Brethren to buy almost $140,000 worth of computers from themselves. In all, the 2007 round of capital grants was worth $502,000 to the sect.

There is no suggestion that any of this is illegal. It is open to any group to apply for any of this funding, set up their own school, and have it registered and funded. The Brethren are simply more organised and more aware than most groups of the possible ways to harvest government largesse. And they have the contacts to help them secure the best possible deal. This behaviour did, however, make Stephen Hales slightly disingenuous when he claimed in a letter to the *Weekly Times* in 2006 that, 'No funding, apart from what is available to any non-government school, is received by Exclusive Brethren schools'.[20]

Funding is not the only aspect of education where the Brethren received favourable treatment from the federal Liberals. In 2004, then education minister Brendan Nelson introduced a national requirement that schools test their students for proficiency in information technology. He said that this was all about standards and that, in the future, 'the only benchmarks that will count are international ones'. But, at that time, the Brethren still had a problem with computers. Through a long-time political ally, Sydney-based Liberal backbencher Alan Cadman, Meadowbank school principal David Stewart arranged a meeting with Nelson to 'seek your discretion for exemption from certain IT conditions'.[21]

With his letter to Nelson, Stewart sent a document entitled, 'School ethos and guiding principles'. This clearly laid out the Exclusive Brethren's objection to information technology. While they conceded in the document that computers were one of 'man's discoveries of what God has put into creation', they argued that IT had become 'a misuse of physical and natural phenomena created by God' and, as with other areas of science, constituted 'interference in God's creatorial rights':

> We believe that occupation with the study of computers is damaging to the proper development of children's minds and only serves to reduce and limit their thinking capacity to be conformed (sic) to programmes and the manipulation of a keyboard and screen .... children become restricted, narrow minded and their creative talent is inhibited.[22]

Particularly of concern was the 'permeating influence of the "world wide web",' which robbed young people of their 'moral judgment'. The internet, they wrote, would 'finally result in the rise of the "man of sin" or "antichrist" who will lead the whole world to destruction. This is well established for anyone that believes in Christian principles'. They said the Brethren would never be swayed in its adherence to these principles because, 'In a changing world, we maintain that God is the same and does not change His standard.'

Two years later, though, the Brethren policy on computers changed. Brethren schools are now full of them, and the sect's elders have made it clear that they will welcome any new computers paid for by the federal Labor government under its 'Education Revolution'. In 2004, however, Brendan Nelson had no idea that the

Lord was about to 'turn a corner' on the question of the evil of computers. He met David Stewart and three others on 21 July of that year, and agreed to give Brethren schools an exemption, based on conscience, from the otherwise national requirement to test students on their IT skills.

The Brethren were delighted and, in a subsequent letter to Nelson, suggested that 'intervening on our behalf for an interview with the Hon. Tony Abbott during this busy period would be valued'.[23] Three days after their meeting with Nelson, Bruce Hales commented in an Exclusive Brethren assembly meeting, 'The government is very favourable; been favourable to us this week, hasn't it, Mr David?' David Stewart responded: 'Yes, very clearly. Those of us who were there had some sense of the Lord having gone before ... the support, very ready support from the Minister for Education federally.' Bruce Hales also referred to it as 'the unexpected recognition of what the saints represent'.[24]

It is not just in Australia that the Brethren have been successful at political lobbying and using the concessions in the system to their own benefit. In the UK, the governments of Tony Blair and Gordon Brown have moved towards a more Australian-style school system in recent years, with generous government funding going to faith-based schools. As in Australia, the Brethren have thrived under this system, setting up 26 all-Brethren schools. But the UK system allows them to go a step further. They have successfully lobbied to not only run their own schools, but also to opt out of the system by which the government school inspectorate, Ofsted, keeps an eye on them. Instead of having to accept government inspectors, the Brethren have followed the elite private schools (such as Eton, Harrow, and Winchester), and some other Christian and Muslim schools, and set up their very own inspectorate.

The Brethren's 'Schools Inspection Service' was set up in 2006, and scrutinises 26 schools under the Focus Learning Trust banner. The government inspectorate, Ofsted, will continue to inspect the inspectorate. In the UK, unlike in Australia, school inspection reports are publicly available; so far, the reports of the Brethren by the Brethren have, with minor quibbles, been very positive about their own schools.

In Australia there is, as yet, no privatisation of school inspection, but the state authorities have consistently accredited the Brethren, saying they have complied with the standards required. However, the foundation principal of Agnew, the Brethren's Queensland school network, warned state authorities to keep a close eye on what the sect was doing. This man, who did not want to be named, was initially hired by the Brethren to help them gain accreditation for a single school with a number of campuses:

> But within two years I was told there was going to be a restructuring of the school and I would no longer be required as principal, and they would re-title my position. In fact, I was effectively being paid for a job that really did not exist, at a reduced rate, I might add.
>
> I made the point that accreditation means it has to be one school, but they said not to worry about that. They said each campus would be run administratively as different schools. The principal was to be a Brethren. The man wasn't an educator. He had no experience. He was a businessman of some sort. They pulled the wool over everyone's eyes. The Brethren are experts at saying something is black when it's white.[25]

Brethren schools in Australia are very rich by comparison with other small Christian schools. Apart from the government funding, parents pay fees set at each campus, but they are very low: at MET, for example, they were about $1800–$2000 for a year 12 student. Families are offered discounts for second and subsequent children, and those who are unable to pay are given further concessions. This puts the Brethren schools among the lowest-fee non-government schools in the country.

The vast bulk of parental financial input comes from fundraising. And the Brethren have no peers in the business of raising money from their flock. In answer to a frequently asked question on their website, the Brethen say that government funding covers less than half of all operating costs of the schools, and that 'the considerable shortfall is made up by contributions from parents and friends'. Assuming that this is true, the Brethren will be looking to raise, from fees and fundraisers, more than $50 million between 2009 and 2012 from their 15,000 Australian members – a prodigious effort.

Since 2006, this fundraising has been done in a systematic way through a system of interlinked trusts, charities, and businesses, which allows Brethren parents to pay money to schools from their before-tax income, saving them thousands of dollars (see Chapter 4). The amount of this income is very difficult to track because it does not appear in the accounts of the central school bodies. But before that system was fully set up, the sect used to raise funds in a way that would be much more recognisable to 'worldly' parents – they held fundraising events, auctions, and concerts, where the children would perform. These events were called 'fun days'.

It sounds normal, but the reality was far from it. To get an idea of the financial resources available to this community, it is necessary only to look at the accounts of the Queensland schools' main fundraising entity, Anchor Fundraising Inc. When the fun days were in full swing in 2003 and 2004, they raised $789,650 at the Brisbane campus alone. That campus had 60 students, from perhaps 30 families. That is $26,000 per family – significantly higher than the fees at the most elite Australian private schools. And there were seven more campuses in Queensland, all doing similar work. In tiny Pialba, north of Gympie, the campus raised $111,418 in one year alone. In total, Anchor Fundraising made $1.4 million clear profit in just two years for its 228 students from fundraising.

The former Brethren principal described these fun days as 'like going to the entertainment at the Birdsville races, all wine and cheese and country and western music'. Another teacher, still at a Brethren school, said, 'It could have been the Sunday school picnic 40 years ago'.[26] Both agreed, though, that the Brethren were 'the best fundraisers you've ever seen'.

'These people will pay up because they're not game *not* to pay up,' said the former principal.

A former member of the Brethren, 'Janie,' explains the excitement when fun days were introduced in her small Australian country town:

> When they came in, they were such a big deal. You can imagine, we were forbidden to have music and have plays and whatever, and now, all of a sudden we're being given permission to have plays, and the kids could all get together and make little bands up. And then they had these auctions.
>
> The items for sale were generally of low value, and the aim is to get a ridiculously high price. Alcohol is popular – a $50 bottle can go for up to $1000. At one of the first fundraisers in Sydney, BDH [Bruce Hales] and his brother Stephen bidded against each other for a pumpkin (apparently left over from the kid's Cinderella play). BDH got it for $100,000 ... I'd say it was a set-up, you know, to give people the idea that this is what they were meant to be doing, because after that everybody said, 'We're having an auction, and did you hear what Mr Bruce did in Sydney? We've got to be generous.' And then everybody was happy to bid stupid prices on stupid things. Some of them were valuable things that you paid way too much for – you might have a $600 barbeque that you pay $3500 for. But I've seen the cap being taken off Mr So-and-So's head and being auctioned – stupid things like that – 'Who wants John Smith's hat for 600 bucks?'
>
> They raised a huge amount of money. Even in a little place like N they could get $80,000 on a Saturday, probably three to four times a year. We were told it was going towards funding the school and paying the teachers' wages and buying courses for the kids, but

really, I don't think so. There were 10 to 15 kids at the school in the year, and five teachers!'[27]

(Through his lawyers, Mr Hales has denied the pumpkin anecdote, saying only $35,000 was raised on the fun night in question.)

Two years down the track, the fun days had begun to wear thin, but by then the money raised was being replaced by before-tax distributions from family trusts, and the central school administration bodies were linked to charities running businesses whose tax-free profits fed back into the schools. This was much less trouble to administer, much more lucrative and tax-friendly, and there was no need for students to work up endless new performances.

At Brethren schools, all the teachers are 'worldly' people, because the 'saints' are not permitted to go to university, and so cannot receive teacher training. All staff agree when they are hired that they will not be members of the union, and they will not encourage any of the students to go on to tertiary education. But, according to one teacher, the 'quality of education is outstanding'.[28]

'I was blown away by the quality of the staff and the curriculum,' she said, on condition of anonymity. As for the equipment, 'I ask and then I receive. And there's parental support like you wouldn't believe; people falling over themselves to help you. You get fabulous family support, and support for the staff.'

Always watching, though, are the school's board of governors, the Brethren men who sit over the top of the teachers and principal: 'There are limits on what you can teach … The concern is to keep the sexual world at bay,' the teacher said. 'There is an old world flavour. English teachers have to read all the texts first to make sure there is nothing overtly sexual.' In fact, as in the strictest Islamic school, all body contact between boys and girls is watched for, and the 2008 national Brethren schools' handbook, says that 'body contact activities will not be included or promoted as part of the school activities'.[29]

David Stewart said that modern fiction was a particular problem:

> We certainly don't promote the reading of novels. It's the imagination of the readers' mind – things that are surreal ... and will direct the mind into areas that are unreal, and you find instances of people trying to go out and do what the novel has written about and get themselves into trouble. I was brought up on Dickens, *Uncle Tom's Cabin*, and there was a certain moral distinction in those novels. The corruption and filth of modern authors, that the curriculum is pushing, was absent. It's the introduction of moral corruption we oppose. That is why we have got the schools, we are trying to prevent the children from being corrupted.

Some former teachers have said that Brethren students find it difficult to do the humanities subjects because they have been taught from the cradle that authority figures have all the answers, and that to ask hard, probing questions, or to disagree, is disrespectful of their elders. One former teacher described students sitting in class during literature discussion, pens poised to note down the right answer, as handed down from the teacher. The notion of debate was foreign to them, he said.

But on this point, MET curriculum coordinator Jacqui van der velde Gilbert strongly disagreed. She is a non-Brethren who has worked for the sect's school system in New South Wales for many years, helping establish it, and she defended it strongly against attack. She insisted that Brethren students were taught all the critical-thinking, higher-order skills, such as debate, composing, and responding, and that they met the English curriculum 'more than adequately'.

'They spend a lot of time dealing with high-order critical thinking skills that are part of any syllabus document,' Ms Gilbert said, 'and all these things are inspected by the (New South Wales)

Board (of Studies).' She agreed, though, that the school's Brethren trustees were active in vetting which titles could be taught, saying, when it came time to renew book lists, 'we consult in that'.[30] In fact, the former Queensland principal said that one of his duties was to oversee Brethren mothers cutting out pages from a prescribed English textbook.

On the theory of evolution, van der velde Gilbert said that it was taught in full. The curriculum documents on the subject for the MET School appear comprehensive, and are apparently fully compliant with the New South Wales syllabus. In New South Wales the teaching of evolution is compulsory, and the MET year 10 science unit, 'Life Goes On', sub-unit 'Evolution', says that students are required to complete an assignment to 'research the two theorists of evolution, Jean Baptiste Lamarck and Charles Darwin'; to 'discuss evidence that present-day organisms have evolved from organisms in the distant past'; and to 'relate natural selection to the theory of evolution'.[31]

But the 2008 parents and students' handbook for all Brethren schools in Australia and New Zealand tells a different story. Its number one 'guiding principle' is the statement: 'The Theory of Evolution is regarded as a falsehood. The Directors see that God as Creator is worshipped in accordance with the teachings of the Holy Bible.'[32] MET principal David Stewart added that evolution was taught, 'as a theory, but we believe the Bible is the literal word of God'.

A former student of a Brethren school in country New South Wales said that, when it came time to talk about evolution, the science teacher vacated the classroom, and the lesson was taken over by the religious-education teacher:

> The scripture teacher came in and covered the whole evolution topic in one period by explaining certain questions that would be asked in the exam, and giving us the answers to them. We were told

to answer the questions by beginning with 'scientists say/claim/ believe', then write the answer supplied.[33]

The supplied answer was correct scientifically, but the topic was not meant to be understood, and was just given 'as a quick outline of what atheist scientists try to claim to prove that the world was not created in seven days. The answer was to be finished with the words, "But I don't believe it." '

In fact, science in general can be a problem for a sect that believes so fully in God's creatorial prerogative. Of science, Bruce Hales told the flock, in a meeting in November 2006, that scientists 'make it up':

> I'll tell you that right here and now, scientists are so intelligent that if they don't know for sure they can make it up so well that you believe them. They keep the world baffled with their nonsense.[34]

Another subject that presents problems, as it does for many hardline Christian schools, is sex education. The 2008 schools handbook says that, 'The Directors uphold chastity as a first principle and the teaching staff and students must conduct themselves in a manner consistent with such principle.' Ms Gilbert said that in New South Wales the teaching of sex education fully complied with the state syllabus; but, according to the former Queensland principal, this was 'not the case' in his state while he was there.

Brethren helpers at the school also teach their children religious education and current affairs. Religious education is not overdone, because the students spend most evenings at church anyway. But the current affairs subject reflects the long-running concern that members of the sect not be too directly exposed to the outside world through the news media and its journalists, who are considered evil distorters of the truth. In current affairs classes, according to Janie, the Brethren 'can put their own spin on it. So if you watch TV you might form your own opinion of George Bush, yet the Brethren might tell you that George Bush is right and we should be praying for him.'

Apart from my visit to the MET campus, the Brethren appear to be particularly fearful of media scrutiny of their schools. The 2008 handbook lists 'damaging media attention' along with terrorist activity, violent assault, death, and students and/or staff members being taken hostage as events that would trigger their 'Critical Incident Management Plan'. If confronted by a journalist or any member of the public, 'including the police', 'no questions regarding the school or the community are to be answered', the handbook says. Names and phone numbers may be taken, but no promises should be made that 'a Director or anyone else will contact them'.

The schools also have strict dress codes for teachers, and do not allow any inter-school sport. Excursions are allowed, under strict supervision, and with the inclusion of parents. The handbook says that teachers are to 'respect ... at all times whilst employed at the school' the 'conscientious objection' of the directors to union membership. One teacher, still in a Brethren school, said that the sect had some difficulty holding staff – not because the classroom environment was difficult, but because it was so different from the average:

> The dynamics of the kids are different; the normal way of disciplining them doesn't work. The whole system is non-confrontational. You can't kick up in the Brethren, so if there's going to be a backlash it will be subversive: an undercurrent of unwillingness, and you will be ignored if they don't like you. It's really hard to deal with.

Setting homework can also be a problem because, from the age of about six or seven, most children are out until 10.00 pm at church on school nights, and all over the weekend. The former Queensland principal said he saw staff, who were initially attracted by the tiny class sizes and clean image of the schools, eventually becoming disenchanted and leaving.

> Within two years there was less than 40 per cent of original staff remaining at all Agnew campuses in Queensland. As a former principal of independent schools, I had never seen such a turnover. They were being questioned. I remember a time when a woman teacher was hauled in and they found her dress was unbecoming. I was called in to be a witness to the discussion. She just left. She'd never been spoken to like that in her life.

But David Stewart disputed that staff turnover was high, saying it was less than 10 per cent in 2007, 'no different from a Catholic or Jewish school'.

Whatever the vagaries of dress codes and contentious areas of curriculum, Jacqui van der velde Gilbert, who designed much of the Brethren schooling curriculum, robustly defends the school and its teaching:

> There is no compliance issue. We teach the curriculum, we don't seek exemptions. And we have children on the honour role for HSC courses, students who achieved 90 per cent or above in their courses, across science, industrial technology, maths, history. One came second in the state in general maths, another seventh in construction. These are not small or insignificant events in any school's life.

But it is on this point that one of the real frustrations for some become evident. Teachers are specifically required to refrain from telling students, no matter how talented and high performing they are, that they should go on to university education, with the exception of technical education. The school motto, listed in the

2008 handbook, is 'Learning to Learn'. Although the Brethren 'want students educated to tertiary education entrance level,' the book explicitly states that any decisions about post-school education are 'not the responsibility of the teaching staff'. It says that, 'Teachers are not expected to influence students on matters of tertiary education.'

Janie has left the sect very recently, prompted by her desire to pursue tertiary education and to escape the role that is demanded of women within the Brethren. This desire was fostered by the encouragement of outsiders – in her case, the teachers she had while completing the government distance-education program. She was one of the last in the Brethren to enjoy this untrammelled influence from educated outsiders:

> They are even introducing primary schools now. Soon these kids won't even know what 'normal' people are like, and it will be even easier to indoctrinate kids with how sinful outsiders are. This really worries me because I know how much I owe the distance-ed teachers I had in high school – they might have been a long way away, but they were the only people I could have real conversations with. They saw potential in me and encouraged me to follow my heart. These kids are being taught by teachers who have signed a contract not to do this.

To another former Brethren woman, 'Sophie', who went to school in the 1960s, this was just part of the pernicious effect of educating children away from the rest of the community. She was educated in the days when Exclusive Brethren children had to rub shoulders with children at public high schools. She believed wholeheartedly in the religion and society she had been raised within, and thought she was the only one in her class going to heaven. But even she could not avoid the realisation that her classmates were fundamentally 'decent people':

And that is one of the tragedies about this education now – at least I could make a connection with normal people, even though I couldn't socialise with them at all ... No amount of brainwashing could blind me to the fact that these were decent human beings, and they showed warmth and empathy.[35]

In fact, when she was thrown out of the sect in traumatic circumstances, Sophie sought out a former classmate from her German lessons, even though she knew next to nothing about her. The good news is that her attempts were successful, and they are now, as women in their fifties, firm friends.

But Bruce Hales sees the children of worldly people differently. They are a danger to his flock, and the education system he has set up will protect them. 'The Lord has carried it forward,' he said in July 2004:

Well, we don't want to lose it ... It was set up to deliver the young people from the world. We don't want to go back to it, we don't want to be stupid enough to go back to the world, otherwise the Lord might take away our liberties; might take away what the government has given us.

CHAPTER NINE

The Family Court

Lloyd Chirnside's letter to the editor of *The Age* on 28 December 2006 said it all. It was, in one brief missive, an almost complete explanation of the official Exclusive Brethren position on family breakdown:

> The accusation that the Brethren break up families is an appalling lie. It is SIN that breaks up families. The Brethren tenaciously uphold the sanctity and purity of marriage as ordained of God and providing the cornerstone of society.
>
> Separation from evil is a principle established in Paul's writings to Timothy (2 Timothy 2 v21) and has long since proven to be a master strategy for protecting the family unit.
>
> Is it not contemptible that persons seeking to discredit the Brethren are themselves attacking the truth established in Romans 1 v21–32? It is the attempt to accommodate evil that is destroying the family unit and bringing confusion into society.
>
> Perhaps Bachelard could consider the facts before continuing his cowardly campaign of vilification against a religious minority group.

When Exclusive Brethren families split up, either because one partner has been excommunicated or has lost faith in the system he or she was brought up in, the Brethren try every tactic they can to keep the children of the marriage in the sect, and to ensure that they have no contact, or minimal contact, with the non-Brethren parent. And Chirnside, a young up-and-comer from Melbourne, has used just about every rationale the Brethren rely on to say why this is justified. In his formulation, those who leave the Brethren are, by definition, sinners. Their sin brings on the need to separate from them, and they – not the sect and its doctrines – are therefore always the ones responsible for the break-up of their own families.

These sinners, by definition, do not have any right to bring up their own children. The 'truth established' in Paul's letter to the Romans, cited by Chirnside, refers to such sinners. They are people who have turned away from God and are consumed by unseemly urges: 'the males also, leaving the natural use of the female, were inflamed in their lust towards one another; males with males working shame'. The Godless are 'filled with all unrighteousness, wickedness, covetousness, malice; full of envy, murder, strife, deceit, evil dispositions; whisperers, back-biters, hateful to God, insolent, proud, boasters, inventors of evil things, disobedient to parents, void of understanding, faithless, without natural affection, unmerciful'.[1] The 30-year-old innovation of no-fault divorce has clearly not penetrated the philosophy of this sect.

No-fault divorce recognises that relationships break down – they just do – for reasons that cannot be attributed to either party. The Brethren's concentration on sin and blame, good and evil, is totally incompatible with this legal notion. In their argument, sinners' marriages fail, but those who remain true to the Brethren have good marriages because they are saved, and because they have discovered the secret of familial contentment. (Push a little further and they will produce a report by Melbourne academic Dr Gary D. Bouma which says that the divorce rate in the Brethren is a fraction, about one-fourteenth, of that in the general population.) This idealisation of the sect's way of life ignores the fact that their very attitude to sin, and the Brethren's central doctrine – separation – have regularly been at the root of family traumas acted out in the Family Court of Australia.

Chirnside also refers to the religious-freedom argument when he calls for an end to 'vilification' of a 'religious minority'. It is not unusual for those with separatist faiths, including Jehovah's Witnesses and ultra-orthodox Jews, to come before judges in Family Court matters. Their argument is almost always that they are exercising their religious freedom when they try to override the rights of non-sect and lapsed parents, and to claim sole custody of children. The Family Court records indicate, though, that the Brethren appear more frequently than most, and that they fight longer and harder for full custody of the children.

The argument in these cases is always the same. On one side is the sect's unbending belief that keeping the children within the Brethren is the right and Godly thing to do, and that the 'fallen' parent must not have access in case he or she exposes the child to corruption and sin. On the other side is the determination of the opposing parent to spend time with his or her child, and the presumption of Australian law that both parents will have access to their children unless the child's safety is in doubt.

In the annals of the Family Court, it is a recurring and, at times, explosive argument. Even before the Whitlam government passed the *Family Law Act 1975*, which established the specialist Family Court and no-fault divorce, the Exclusive Brethren were fighting these cases. In 1960, the sect's American leader, James Taylor Junior, made the doctrine of separation stricter than ever before, prompting a rash of cases in courts around the world. Just three years later, the first Brethren test case hit the courts in Australia.

In *Ex parte Paul; Re Paul*, in 1963, Justice David Selby granted custody of the child to the non-Brethren father, in the face of the Brethren mother's application. Justice Selby, later the deputy chancellor of the University of Sydney, said in his judgment that a mother might be unfit to be awarded custody on the basis of being 'an unnatural or immoral mother' because of 'fanatical religious beliefs'.[2] The Brethren's beliefs, he found, 'if applied in the upbringing of her children, are likely to leave them ill-prepared to take their places as citizens playing their part in the hurley burley of the modern world'.

Three years later, in 1966, the case of *Mauger v Mauger* was heard in the Supreme Court of Queensland, and Justice Graham Hart decided it was 'very much against the children's interests to allow them to be brought up in the tenets of the [Exclusive Brethren]'.[3]

The Brethren appealed the decision to the Full Court of Queensland, where the Chief Justice, Sir Alan Mansfield, observed, 'If any religion or religious belief is such that it would cause the breaking up of a matrimonial relationship ... then the tenets of that religion are contrary to public policy.' The Brethren applied for special leave to appeal again, this time to the High Court of Australia, and then to the judicial committee of the Privy Council in Britain. Both applications were refused.

In 1972, New South Wales Supreme Court Justice Carmichael was hearing a similar case involving 'dis-fellowshipping' from the Jehovah's Witnesses, and he looked over a number of these old religious cases to try to establish some general ground rules. He considered a number of disputes: two cases involving the Brethren; one between a Jehovah's Witness and a former member of the sect; one between a Roman Catholic and a Protestant; another involving an Anglican and a Catholic; and one between a Jew and a gentile. Having done this, he singled out the Brethren for special mention. Their doctrine was the most extreme of all, he found, because of their insistence that a husband or wife who is a member of the sect must 'desert his spouse if that spouse is not also a member'.[4]

Far from the Brethren, in Chirnside's words, having discovered a 'master strategy' for protecting the family unit, according to Justice Carmichael, it was 'necessary for the protection of the community' and 'in the interests of social order' for the Brethren to be prevented from erecting barriers within families and imposing on children their rules of separation from the world.

Justice Carmichael wrote:

> The time will come when the children will be required to take their place as responsible members of the community. Deprived of the advantages gained by intermingling with their contemporaries, denied the opportunity of character building conferred by sporting activities, they must necessarily suffer when the time comes to play their part as citizens. These matters, I consider, directly concern some of the most important elements in the child's welfare, and the way of life to which their mother would condemn them can only redound to their disadvantage.

After the Family Law Act was passed in 1975, the Brethren cases continued in the new forum, as did the adverse judicial commentary. In *K v K* in 1979, Justice Paul Toose, in the New South Wales Supreme Court, referred to the 'anti-social character' of the Brethren, saying that the evidence put before him by the sect's witnesses had made his view of them even worse:

> It ... demonstrates them to have a self-righteous and arrogant attitude. While they claim to be Christians they do not appear to follow the ordinarily accepted precepts of Christian conduct ... what is ordinarily referred to as Christian charity appears to form no part of their belief.[5]

The judge gave joint custody to the father (who was 'withdrawn from' by the sect) and the mother (acting in an impeccably pro-Brethren fashion because she wanted to be readmitted to it), but he restrained her from taking the children to religious meetings, or from making any decisions regarding their education or religion.

A recurring argument in these cases, not just with the Brethren, but with other strict sects, is the one which Chirnside alludes to – the claim for special consideration from the courts because to deny them what they seek would be to prevent them from practising their religion. Section 116 of the Australian Constitution guarantees that 'the Commonwealth shall not make any law for establishing any religion, or for imposing any religious observance, or for prohibiting the free exercise of any religion'. Lawyers for the Brethren and other religions have often relied on this provision to argue that judges should not trammel the rights of the sect's members to fully participate in their religion according to its own rules. (This is a similar argument to that used by Exclusive Brethren lobbyists to convince politicians to give them special consideration and legislative exemptions.)

The judicial view of this has been consistent: it is not the court's job to prefer one religion over any other, nor to suggest that a religious household is better than a non-religious one. Importantly, though, this does not mean that religion is a no-go zone for critical thought. For one thing, what constitutes a religion can be difficult to define, as memorably put by the Full Bench of the Family Court in 1979:

> There may be many paths to the top of the mountain. Some would say there is only one. Some would say there is no path. Some would say there is no mountain. It would be presumptuous, vain and temerarious [reckless] for a judge to make a finding of fact on such an issue.[6]

But the court also found in this case that some faiths or doctrines are simply, objectively, beyond the pale. Some, 'albeit given a veneer of religious justification, are in fact ... [so] positively harmful to the welfare of children that they must be removed from the influence of those who advocate in such practices'.

In 1988, the court again confirmed this finding, ruling that, once religious factors are weighed up, 'together with all other relevant factors', and the court decides it is 'detrimental to the welfare of the children for them to be brought up adhering to such practices', then 'this does not constitute a breach of section 116 of the Constitution'.[7] Hinted at, but obscured by the legal words of all these judgments, is the sheer psychological turmoil of family breakdown in a sect such as the Brethren. 'Assembly discipline', accusations of the 'sin' of splitting the family, children being told that their parent is leprous, wicked or 'of the devil', and separation from all family and support are the conditions under which sect members and ex-members come to the door of the court.

In 1980, a young mother, Mrs G, was withdrawn from for having made a number of verbal outbursts against senior people within the Brethren.[8] These outbursts suggested that she had some untreated psychological illness – an impression confirmed by later events – but, instead of being cared for, she was excommunicated for being troublesome and for questioning authority. Her husband had been 'withdrawn from' a few years earlier; now, outside the sect and alone, she could not cope. She sent her two children to stay temporarily with her Brethren brother.

Three weeks later, her brother told her that if she signed a piece of paper giving him custody of the children, 'it would be in her favour with God'. She took this to mean that temporarily signing over custody of her children would help her bid to return to the sect. Mrs G signed the paper and then waited for the Brethren to visit her and 'release her' from assembly discipline. When she asked a priest when the visit might happen, he said, 'We are not saying whether we are going to come in three weeks or three months.'

For six months, nobody came. With increasing hysteria, Mrs G tried again and again to get her children back, but nothing would move the Brethren. She even went with police to her elder son's school to try to bring him home. But the boy was visibly upset, and tried to escape from her through a window, saying that she was 'a wicked woman' and a 'lawless woman'. The boy told her ,'That bit of paper you gave Uncle J, you know, you have given me to Uncle J.'

Shortly afterwards, Mrs G lodged proceedings in the Family Court to try to get her children back from her own brother. The lawyer she found, a junior barrister called Paul Guest, was up against one of Melbourne's top QCs of the day, Abraham Monester, in a trial that was to become the longest held in the Melbourne court until that point.

Mrs G was, according to the judge, 'a particularly intelligent young woman with an extraordinary sense of responsibility towards her children'. But, during the hearing of her case, her behaviour became more and more erratic. One day, she went to the Brethren assembly hall and sat in the gutter outside for an hour, screaming at the people going inside and raising two fingers at them. She produced dolls and a chisel, and started stabbing the dolls with it.

(Another woman was herself withdrawn from, and kept out of the sect for some months, for saying to another member of the congregation, 'That poor woman!' on the day Mrs G sat in the gutter.[9] At the time, the Brethren were praying against Mrs G and her lawyer, and praying for a 'righteous judgment'.[10])

But when Mrs G brought her chisel into the courtroom one day, and then, during the case, leaned forward towards her brother, pointed the chisel at him and said, 'I will stick this through your guts', her case nearly collapsed. Guest, who later became a Family Court judge, and retired in May 2008, remembers it well: 'We were winning and I thought my world had come to an end – the judge was onside, and then this happened. It was terrible.'

The hearing was adjourned, and psychiatrists called in. They diagnosed Mrs G with bipolar disorder, which no doubt had contributed to the erratic behaviour that had led to her being withdrawn from in the first place. The doctors said it had been exacerbated by the stress of the case. After a long assessment, they agreed that she could cope with custody of her children if she were properly medicated. Despite Mrs G's behaviour, Justice Walsh's judgment could not have been more categorical. Almost a year after she had come to the court seeking its help, he awarded custody to her, and aimed a broadside at the Brethren, saying that their doctrine of separation was opposed to every single one of the Family Court's principles:

> The 'institution of marriage' appeared to me to be, from the point of view of the Brethren, secondary to their beliefs, specifically their belief in 'eternal salvation'. Marriage between members of the Brethren, in my view, must be at abnormal risk, because of the risk of either party being withdrawn from ... There can be no doubt that the disintegration of the 'family' of the husband and the wife and their children has been primarily due to the practice of withdrawal, practised by the Brethren. I am not generally disposed towards the use of strong words, but I can find no other more apt words to describe the conduct of the persons involved in the circumstances of the wife's withdrawal and the removal of the children from her, than as 'vicious and cruel'.

Justice Walsh said Mrs G had been 'deceived into believing that her withdrawal may only be for a short period and that the removal of the children from her would similarly be for a short period':

> To use the vernacular, she was 'strung on' for almost five months, and watched in her crying ... grovelling and pleading, shouting and desperation, without any hand of fellowship being extended. All this, it seems, was justified by those involved on the basis that the wife was 'iniquitous' and 'lawless' because she had been withdrawn from.

The basic notion of these practices is to stand aloof from that community and to nurture their children only to serve and meet the demands of their own minuscule community. Their expectation that their children will grow to responsible and consummate adulthood, given that type of background is, in my view, naive in the extreme.

Justice Walsh ordered the police to remove the children from Mrs G's brother and to deliver them to her. The Brethren appealed, and the Full Court overturned Justice Walsh's decision, on the basis that he had concentrated almost solely on the religious dimension of the case without properly weighing the balancing factors. The case was sent back to be heard again. The new judge, Justice Strauss, found in her favour again, awarding the children to the mother, using language that was almost as vehement:

Measured by the standards of the right thinking members of this community ... the determined attempt made by [Mrs G's brother and his wife] to deprive the children of their mother's love and affection and care and a loving and caring relationship with their mother, approaches far more nearly the connotations of the terms wicked and evil as they are understood generally in this community, and as I understand them.[11]

Despite the declared wishes of both the children, the judge left them with the mother, and said that the Brethren were not to have visiting rights. Paul Guest, who retired in May 2008 as a judge of the Family Court, represented Mrs G through all the appeals, against two different QCs brought in by the Brethren – for whom, he says, 'Money was power'.

In his career as a Family Court lawyer, and then a judge, Guest has seen almost every kind of bad behaviour, but the case of Mrs G left a lasting impression: 'It had a severe effect on me,' Guest said:

I was young in those days and I was absolutely amazed at how a family could treat another member of the family with such disdain and arrogance. It was an appalling exercise in human behaviour. I remember the term, 'withdraw from' – it was as if she was dirty, repulsive, not clean. The way they moved away and left her alone. Every element of compassion and human understanding, every fundamental element of goodwill was absent. She was robbed of a life, stripped.

He added that the way the boys were influenced against their mother by the Brethren was 'contrary to all good parenting'.

Guest did not know what happened to the family after the second judgment. There was some talk that the mother might move away from Melbourne with her boys. But, about a decade later, when he himself was a QC, he was approached by two 'very fine, good-looking boys' in the precincts of a court where another Brethren case was being held.

'And they said, "Mr Guest?" I said, "Yes." And they said, "We're the G boys. We'd just like to say how you ruined our lives." They had got away from their mother and were now part of the Brethren again, and they said the court ruined them, and that I was part of that, and I was associated with the devil.'

The bitterness, the length of the G case, and the money spent on it is a common feature of Family Court fights involving the Exclusive Brethren. Former Chief Justice Alistair Nicholson remembers that the Brethren 'fought grimly, and really not too much quarter given'. If they lost, they appealed, 'no matter how hopeless the appeals were'.[12]

Funding all this legal work is a vast pot of money, drawn from the congregation at monthly meetings, which is specifically procured for legal cases – particularly for cases in the Family Court. It is known within the Brethren as the 'fighting fund'. 'We knew what this fighting fund was for, and we thought it was pleasing the Lord to get these children out of the hands of wicked parents,' recalls one former Brethren member Alison Alderton, with profound regret.[13]

Elderly Brethren are even known to have been encouraged to contribute money to this fund in their estates. The will of one woman, which appears to be modelled on a template, gave a large amount of money to her trustee to 'use such bequest for payment at his sole discretion to any trust or other fund existing at my death or subsequently for the purpose of meeting legal costs and expenses related to actions in the courts'.[14]

Former Chief Justice Nicholson said that the existence of this money supply often tipped the balance in favour of the Brethren in such cases. 'There seemed to be unlimited money in terms of paying counsel for the purposes of conducting appeals, no matter how hopeless the appeals were ... [The non-Brethren parties] were put in a very unfair position,' he said.

The non-Brethren parent also had 'no real prospect of recouping costs that they'd incurred in fighting the Brethren-supported partner' because 'there are legal difficulties about making costs orders against third parties,' Nicholson said. Very often, the parents who have been subject to the endless legal proceedings brought by the Brethren have pulled out before the case has been finally settled, broken either financially or psychologically, or both, by their long ordeal.

A.B.'s was just such a case. He lost a wife and two young boys when he could no longer bring himself to be part of the sect, and quit it in 1988. From the time his family was removed from him, A.B. was forced to endure long months in the Family Court in an attempt to gain access to his children. The Brethren instigated the first court case in the Albury Court and then continued through about 30 more cases, motions, appeals, applications – the full panoply of what the court has to offer in Albury, Canberra, Melbourne, and Sydney. The case went to the Full Bench of the Family Court more than once.

'They tried every trick in the book,' A.B. says. There was even a failed attempt at removing one of the many presiding judges, after then world leader John Hales said at a meeting in the UK in September, 1990, 'They should impeach the judge' (Justice Strauss), because he was 'blatantly strongly asserting that a child of six would not have the capacity to come to a moral judgment' about which parent he should stay with. In the same meeting, Hales also said that the children of A.B. 'should flee' – meaning that, when time for access visits came, they should run away.[15]

A.B.'s younger child was six at the time. In the Brethren's usual formulation, a child of eight is able to make the 'moral distinction' between 'good and evil' and to therefore choose which parent and which lifestyle he or she should live with.

A.B. won every case. Even so, the only time he got to spend with his sons was 'a little access' in the first three months after they had been taken away from him. Former members say that the Brethren are told that the assembly is the highest court, higher than any worldly court, and therefore that the orders of other courts do not matter so much as the judgment of the assembly.

In one of the judgments in A.B.'s case, in 1991, Justice Stephen Strauss said that A.B. was 'a gentle and altogether honest man':

> He is much distressed by these proceedings. I have no doubt that he loves these children and indeed he still has great affection for the wife as well. He found it difficult, if not impossible, to speak ill of her. He blames the Brethren for her failure to give access and he is probably right in this. I have no doubt at all that if it could be arranged, he would be a most valuable parent to these two boys. He will give them his love, devotion and affection in every way that he can give it to them. To deprive these boys altogether of the filial bond with him, as is now attempted, would be a most grave step and I believe a grave wrong to these children.

Justice Strauss also made an important finding about the credibility of the witnesses:

> Importantly, for the purposes of this case, I have no doubt at all about his honesty, integrity and veracity as a witness. He was frank and truthful. The wife is much more difficult to assess. I do not believe that she would tell an outright lie. However, I found her to be evasive and lacking in candour. To a certain extent she gave me the impression that she was labouring under some sort of control and that she had been tutored.[16]

But, as the cases dragged on, and A.B.'s money began to run out, the children themselves increased the pressure on their father as they were progressively being turned against him. They wrote A.B. heartbreaking letters to tell him that they would not see him any more unless he 'got right'. Under the financial and emotional pressure, A.B. eventually gave up the case. He has seen the children only fleetingly in the almost 20 years since.

There are many examples of this pressure being brought to bear on grieving parents already suffering from the separation from their children. During the hours that the Brethren parent, extended family, and priests have access to the children, they have time to tutor them in how evil and devilish the estranged parent is, how they have deserted the mother and children and left them penniless, how they do not love the children and, particularly, how dangerous their estranged parent is because they are going to hell.

The longer the Brethren can string out a court case – through new cases, applications, appeals, motions to disqualify the judge, and so on – the more time they have to influence the child, and the more their ability to out-spend their opposition begins to bite. If they must give the child up for access visits with the non-Brethren parent, the children are rewarded and praised when they get home from the visit if they have behaved badly towards him or her.

Vincent Field, a former member of the Brethren in New Zealand, was separated from his parents and moved to his grandparents' house as an eight-year-old in 1990. He remembers very well the psychological pressure put on him to reject his mother and father:

> There is a point where you actually start to believe that because your parents 'aren't right with the Lord' that you don't want to see them. It's continually reiterated by all the people in the church, especially when they pray in their meetings ... Initially we would have loved to see our parents, but just the methodical phrases and the way they talk about your parents made you not want to.[17]

Former Chief Justice Alastair Nicholson says that to 'brainwash' children in this way 'is abusive of them, and it's psychologically very damaging to the child'.

'It's in effect telling the child that their parent is worthless, and is someone that they're not entitled to let the children see. And that really is quite unacceptable.'

The children's reaction to all this is understandably strong. Louise Samways, a psychologist experienced in dealing with the effects of strict religious organisations, says that sects who say the lapsed parent is of the devil 'deliberately use this to create an absolute terror of a parent who may have been expelled. This is child abuse'.[18]

Nevertheless, it sometimes has the effect of putting pressure on the judge, as well as on the non-Brethren party. In the case of *Litchfield v Litchfield* in 1987, Justice Graham Mullane agreed with the Brethren mother's application that her child should have no contact with her father because of the strain caused by the visits. The effects on the child included insomnia, insecurity, and bedwetting – evidence, according to the judge, of 'extreme stress and anxiety'. The mother in this case had given evidence that she and her child both believed her ex-husband was 'evil' and an adulterer.[19]

The Brethren version of what is happening to the children in cases such as this is that the trauma emerges not from the way they are treated within the sect, but from 'the children's exposure to this diametrically opposed lifestyle' of the non-Brethren parent.[20]

Former members of the sect who are trying to enjoy access with their children also face another real, practical difficulty in cases involving the Brethren: the children simply do not turn up for access visits. The Brethren's official line on compliance with court orders is that 'the Brethren urge members to abide by the court's decision in relation to access and other matters'.[21] But, according to Nicholson, this is not the case in reality:

> When decisions were unfavourable and they appeal, then there was often difficulty in relation to complying with terms of orders, in that either they would be refusing to comply, or begrudging compliance, or partial compliance ... that's not uncommon in Family Law, but this was very much a pattern in cases involving Brethren people.

Supporting the Brethren parent in these cases is their firm belief that the 'worldly' court system is inferior to the Brethren's own judgments: 'Of course, the assembly is the highest court, so that's a matter that we can take comfort in,' said Hales in 2003. 'It's a very great matter, I think, to know that this place, the assembly, is the highest court. It's the area of God's direct dealings, and it's got the power to overrule other judgments if there's a righteous basis for it.'[22]

Of course, the worldly courts have a very different view, and the Family Court has, in general, been quite unsympathetic to the Brethren's arguments. In fact, the rash of unfavourable Family Court judgments through the 1980s, and the feeling that judges and counsellors were not paying sufficient heed to their arguments, so upset the Exclusive Brethren leaders that, in 1991, a group of the sect's marriage celebrants went over the judges' heads. They complained to the Chief Justice.

'We know of no other institution or group which has been the subject of such repeated criticism or comment by your Bench,' they lamented in a written submission to then Chief Justice Alistair Nicholson. The judges' comments, 'if repeated in a non-privileged forum, would give us no option but to pursue our rights under the ordinary laws of defamation'.[23]

The main complaint of the delegation was that Family Court judges' rulings appeared to them to be aimed at 'liberating children from the Brethren lifestyle, and to turn them against the church ... Members of our community do not feel that they face an impartial and unbiased bench when they come to the Family Court.'

Judges should have the role of 'the upholding of fixed principles regarding right and wrong, good and evil', which meant in practice that children should always be brought up in the Brethren:

> The welfare of the children is best preserved by being maintained within the lifestyles and belief systems which they have been brought up in since birth. We see the Court as being more concerned to protect the interests of the non-custodial parent than in promoting the best interests of the children concerned. Much of this attitude flows from the judicial determination to minimize the weight to be given to (or even ignore) the wishes of the children.

They stated that, where contact had been ordered with a non-Brethren parent, 'this has been respected and obeyed by the Brethren parent', though doing so was 'stressful'. And they added that there was 'no pressure brought to bear on any member'. They also made an argument for the traditional family. 'The cornerstone of a healthy society,' they said, was the 'regulation of order in the family home in accordance with the creatorial status of man and woman ... Numerous social studies confirm the enduring value of the dedication of the mother to the home setting and the tender care of children.'

Eleven years later, in 2002, matters from the Brethren's perspective had not improved. So they tried again, making another submission to Nicholson and visiting him again. In this second letter, they said that in every single case where custody of children was involved, the children's wishes were to 'reside with the parent among the Brethren; to refrain from contact with the former members; to remain together as a family unit with the Brethren parent'.[24]

The intention of the Family Court Act to take into account the child's best interests, the sharing of responsibility and care between both parents, and the right of contact 'each impinge directly on our practice of separation where there has been a marriage breakdown', they wrote. Contact should never be awarded to the non-Brethren parent because, where it had been,

> the conflict has always been very severe, emotionally traumatic, and damaging; the children have ultimately themselves terminated the contact and remain among the Brethren, but with very damaging and unhappy memories which continue to traumatise them in later life.
>
> With all Brethren children, their religion pervades their entire way of life ... Where one parent has left the Fellowship it IS NOT in the child's best interests that they: 1. reside with that parent, 2. have contact with that parent or 3. are subject to the jurisdiction of that parent ... It IS in the child's best interests that it remain in the spiritual and secular environment into which it has been born.

They also reiterated their argument that children had a right to make up their own minds about 'good and evil': 'It is well-recognised that a child of eight years normally has a moral judgment of right and wrong and knows who can be trusted and who they are uneasy with. Their instincts should be respected.'

Almost invariably, the children of cases involving the Brethren who have come under the kind of pressure described by Vincent Field will make strong statements that they want to remain in the sect, and that they choose the parent who is 'in fellowship' rather than the one who is 'of the devil'. The sect relies on this reaction by its children, both in court cases and also in the public sphere, to claim that the child has the ability, and therefore the right, to choose which parent they should live with. This argument is an opportunity for the Brethren to try to turn an argument about rights – in this case, the supposed right of the child to choose its preferred parent – to their advantage.

But Chief Justice Nicholson said that, when he was confronted with these submissions, he had told his Brethren interlocutors that 'you can't just influence the system in that way', and that his judges needed to apply the law of the land as it stood. Disappointed, twice, by Nicholson, the Brethren sought a remedy even higher up: among the politicians who made the law.

In 2005, attorney-general Philip Ruddock was conducting a major overhaul of the Family Law Act, and during the drafting process the Brethren took the opportunity to try to influence Ruddock to their way of thinking. They sent copies of their 1991 and 2002 letters to Nicholson to Ruddock, made a submission to the parliamentary inquiry into the proposed laws, and went to see the attorney-general himself. In each submission, the argument that the Brethren put at centre stage was the 'right' of children to choose their custodial parent.

In their submission to the parliament, the Brethren reiterated their argument, referring to the government's proposal to strengthen the child's right to be known and be cared for by both parents. 'The nature of this "right", however, needs to be articulated,' the Brethren elders argued. 'Is it some abstract right or is it a more tangible right ... the concept of the "right" of a child extends to a child of suitable age being able to have substantial weight, sometimes decisive weight, placed on what his or her wishes are.'[25] In a separate letter to Ruddock, the Brethren lobbyists said that, 'A child should not, without adequate and compelling grounds, be subject to a radical lifestyle change. Why should this not be a "right" of a child?'[26] Their plea was rejected.

One of the innovations of Ruddock's legislation was to create a new device, called 'Parenting Plans', which gave legal weight for the first time to the agreements made between divorcing parents about how their children's time should be split up between them. In this, the Brethren saw another opportunity: they argued that parenting plans should be available to be 'entered into at any time before the marriage breakdown'.

It is clear from their submission to the parliamentary inquiry that the sect's elders were proposing a kind of child-custody prenuptial agreement to covered 'health, schooling, religion and so on'. Their plan was that, while two Brethren parents were happily married and ensconced within the sect, they would be required to sign a 'parenting plan', perhaps at the same time as the wedding contract, which agreed that the children of the marriage would be brought up exclusively within the Brethren, in perpetuity, even if one party left the sect.

'If, for example, at the time of marriage both parents have a common purpose as to one or more aspects of the lives of their children, why should this not be able to be put into a parenting plan?' their submission said.[27] The Brethren lobbyists hoped to convince Ruddock to make these plans enforceable in law, a 'rebuttable presumption' – something that anybody arguing against it would need to shoot down in court. Thus, children could be legally secured within the Brethren. They also failed in this.

The Brethren's political lobbyists also objected to the proposed new Act's presumption of 'equal shared parental responsibility', which would give both parents an equal right to make decisions for the children, except when there was evidence of 'violence, abuse or entrenched conflict'. In their submission, they wanted to redefine 'abuse' and 'entrenched conflict' to help them reject someone who had left, or had been evicted from the sect, by accusing them of causing the said 'entrenched conflict'. 'For instance,' they asked, 'is entrenched conflict meant to refer to some long standing conflict, or could the nature of the issue in relation to which the conflict exists [that is, a conflict between someone in the Brethren and someone leaving it] be sufficient to make it "entrenched"?'.

Again, they were refused.

Their submission also gave a clear indication that Brethren parents had no intention of complying with one proposed element of the Act: the compulsory requirement of attending mediation sessions. Since they clearly had no intention of settling their disputes with any kind of compromise, they asked that a financial penalty for failing to attend mediation should be the 'the only possible downside to a parent who does not attend "Dispute Resolution".' In other words, they could simply pay money to avoid having to attend mediation to negotiate a solution.

In May 2005, four Brethren lobbyists met Ruddock to discuss these issues. Among them were two of the sect's chief political flag carriers, Warwick John and Phil McNaughton. The minister politely heard their arguments on parenting plans, innocent parties, and drastic lifestyle changes. Ruddock's letter in reply to this meeting is delightfully deadpan. It reads like a press release, pushing the government's policy and failing to directly address any of the Brethren's issues.[28] Ruddock told me he had been happy to meet the delegation, but had not put into practice any of their suggestions:

> When the Exclusive Brethren have a view, I'm perfectly happy for them to put it, and to have it heard. But the fact that you hear it doesn't mean you adopt it. My view is that children have an entitlement, and it's now effected in the law, provided they are safe

and secure, to know both their parents ... to know something of their genealogy. I don't think children are well served if one person determines a relationship should no longer exist.[29]

He added that the Brethren's belief that 'if you put yourselves outside the church, that you put yourselves outside any relationship with your former partner and your progeny – that is something I find difficult to accept,' he said.

In developing his family law legislation, Ruddock said he had also been approached by fundamentalist Jews and Muslims arguing for a religious twist on the law to suit their purposes. 'In each case, I took the view that the normal law of Australia should take precedence.'

In practice, though, Brethren parents are still avoiding the normal law of Australia in the Family Court. Many things have changed within the Brethren in recent years: they are fighting far fewer court cases because it is much less likely that members will be excommunicated; and strong efforts are being made to keep in the fold those who are contemplating leaving the sect. But when they do engage in legal battles, they are as trenchant as ever. Two sets of non-Brethren parents who were fighting with the Brethren over access at the time of writing have painted exactly this picture.

'They are just as bad, as controlling, as they ever were,' said one father. His young daughter is reluctantly given up by the mother for access visits with him, but he is sure she is being schooled to dislike him – she treats him as if he were dirty, untouchable. 'They're going to try to stop her coming to us ... when she gets to a certain age, they'll just stop her coming. They can take everything off you and then hang their hats on freedom of religion,' the man said.[30]

The Brethren say, categorically, that 'our members are committed to obey court orders and comply with such orders'.[31] But a Tasmanian case, *E v P*, in which the mother had access to $50,000 from the Brethren fighting fund, suggests that this is not the case.

At the time of writing, *E v P*, a tragedy in a dozen acts, was still going on. It involves all the human misery capable of being inflicted by any family breakdown, with a few extra miseries inflicted by the Exclusive Brethren. In this case, the father, who became disillusioned and left the Brethren in early 2003, sought orders that the three youngest of his eight children should live with him, but that his ex-wife have time with them and share equal parental responsibility. The mother, still a member of the sect, sought sole custody with no access to the children by the father.

By the time the case came to court in 2006, the Brethren mother had had custody of the children for the three years following the couple's separation. After nine days of exhaustive hearings, Justice Robert Benjamin concluded that the children had been 'the subject of comment and influence by member/s of the Brethren', and were 'discouraged from enjoying or taking benefit' from the two visits they had already had during the case.[32]

He also accepted the evidence of a court-appointed psychologist that these actions by church and family members 'amounted to psychologically cruel, unacceptable and abusive behaviour' that was at 'the highest end of psychological abuse of them'. But he found this was not malicious – just the product of the mother's sincere and real belief in the Brethren religion.

In his judgment, Benjamin tried to be scrupulously fair to both parties, and considerate of the Brethren's sincerely held beliefs. He ordered the wife, who stayed within the Brethren, to have custody, so as not to disturb the children's living arrangements, but he also ordered that the father have significant time with them. The father was under strict instructions not to try to influence them against the Brethren, nor to introduce them to television, radio, or computers. The mother was ordered not to try to sway the children against the father, and to make sure they were prepared for the access visits at the appropriate pick-up times.

But the judge went a step further. In a special coda to his

judgment, he called the children, the family members, and sect elders to the courtroom, and read out a sternly worded warning. He said that they must not apply any pressure to the children to try to alter their relationship with their father. He said, pointedly, that abuse of a child, physically or psychologically, meant that 'prison is a proper consideration, particularly when it also involves contravention of a court order':

> To the elders of the Exclusive Brethren, a review of the authorities shows that these difficulties have been going on for thirty years ... it must surely not be beyond your intellect and wit to find a dimension in your beliefs so that they may reconcile with the law of this country and the need for children to know both of their parents.

But, apparently, it was. Four weeks after the judgment, when the father went to collect his children, their bags were packed and sitting on the front porch. But the children stood in the doorway, flanked by two adult male members of their family with their arms crossed (an older brother and brother-in-law of the children). The children refused to go with their father, and the father gave evidence that this seemed to meet with the approval of the Brethren adults in attendance. The police were called and interviewed the children, with the Brethren family members hovering just outside the door to the room. The police also had no luck convincing the children to go. The father gave up and left.

Shortly after these events, Bruce Hales visited Tasmania and spoke to the mother about the case. The mother later described the Man of God as a 'family friend', and denied he had influenced her on the subject of custody, nor that they had discussed financial aid. But, back in court, as the father tried to get redress for the children's failure to show, the mother appeared for the first time with one of Australia's most expensive Family Court lawyers, Melbourne QC Noel Ackman. The mother gave evidence of a $50,000 'loan' in her bank account that had been placed there by unidentified 'friends' to help with her legal bills, but which she was expected to pay back. Cross-examined by her ex-husband's lawyer, she said, 'It's a system of society of love that you probably don't understand.'[33]

Ackman tried to get the judge to dismiss himself on the grounds of bias. When this failed, he argued that the children had declined to visit their father of their own free will, and that this should be respected. The judge concluded otherwise, saying that the Brethren had pressured the children again. Out of patience, Justice Benjamin convicted and sentenced the mother, her son, and her son-in-law to four-month suspended jail sentences for breaching his painfully explicit orders of only two months earlier. 'These children are entitled to have a relationship with their father, and the steps that the respondents have taken to prevent the relationship are extraordinary and appalling,' he said.

During evidence in the case, the mother laughed when asked if there was a photograph of the children's father in the house. Asked if she had told her ex-husband that he had become a grandfather, she said: 'That's not my responsibility.'

'That's extraordinary,' the judge responded. 'How sad it was that this house was so poisonous to the father that they could not even have a photograph of the father in their home.'

Still, that was not the end of the mother's resistance to the judge's orders. The children turned up, for a time, for their access visits, and the father was certain that the two younger children thoroughly enjoyed them – once they had overcome the journey to his house and the awkwardness of the hand-over. But the Brethren did not let the matter rest there. More court applications were lodged. The mother and the children's older brother and brother-in-law appealed against their suspended jail sentences, and won. Then the children started not turning up for visits again. Once again, the father sought the court's time to enforce its own orders. Then the mother's lawyers moved that, for the hearing of the new cases,

Justice Benjamin should disqualify himself on the grounds that he had given the impression that he was biased against her. This time, Benjamin reluctantly agreed, and quit the case, saying it was a 'finely balanced' judgment.

Complicating all of this was that, during the case, the mother was diagnosed with terminal cancer. Under these circumstances, none of the parties was willing to push the children away from her. At the time of writing, the father was simply biding his time in the hope that, someday, he would be able see his children again, and that, despite all the time the Brethren will have had to work on them, they will still want to see him. If the mother dies, he will have a good argument for custody of the children, but there is every likelihood that he will then have to fight the other Brethren relatives for custody.

Despite clear evidence of substantial financial support in this sad case, the official line of the Brethren is that they 'feel for both parties, and in particular the children in this situation, and have offered their prayers and support', in the words of spokesman Tony McCorkell.[34] They refer to it as a private affair, having nothing to do with the church.

This is the old argument that the Brethren use about political advertising, and in other cases where the sect is challenged over the excesses of its behaviour: they steadfastly insist that individual Brethren members have acted independently, without the influence, control, or guidance of the church. The long history of Family Court cases involving the Exclusive Brethren provides plenty of evidence to contradict them.

CHAPTER TEN

Silencing Criticism

For a group that maintains it is separate and aloof from the concerns of the world, the Exclusive Brethren are inordinately sensitive about what the world says about them. Three times since 1998, former members of the sect have set up websites that have attracted large numbers of ex-Brethren people to them. These sites have acted as meeting rooms for former members, where they could make contact, share information about missing families, criticise the sect in which they were raised, and conduct a kind of online group therapy.

In two of these three cases, Brethren legal action, or the threat of it, has closed the sites down; and, at the time of writing, the third and by far the largest of those sites, www.peebs.net, was battling a Brethren application in the American courts that threatens to achieve the same end.

Since people who are members of the Exclusive Brethren are supposed to have no regular access to the internet, these attacks can only be interpreted as an attempt to eliminate public criticism of the sect, and to try to minimise bad publicity. In the latest case, the Brethren's publishing arm, the Bible and Gospel Trust, has taken action against www.peebs.net on the basis of an accusation of copyright infringement. Copyright is a familiar jurisdiction for other religious sects, such as Scientology and the Jehovah's Witnesses; in an attempt to silence critics, both sects have used the accusation that their proprietary material has been stolen.

In the past, the Brethren have also used defamation writs to limit discussion of their practices. They have sued an academic who wrote a book about their history, journalists who criticised aspects of their behaviour, and even a former member who pinned his objections to the sect on a town notice board. Some of these cases make it to the courts, but they rarely, if ever, go to judgment. So far, the Brethren seem to have preferred to flex their legal muscles enough to give ample warning of the scope and potential expense of the case and then to settle out of court. Part of the settlement has been an agreement by the defendant to close down the website or to limit the scope of his or her further criticism. In these kinds of cases, it is the threat of legal expenses more than the quality of the argument that wins a favourable settlement for the Brethren.

Dick Wyman was the first of the owners of the websites that sought to expose the Exclusive Brethren. A former member of the sect himself, Wyman started a site in 1997 that eventually became www.exclusivebrethren.net. At its heart was a simple guestbook, which allowed former members of the Brethren to make contact with one another, seek out lost members of their families, and to tell their stories. Wyman also used the site to publish short biographies of the various leaders of the Brethren over its 170-year history.

This was in the early days of community activism on the internet, well before social-networking sites began, but members of this unique and traumatised community eventually found Wyman's site and began using it with enthusiasm. For many of them, it was the first time they had found anybody else who had gone through similar experiences, and the first time they felt that they were not mad or alone.

According to Tim Twinam, a former Brethren member from the UK who contributed his own stories to the site, Wyman was not a particularly militant ex-Exclusive Brethren member. But the more that Wyman read about the Brethren and its effect on the people contributing to his site, the angrier he grew:

> Dick had left before the Brethren really got bad in 1960s. He was a fatherly man, a very thoughtful man, with an academic kind of approach, who simply started a guestbook. And that's what took off. He was searching for himself, asking 'What am I, what's my background?' And he was creating an online story and allowing other people to put theirs up, too.[1]

But for the Exclusive Brethren, Wyman's exercise represented an enormous danger. They feared the site would be used by former members who had left, or been kicked out, to organise themselves so they could spread knowledge about the truth of life inside and outside the Brethren. Many of the entries on the site insulted the sect and, importantly, threatened its public image. In early 2004, through its lawyers, and describing itself as an 'unincorporated association', the Brethren filed a defamation suit against Wyman in the Minnesota district court in the United States. If the aim was to shut down his site, it succeeded. Faced with the potential of massive legal costs to fight the case, Wyman decided to settle. The agreement is telling, acknowledging that the Brethren and Wyman both 'wish to avoid the expense of continued litigation'. They did so by 'settling all of the Brethren's claims'.

Wyman states in the settlement document that he has complete defences to all the Brethren's 'claims and allegations', although he acknowledges that some of the comments on the site were 'capable of being construed as defamatory', and that he regretted any pain these comments caused. (Later case law in the United States has found that a website owner is not responsible for the defamatory statements posted by a third party contributor.[2]) The Brethren acknowledged and regretted the 'pain, distress and offense to Wyman and members of his family' caused by their lawsuit.

Wyman agreed to take down his site and to never start another one. He agreed not to pass the information to anybody else, and to transfer the ownership of the domain name to the Brethren; in turn, the Brethren agreed to pay him $10,000 and to 'encourage Wyman's mother in writing to meet with him' and to 'not interfere with or monitor any contact between them'. Wyman also agreed to answer 'no comment' if any journalist asked to speak to him on the subject of the Brethren.

Now hosted on Wyman's web address, under the heading, 'Richard Wyman Regrets Pain, Distress and Offense to the Brethren', is a selective quote of the parts of the settlement that are favourable to the Brethren. And it redirects traffic to the official Brethren website, www.theexclusivebrethren.com.

During the Wyman case, another former Brethren man, Daniel Little, tried to take up the cudgels. He put Wyman's guestbook up at www.withdrawnfrom.com, but he was immediately joined to the Wyman case and was also forced to remove it. That site lasted just months in its original form, and now has a message in the same vein as the former Wyman site.

Tim Twinam remembers what it was like when these sites disappeared:

> I felt terrible. I was meeting people who'd been through things that I'd been through, and there's a language which we understand – it's a language that, when someone says Minister of the Lord in the Recovery, and separation, and withdrawn from, I know what they're talking about. I can't talk to a psychologist about what they mean without explaining everything, so there was a very important therapeutic component in being able to have a community of people who understood.

The need among former members of the Brethren for an open-discussion forum was enormous. Moved to answer this need, Twinam decided to set up his own website. In many ways, Twinam was the perfect candidate for the job. Unlike most former Brethren, who are brought up knowing nothing about computers, and are taught to regard them as conduits of evil, Twinam was a database specialist. Most importantly, though, he had been practically bankrupted when his business had been caught in the technology bust of 2000 and 2001. This meant he had no property. Unlike Wyman, he had nothing financially to lose from a Brethren lawsuit.

In 2004, he created a new website and registered it in California, after it became possible for the first time to register new domain names anonymously. Over the next four years, peebs.net has become by far the largest of any of the ex-Brethren sites. It has a front page that summarises the Exclusive Brethren and points to more information inside. It hosts a detailed history of the Aberdeen incident (described in Chapter 1), including tapes of the infamous Saturday meeting. But at the heart of this site are the forums, where members and guests can discuss any aspect of the news, history, and philosophy of the Brethren, and freely relate their personal experiences.

Those forums have member-only sections and public sections, and there are several layers of security that, at their deepest, allow for high levels of privacy. The forums have become the repository for a vast amount of discussion and debate. They also contain a large number of excerpts of Brethren ministry from recent times.

Other sites, including Stem Publishing[3] and MyBrethren,[4] openly publish the utterings of earlier world leaders of the sect. But ministry since about 1960, when Taylor tightened the doctrine of separation, is much harder to come by. The Exclusive Brethren now argue that it is subject to strict copyright protections, suggesting that they are now more sensitive about it. However, as former members have left the sect over the years, they have carried the books of transcribed meetings with them, including the teachings of the Men of God, and these books provide a window into what the Brethren are being told in the modern era. This feature of the peebs.net site has been an invaluable source in the writing of this book.

According to Twinam, there are 597 members of the site; some post anonymously, while others list their full names and several phone numbers. Each is vetted to ensure they are genuine. He said that about 200 of these are active at any one time. It is a rowdy, sometimes aggressive, sometimes reflective, forum. Twinam said that many use the site as therapy.

'One of the side effects of a cult is that that they suck *you* out of you and replace you with a template,' Twinam said. 'And these empty people come in, they're angry and they don't even know why, and gradually they find themselves. It's not a religious concept; it's literally a psychological one':

> At any one time there are 200 to 300 who are in different phases of recovery from their experiences ... many join, become shocked at where the Exclusive Brethren have gone and leave again. Some rage at the world, God and the Brethren. Others go crazy, saying, 'I'm amongst folk who understand me!' They hit a peak, and then they start to heal, find their feet, gain confidence in who they want to be. That's the therapeutic context; finding people who understand, who know you're not nuts, and then you see people gain their personality. And I get comments in my inbox almost every day saying, 'Thanks so much, I don't know what I'd do without you being there.'

Peebs.net has an emergency button, whereby people in the Brethren or the ex-Brethren community who are contemplating leaving the sect, or who are contemplating suicide, can be put immediately in contact with volunteers around the world who are willing to help them with accommodation, support, even jobs. When they have grown up entirely sequestered from the world, with only other Brethren for friends and confidantes, these simple things are often the most difficult for a member who is leaving to find. The emergency button had been used 17 times since the site was established, and the helper network of almost 100 ex-Brethren people in ten countries has been used many more times.

It is also a worldwide clearing-house for newsworthy items concerning the Exclusive Brethren. Since Bruce Hales led his sect into the snake pit of worldly politics in 2004, hundreds of news items have sprung up in media around the world. Collecting, hosting, and commenting on these news items, gleaning information from them, and adding to the general store of information publicly available about the Brethren has been a key part of the work of the contributors to the site.

The Exclusive Brethren hate it. Within the Brethren, those who are active on the site are dubbed 'the bitterness crew' or the 'opposers'. If there genuinely is a thaw underway in relations between those still inside the sect and those who have left it, those who post regularly to peebs.net – the 'opposers' – complain that they have been left out.

For almost four years, Twinam presided over this anarchic conglomeration of contributors, and succeeded in remaining anonymous himself. Suspicion naturally fell on him because of his IT expertise and the fact that he had participated on Wyman's website. At least one man, linked with the Brethren but not a member of the sect, came close to unmasking him, but did not manage to do so officially.

In 2005, the Brethren embarked on an apparent fishing expedition to try to find out who was tormenting them. In April of that year, while she was in the middle of preparations for her first-year university law exams, Sheila Seesahai was sent a detailed, 25-page threatened lawsuit (a 'draft' suit, which had not been filed in any court) by the Brethren, and a letter containing six demands. The legal action directed against Ms Seesahai, and two others, accused them of running www.peebs.net and also of helping Dick Wyman and Daniel Little to run their sites.

The Brethren claimed both defamation and copyright infringement, and the document included 'pages and pages of quotes from various contributors to all three websites,' she said later.[5] According to Ms Seesahai, the copyright-infringement allegation was 'based on some Bruce Hales Ministry which had been posted on one of the sites'.

The complainant was the Bible and Gospel Trust, the body with offices in each country around the world in which the 'saints' live, and which transcribes, prints, and sells the 'ministry' of the great men to Brethren around the world. The Bible and Gospel Trust has a truly comprehensive and threatening copyright notice at the beginning of each piece of its printed ministry:

> No part of this publication may be copied, reproduced, scanned or stored in any electronic database, whether in whole or in part, in any form or by any means. Bible and Gospel Trust will not hesitate to take appropriate legal action if its rights in this respect are infringed. This publication contains material that is not to be disseminated to anyone outside of the Brethren.

Copyright is a well-established legal concept, and is similar in most Western jurisdictions. It is intended to allow the creator of a work (such as a journalist, author, musician or, theoretically, the Minister of the Lord in the Recovery of the Truth) the exclusive right to sell that created work. But copyright law also allows others to use that work, particularly for the purposes of education and critique. These 'fair use' provisions are crucial free-speech protections, and they allow for all sorts of discussion about works that are otherwise copyrighted. The Exclusive Brethren's strongly worded statements of copyright almost certainly do not over-ride these national laws.

The Brethren's other threatened lawsuit was over defamation. In most jurisdictions, truth is a defence, either partial or total, to such an action – so the contest usually revolves around whether the statements alleged to be defamatory are true. But in the case against Ms Seesahai, the Brethren had an even more fundamental problem than proving the truth or otherwise of certain statements, or whether she had infringed their copyright. It was that she had nothing to do with running any of the websites in question. She wrote:

> Although I am friends with Dick [Wyman] and Daniel [Little], I never helped run their websites and I have no connection to peebs.net other than making the occasional posting of my own ... I am rather a total idiot with computer technology and the idea that I could run a website is kind of hilarious. I can barely run a word processor and download PDFs properly.

Ms Seesahai briefed lawyers and hit back, threatening the Brethren with damages for any loss she suffered as a result of their vexatious lawsuit. But still the Brethren hung on, with Seesahai becoming more and more concerned that an adverse finding of some sort, particularly in the defamation case, might affect the legal career she was intent on pursuing:

> I believe that the Brethren well knew that I was not running peebs.net, but they thought that I might know who was. Although I had not been in the practice of airing my views about the Brethren publicly, they appeared to want to pre-emptively muzzle me. They sent several proposals of documents they wanted me to sign, with things like this: 'I will not participate in the publication of statements of a derogatory nature concerning the Brethren and related entities on the internet or in any other form including, but not limited to, books, magazines, newspapers, radio, television, printed communication or electronic media of any kind.'

She refused to sign, though two co-defendants (whom she does not name) did express regret. Eventually, the Brethren backed off. In her case, the lawsuit has backfired because it has encouraged Ms Seesahai to become more outspoken in her attacks on the Brethren. It has also ruined whatever remaining links she had with her parents, who remain in the Brethren, because she found out that they had known about and supported the Brethren's legal action. Her parents informed her that, if the elders were pursuing it, it had to be right, even if it was against their own daughter.

The early attempt to identify the owners of peebs.net had failed. According to Twinam, the Brethren then decided to use other methods to try to shut down the site. An Australian man, a former Brethren member, spent some time trying to find out who the owners of the site were. According to Twinam, the man contacted him and 'let slip that he had conversations with the Exclusive Brethren, and that they were, at one time, prepared to pay me almost anything to close the site down'. The man, whom I will not name, denies this is the case. He says he did do some work for the Brethren, but not on the subject of the website. He says that he investigated Twinam's involvement out of curiosity alone, not because the Brethren were paying him. He acknowledges that he informed them of Twinam's identity, but denies he made any suggestion that Twinam would be paid to switch the website off.

Either way, in 2005, the threats against peebs.net began to become more serious. In that year, the Exclusive Brethren themselves had taken to the internet to put the official version of their story online. 'An Open Documentary of their Life and Faith' the 'only site endorsed by the Exclusive Brethren', appeared at www.theexclusivebrethren.com.

The domain name was registered by Chipeur Advocates, the law firm of a pro-Republican, anti-gay-marriage Canadian lawyer called Gerald Chipeur. The members of peebs.net seized on this fact, exposing it on their site, and naming and identifying Chipeur. They also researched elements of Chipeur's background, and invited other readers to contact his law firm. In response, Gerald Chipeur sued Twinam as well as the holding company of the web registrar, the web-hosting company, and a former employer of Twinam's, claiming damages of $500,000 plus special and punitive damages.

The lawsuit said that, on the site, Chipeur Advocates had been 'defamed and severely and irreparably injured in their credit, character and reputations as citizens, in the practice of their profession, and have been brought into public scandal, odium and contempt'.

Twinam had still never admitted to running and owning the site, and he essentially ignored the Chipeur legal claim in the Canadian court. Citing the lack of a passport, he said he could not travel to Canada to answer the suit, even though Chipeur Advocates sent him thousands of dollars to pay for tickets. Twinam simply strung the case out, answering motions when he could, but without legal advice, and never showing up to court. Eventually, he was found in contempt of court in Canada.

It is not clear whether Chipeur had any current financial link to the Exclusive Brethren; but, even if there was a link, the Brethren were apparently not driving the suit. According to Twinam, the impetus seemed to come solely from the law firm, for reasons he can only guess at. He regarded it as little more than an irritation. But the potential liability of that case, and the contempt finding, finally pushed Twinam's precarious financial situation over the edge. In 2006, he declared bankruptcy. This, however, he regards as a good thing.

'Bankruptcy is actually protecting me,' Twinam said. 'The Brethren can't hurt me financially. All they can do is get an injunction to stop me from doing what I'm doing ... In Dick's case, he had a lot to lose, in Daniel's case too I assume it played a part. In Sheela's case it played a part. In my case it does not at all.'

In late 2007, another attack was mounted on the site, from an entirely different quarter. An unidentified person or group of people began a series of what are called 'denial of service' attacks on the computers hosting it. In such incidents, a website is bombarded with so much traffic from a number of different computers that the server cannot cope, and stops handling normal web requests. The first attack against the peebs site began in December 2007, involving multiple computers from a 'masked' or hidden origin. It lasted four days.

The site survived the first volley but, in January 2008, a much larger attack began. 'This time it could not be contained and it was relentless,' Twinam said. It forced the site to close down, though most of the information on it was saved. The domain was moved offshore to try to protect it, and other emergency procedures put in place to ensure that, in the face of another attack, peebs.net could save its information and keep operating.

There is no proof that the Brethren were behind this attack, and it could simply have been a set of teenage hackers attempting to shut down a high-profile site. But, meanwhile, the proper lawsuit had arrived. In January 2007, the Exclusive Brethren publishing arm, the Bible and Gospel Trust, through the Brethren's Washington DC law firm, Fulbright & Jaworski, filed a suit in the court in Twinam's home state of Vermont. It alleged infringement and threatened infringement of the copyright of Brethren works. It also alleged that peebs. net had breached the settlement agreement with Richard Wyman by communicating with the sect's former nemesis and sharing information. Both Twinam and Wyman deny that they made any contact at any time while Twinam was running peebs.net.

The legal action focuses on two pieces of old Brethren ministry that the Bible and Gospel Trust claim appeared on the Wyman site and which, according to the suit, Twinam published or threatened to publish. The first is an address at Leicester by R. Alan C. Ker (the husband of Madeline Ker, who was famously found naked in bed with the former Man of God, James Taylor Junior, in 1970), in which he gives his version of events. The second copyrighted document was an address by Bruce D. Hales from 2002. The Brethren claim in the suit that they enjoy 'certain exclusive rights with respect to the materials, including the exclusive right to copy, distribute, display, publish and prepare derivative works'.

Twinam denies that he ever published those pieces of ministry on the site. But, whether or not they were published, this suit is a proper attempt to drag him through the courts in his home state, where he cannot dissemble or escape. It was backed by a full motion for discovery of documents.

The discovery motions and this suit finally forced Twinam to reveal to the world who he was. He could no longer deny it because, legally, he was unable to. On 17 February 2008, he and wife Sallie introduced themselves to the world via a new thread on peebs.net, and they finally revealed the extent of the legal action against them.

The Bible and Gospel Trust wants a permanent injunction on the copying or distribution of the copyrighted materials, and a retraction and apology to be published by Twinam. The suit also claims 'compensatory damages in an amount to be established at trial', as well as punitive damages and costs.

It is interesting that the Brethren have chosen, at least initially, to sue over a couple of quite obscure pieces of ministry, when so much more recent and more controversial Bible and Gospel Trust material is available elsewhere on the site. Even if the Brethren were to win the suit, it would not have any effect at all on the peebs.net site – because, if these pieces of ministry ever were ever published on it, they are now not. Twinam fears that the initial suit was simply intended to open the door, to confirm that he was the owner of the site, and then that a much larger suit would be filed to bring him down.

'Both of those documents were of utterly no interest. I mean, Alan Ker is who he is, and he is trying to compare JT Junior to Jesus Christ,' Twinam said:

There is no other significance. So why pick two documents, copyright them, and use it as leverage for the suit? I think it's a process they are planning to do with all the material they can lay their hands on, because it is the only route they have. Defamation is probably going to fail; with defamation, the onus is on the plaintiff to prove damage caused by statements. Copyright is, by comparison, very straightforward. Also, copyright is a federal offence, and the Federal Court has far more blast than a standard district, so it can bring the full weight of discovery to bear. And that's what they wanted – to find out who peebs.net was – and they've got it!

After initially trying to fend off the lawsuit on his own and without legal advice, Twinam has raised some money, briefed lawyers, and begun to fight the Exclusive Brethren in the courts with a motion to dismiss the case. According to Twinam, it is a classic SLAPP ('Strategic Litigation Against Public Participation') writ – an attempt, in other words, to use a vexatious claim to shut down debate about a particular subject by tying up the defendant in the court until he has run out of money.

In some western states in the US, such strategic litigation is illegal, on the basis that it is an infringement of free speech. In Vermont, where Twinam lives, it is not illegal in that precise form. But Vermont does have a previously unused piece of state law on its books, which he is hoping to rely on. It gives defendants the right to apply to the court to strike out lawsuits that attack free speech when it is exercised 'in connection with a public issue'.[6]

'It is intended to protect people when they are reporting on something that is a newsworthy matter. And one of the strongest pieces of evidence on our side is the list of 400-odd news articles on the website,' Twinam said. 'Bruce Hales made it news. By taking the Brethren into politics, he has generated all these news stories and, because we had all this material, on a daily basis, this was a newsworthy event.'

The legal action was continuing at the time of writing but, in a piece of good news, the state of Vermont joined the case as a 'friend of the court' to argue on Twinam's side. However, it, and the cost of legal fees, remained a serious threat against the open discussion of ex-Brethren issues on the internet. But Twinam believes that, whether or not he loses the case, the site will be able to survive. 'They can't hurt me financially,' he said. 'All they can do is get an injunction stopping me from doing what I'm doing. We obviously planned to cover that. We've got 50 people who can jump in, and they will get the site back up.'

But it is not just the internet that the Brethren have tried to keep silent: it is critics of all kinds. In 1984, the renowned Dutch theologist Willem J. Ouweneel published a book about the history of the Brethren movement. Ouweneel is a member of the Open Brethren, not the Exclusives, but his book canvassed the most sensitive part of Exclusive Brethren history, the 'Aberdeen Incident' (which is briefly related in the first chapter of this book).

Ouweneel's book was published in the Netherlands, and he was planning to translate it for a German edition. But before this could be done, the Exclusive Brethren brought a lawsuit against him in the Dutch courts for defamation. According to Ouweneel, the sect's complaint was that he 'did not properly describe their history and theological position' and that 'they felt offended'.[7]

In their prayer meetings, the Brethren referred to this legal action in The Hague as 'the Dutch Book Case', and offered a prayer to God asking, 'may the man behind the Book Case be squashed'. David Shorto remembers the case well. A former member of the Exclusive Brethren, who had been at Aberdeen on the weekend of the fateful three-day meetings, he was called by Ouweneel to give evidence for the defence, to testify to the accuracy of his account of Taylor's behaviour. 'This was an excellent opportunity to tell out the truth of what we had witnessed while still in, and what we had found in terms of real Christianity since leaving, and nobody could interrupt!' Shorto later wrote:

The judge was very fair and asked reasonable questions. The counsel for the Exclusive Brethren challenged my statement that Taylor was seen inebriated in meetings, and asked if I could prove that he was. I replied that I could only testify to what I had seen; all the evidences of a man seriously affected by alcohol who continued to drink a brownish liquid during the meetings. Either he was drunk or a consummate actor![8]

The case was heard, and evidence produced on both sides. Even the Kers – Madeline, who had spent time naked in Taylor's bed as part of his alleged 'trap', and her husband Alan – were in attendance and gave evidence. But, as with many other cases by the Brethren, the case was settled prior to the verdict, out of court. The settlement included an agreement that Ouweneel would show the Exclusive Brethren representatives 'any further edition of the book in whatever language'.

Ouweneel remains convinced that the book was not defamatory, saying, 'I just told the truth as I had come to understand it – and they did not like that.' But he did not go ahead and publish an edition in any other language. 'After the law case of the Exclusives I refrained from a planned German edition. I also had other reasons for not publishing the book beside the difficulties with the Exclusives: I was not happy with certain other parts any more,' he said. Ouweneel did not agree that it was an attempt to shut down free speech. 'That was not the point. They felt offended, and if someone feels offended he can always go to court.'

The Brethren used the defamation law ten years later against a politician, in a reversal of the Brethren's usual style of political lobbying. Brethren members in Nelson, New Zealand, took exception to local MP Nick Smith's dogged questioning of their behaviour over another tragic family dispute in 1992. The dispute involved a young boy, Vincent Field, being separated from his excommunicated parents and sent to live with his grandparents. The Family

Court case for the Field family went all the way to New Zealand's High Court (with the boy eventually being restored to his parents), and Smith raised the issue in the parliament and in the press.

In response, the Brethren slapped a $3.2 million suit on the MP for comments he had made outside the safety of the parliament. The case was eventually settled with a joint statement and no payout. A few years later, the Brethren apologised to Smith for the action, saying it had been wrong, and that family disputes were now handled differently.

In 1997, a similar situation arose in Western Australia, where some Exclusive Brethren children were prevented from going home after school to parents who were under discipline or who had left the sect. John Wallis, a former sect member, became angry at what was going on: he wrote a letter in February 1998 demanding that the children be brought back to their families, and that the Brethren put an end to the break-up and dividing of families.[9] Wallis criticised the Brethren leadership, including some local leaders in Dalwallinu, and he posted copies of his letter to the leaders, the local police, and others, and posted it on the town's public notice board.

The Brethren sued him, prompting years of legal wrangling which led almost to the door of the courtroom. But, just three days before the case was to be heard in court, the Brethren dropped their action. Instead, they settled out of court. Wallis refused their demand that he pay them $50,000, and instead demanded they pay him, without at all resiling from his criticism of the sect and its leadership. According to Wallis, the Brethren agreed to pay him $25,000. A spokesman for the Brethren later told *Sunday Times* reporter Jim Kelly that it was better to pay John Wallis off, rather than allow him to 'publicly air misleading and damaging claims about the church'.[10] Wallis is now a contributor to peebs.net.

In late 2007, the Brethren engaged in a pre-emptive threat of legal action. The sect in the United States became aware that one of their former members, Don Monday, was about to contribute to an

Australian documentary to be screened by current affairs program *Four Corners*. According to Monday, they threatened to sue him. He spoke nonetheless, and no lawsuit was forthcoming. The Brethren did, however, issue a press release put out around the time that the broadcast went to air, saying that Monday was making 'blatantly untrue statements, fabricated for what could be personal financial gain,' and calling him 'an unreliable witness who has no credibility'. The Brethren used the threat simply to prevent Monday from disclosing what he had experienced as a member of their sect.

In the course of reporting on the Exclusive Brethren, I have had a number of legal letters, threatening everything from actions for trespass, apprehended violence orders, complaints to the Australian Press Council and, of course, actions for defamation. Brethren leader Bruce Hales, through an intermediary, also offered me an all-expenses paid trip to Noumea with my wife. I assumed this proposed Pacific island getaway was an attempt to compromise me or to induce me to stop writing about his organisation. I refused it.

In 2007, as the scrutiny of the Brethren increased, and their tactic of threatening people who quizzed them was clearly not working, they began to be more open to the media, to put their spin on events. They appointed a media professional, Tony McCorkell, to speak on their behalf, and began offering senior Brethren members to journalists for interviews. They also briefed a public relations firm, Jackson Wells Morris, to advise them on such matters, and to give them media training.

Some in the ex-Brethren community believe that these innovations have merely served to put a superficial gloss on the organisation to more effectively hide its flaws. Others hope that, perhaps at last, it is beginning to engage more openly with the world. If that is the case, though, suing a website for hosting an open discussion about it constitutes a big step backwards.

Conclusion

When Bryan R. Wilson, PhD, DLitt, FBA, reader emeritus in sociology at the University of Oxford, was asked to write a sociological appraisal of the Exclusive Brethren in 2000, his report was so complimentary of the sect that it retains a prominent place on their website:

> Since the sect is a voluntary body, the members of which are self-selected, and the leaders of which may exercise only very limited sanctions (i.e. discipline to which members themselves consent) there are always limits to the measure of 'coercion' that can obtain within the movement. The popular press disseminates many misleading impressions concerning the power wielded within sects, and these, unfortunately, are often the only information available to the public, giving rise to general misunderstanding of the nature of sectarianism. So long as a movement operates within the framework of the law, it must be acknowledged that members voluntarily commit themselves to sect discipline, and they look to their acknowledged leaders to set forth the appropriate requirements of scripture to enable them to maintain moral and doctrinally prescribed patterns of behaviour and belief.[1]

This analysis may please the Brethren, but it reveals some naivety. Members of the Exclusive Brethren hardly self-select – they are born into it – and you can't choose your family. Many stay because they like it, and because the life is generally comfortable, well funded, and safe. But others stay, in spite of their lives of claustrophobic insularity, because of the considerable coercion and severe sanctions they face if they leave. Some do leave, and then experience the agony of learning a new way of life without any support from family, friends, or church.

Wilson, like many others, including some politicians, has probably made the mistake of speaking only to the male Brethren elders about their sect, and has come away with the impression of an old-worldly group whose members, in his words, lead rather simple lives of 'exemplary moral demeanour'.

On this view, any criticism of the Brethren is inexplicable and offensive. Those who ask questions of this lifestyle are told that a tolerant society should extend religious freedom to all the groups who live within it, whether or not it agrees with their views. The argument is simple: we must leave them alone until they break the law; if they do transgress, let them be investigated and punished, like any other law-breaker, by the police and criminal justice system.

Almost six months after his election as Australian prime minister in late 2007, and after months of consideration of this very issue, this was also the position that Kevin Rudd adopted. Responding to the requests of aggrieved former members of the Brethren that he instigate a broad-ranging inquiry into the sect, he said that religion should not be a shield behind which criminal activities could hide, and urged people with knowledge of criminality to step forward.

In the meantime, he stated: 'The Government has not acceded to continuing requests for a wide-ranging inquiry into the Exclusive Brethren. The Government believes that such an inquiry could unreasonably interfere with the capacity of members of the Exclusive Brethren to practise their faith freely and openly.'[2]

Religious freedom and tolerance is a powerful hand in any debate, and the Brethren and their supporters play it remorselessly. But it should not be a trump card. A secular, multicultural society should be constantly aware of circumstances in which religious belief comes into conflict with civil laws and conventions. Courts and governments will sometimes be called upon to adjudicate upon these difficult arguments, particularly when religious minorities demand special treatment under laws that govern the rest of us.

Those claiming immunity from general laws or values on religious grounds must, at the very least, be open to their motives and practices being examined. If they dissemble about this, if they avoid scrutiny, their motives can be called into question. And if the beliefs they pursue entrench unreasonable discrimination, or are motivated primarily by political or financial considerations, they should be seen for what they really are. Religions should not expect the broader society to accept bad behaviour from their members simply because they claim it as a matter of conscience. This is a point that John Howard himself made when, in 2006, he exhorted another religious minority to leave behind some of its cultural and religious baggage and become part of his 'mainstream':

> What I want to do is to reinforce the need for everybody who comes to this country to fully integrate, and fully integrating means accepting Australian values ... And it means understanding that in certain areas, such as the equality of men and women, that the societies that some people have left were not as contemporary and as progressive as ours is. And I think that people who come from societies where women are treated in an inferior fashion have to learn very quickly that that is not the case in Australia; that men and women to have equality and they're each entitled to full respect.[3]

He was, of course, talking about Muslims. But in the case of the Brethren, their 'conscience' has always made women inferior to men. In fact, they claim it as a religious and social virtue – an attitude that did not damage their relationship with Howard, nor did it ever draw any criticism from the former prime minister.

As this book has shown, it is not just in their treatment of women that the Exclusive Brethren stand apart from Australian norms. Religious conscience has won them fabulously generous school funding, as well as exemptions from workplace relations laws and the need to be responsive to organised labour. They have won exemptions from military service and voting, and have skated very close to the line on electoral-law disclosures. They claim rate exemptions on their meeting halls, but deny public access to them, contravening the law in several states. They have made persistent attempts to sway politicians on any number of issues, as well as repeated applications to courts, parliaments, and politicians to have the Family Court recognise practices that lie well outside the law, but which they claim as inalienable rights.

The Australian Greens and a group of former Brethren members argue that any group which pushes this hard at the boundaries of what other Australians find acceptable should be fully investigated to find out what concessions they have gained, and to have those exemptions overturned, or at least exposed. But because they are a religion, every other political party has twice joined together to deny any attempt to instigate such an inquiry through the parliament. Like Rudd, they have said that the Brethren should not be investigated until they are investigated by the police.

This may well be the right outcome. Governments cannot legislate for reasonableness, or modernity, or treating people nicely, and they should not attempt to control every activity of small portions of society.

But leaving it entirely to the police probably means, in effect, that little more will be heard of the Exclusive Brethren. The taboo within the sect against its members reporting crimes that are perpetrated by their fellows means that the police will rarely hear of any serious criminal activity. Occasional cases emerge, most recently of child sex abuse, as described in Chapter 6, but we do not know the extent to which, in this closed group, there are more criminal cases that we never hear about. There is no evidence that the incidence of any crime is any higher within the Brethren than in the general community; but perhaps it is no lower either.

This book, however, has thrown up a number of areas where the government should look closely at aspects of the law to protect the national interest against the kind of exceptionalism pushed by the Brethren.

The first is in Family Law, where this sect acts as a cashed-up, vexatious litigant, misusing the goodwill of the system to thwart the wishes of parents to have access to their children. Our law should be able to find a way to stop the Brethren ignoring court decisions and using apparently endless appeals to frustrate society's determination to give children time with both their parents. Perhaps it is time to look again at the somewhat more no-nonsense approach of the courts in the 1960s, which found that the tenets of this particular sect were 'unnatural' and 'contrary to public policy', and tended as a result to award custody to the non-Brethren parent.

In education, any funding system that allows one of the richest, most employed, and least disadvantaged groups in the nation to receive the highest level of government subsidy for schools which sequester children from the world is a system in desperate need of review. The Brethren example also reveals that the curriculum taught in religious schools should be much more openly monitored. In Victoria, at least, the state bureaucracy rejects any requests for information about which non-government schools have been subject to inspection – much less the inspection reports themselves. They do this by citing the Privacy Act. This is ridiculous. Privacy should be a protection for individuals, not for school systems. No-one's privacy would be trammelled if inspection reports were released. In Britain, they are posted on the internet.

The British also allow virtually free online access to the trust deeds and financial accounts of charities. In Australia, by contrast, these records are difficult and expensive to access, which makes it almost impossible to mount any systematic inquiry into the tax-free benefits that the Brethren or other religious groups are reaping from their schools, and associated charities and businesses. Billions every year goes, tax free, into charities; opening up scrutiny into these organisations would be an enormous public benefit.

Our electoral-disclosure law should also start from the presumption that voters are entitled to know who is trying to influence the political process through donations. Too often, this law has been used to obscure the ultimate source of the money pumped into politics, and the Brethren have used the letter of the law to continue to deny that they have had any role in bankrolling election campaigns. If the loopholes prove impossible to close, perhaps donations should be banned altogether, or seriously capped, as is the case in some other countries.

Finally, Australia should investigate legislation to rule out so-called 'Slapp' lawsuits – Strategic Litigation Against Public Participation. This is legal action taken by powerful interests, including religious ones, to stymie public debate. These legal actions are usually not intended to win in court – some of them have so little foundation that a judge would not hesitate to throw them out. They are designed instead to intimidate people into withdrawing their contributions from the debate in fear of the massive legal fees they would amass if they chose to fight on in favour of free speech.

The thread that runs through all these prescriptions is openness. Transparency is a tonic; it cleans out the toxic residue of secrecy, political lobbying, and a culture of favouritism. If we are not to conduct a comprehensive inquiry into the Exclusive Brethren, we should have a legal and political system that allows regular, everyday inquiries to be made – not just of this sect, but of every group that seeks and receives special treatment.

Acknowledgements

The personal stories of former members of the Exclusive Brethren are the backbone of this book. Many of them I cannot name, and each of these people took the risk of trusting a journalist with their stories on the promise that I would keep their identities confidential. It's always a leap of faith, and I thank them for taking that leap.

Of these people, I want particularly to thank 'Janie'. You are a brave and level-headed person, you gave me more insights than you realised, and were an invaluable sounding board. I also want to thank 'Sophie,' whose terrible experiences show what it was like for a whole generation of people who grew up in fear.

Some ex-Brethren can be named. I want to thank Warren McAlpin, who led me through the intricacies of this topic. Thank you also to Alison Alderton, whose account is so powerful and so revealing, and to her daughter, Priscilla, whose story embodies defiance and strength of spirit. Bruce Suggate, thank you for your story: may you heal and be free; and to Tim and Sallie Twinam, may free speech win in the end. Many thanks also to Iain Gibb, who was there at Aberdeen and who remembers it all.

There are also some non-Brethren who trusted my discretion. I shall be too discreet to mention you by name, but thank you.

David Poulton gave generously of his time and expertise, as did Julian Burnside and his formidable crew. David Marr's comments immeasurably improved this book. I also thank Dr John Hennessy, Senators Bob Brown and Christine Milne, and Prue Cameron for their help. Justice Paul Guest, Lyndsay Connors, Jim McMorrow, Alison McClymont, and Quentin McDermott will all see their footprints in various places. I also thank Henry Rosenbloom, Scribe's publisher, who convinced me that doing this was a good idea, and who then shepherded it into being with his diligent (and endlessly patient) editing.

Two current members of the Exclusive Brethren deserve thanks: Tony McCorkell and Chris Shore. You were generous with your time, and your words gave me pause for thought. You put your case strongly.

Finally, I thank my wife, Sally, who did not really want this book, but who got it anyway, and who has been a tower of strength, a pillar of support, a font of useful advice, and a well of hot drinks.

Notes

All quotes from the Exclusive Brethren are taken from its ministry, transcribed and distributed to the Brethren worldwide. The Exclusive Brethren, through its publishing arm, the Bible and Gospel Trust, asserts strict and exclusive copyright over this material. Most ministry quoted can be viewed at www.peebs.net.

Where sources are not divulged in these notes, it is to protect my sources. As well, in some cases it has not been possible for me to provide full details of printed source material.

Introduction
1. Letter from Warwick John to ABC *Four Corners* presenter Quentin McDermott, 12 October 2007
2. Bruce D. Hales, press release, 15 October 2007
3. Bruce D. Hales, White Book 161, p. 11, 18 March 2006
4. Interview with the author, 1 April 2008

Chapter 1: The Making of a Cult
1. From a document, 'If We Walk in the Light ...', produced by Robert Stott, November 1970
2. Louise Samways, *Dangerous Persuaders: an expose of gurus, personal development courses and cults, and how they operate*, Penguin Australia, 1994
3. Thomas Matthew Bennett was a working-class Brethren member from Edinburgh. When the split came, after the Aberdeen incident, he was one of only two men from Edinburgh who remained loyal to Taylor Junior. Later, he

was purged by Taylor's successor, James Symington.

4 George Strang was also from Edinburgh. An upright man, witnesses recall he was subject to 'constant humiliation' during the 1960s from Taylor, who called him 'Mr Strange'. Strang became leader of one of the splinter groups that formed after they left the 'Taylorite' Brethren.

5 George Brown was from London. An older man, he was apparently bemused by the direction in which Taylor had taken his beloved assembly. After Aberdeen, he was firmly in the anti-Taylor camp, and left the sect.

6 Letter to Robert Stott from William T. Petersen, 5 October 1970, included in 'If We Walk in the Light …'

7 Letter to A.B. Parker, New York, from James Alec Gardner, Aberdeen, 30 July 1970, included in 'If We Walk in the Light …'

8 Letter to Elizabeth M. Hindle from James Taylor Junior, 7 August 1970, included in 'If We Walk In the Light …'

9 Letter from Magnus Dawson to George Scott, 21 August 1970. Despite this loyal display, Dawson, an art teacher, was himself excommunicated, in 1972, by Taylor's successor, James Symington

10 Biographical details of John Nelson Darby sourced from www.mybrethren.org/bios/framjnd.htm

11 Darby letter to the Archbishop of Dublin and the Clergy who signed the petition to the House of Commons for Protection, 1827. Darby letters found at www.stempublishing.com/authors/darby/

12 Bryan R. Wilson, *The Brethren: a current sociological appraisal*, 2000, see www.theexclusivebrethren.com/documents/academicstudy.pdf

13 From James Grant, 'The Religious Tendencies of the Times'. Reproduced in *Sword and Trowel*, June 1869. See www.spurgeon.org/s_and_t/dbreth.htm

Chapter 2: The Australian Succession

1 W.R. Dronsfield, 'The "Brethren" Since 1870', www.biblecentre.org/topics/wrd_brethren_since_1870.htm

2 Gordon Rainbow, 'F.E. Raven (1837–1903)', www.mybrethren.org/bios/framfer.htm

3 'Ministry by F. E. Raven, 6: 244–45', cited at www.mybrethren.org/bios/framfer.htm

4 Memories of Mary Markham, cited at www.mybrethren.org/bios/framjt.htm

5 Quoted at Taylor's funeral by Stanley McCallum, 1 April 1953

6 W.R. Dronsfield, 'The "Brethren" Since 1870', www.biblecentre.org/topics/wrd_brethren_since_1870.htm

7 Gordon Rainbow, www.mybrethren.org/history/framhymn.htm
8 Transcript of London special meetings, 1959, www.mybrethren.org/mygrcol/frgcos.htm
9 'J. Taylor Jnr Letters', vol. 3, p. 16, 16 September 1960
10 Interview with the author, 21 February 2008
11 Email to the author, 23 December 2007
12 'The Importance of the Directives,' Reading, Barbados, 1967, 'J. Taylor Jnr Letters', vol. 72, p. 1
13 Alan Robertson, 'The Life of a Nobody', (unpublished manuscript), 2008
14 Iain Gibb email to the author, 23 December 2007
15 '"Matters consider in Assembly in Sydney", 13 October 1987', John S. Hales, Reading, Neche, vol. 516, October 1987
16 Interview with the author, 27 March 2008
17 'Frequently Asked Questions', www.theexclusivebrethren.com/update/faq.htm
18 'Suggested Approach to Administrative Reviews' (undated document)
19 Interview with the author, 27 March 2008
20 Former Brethren member Russell Dent, 'Bruce Hales Era' (undated)

Chapter 3: Life in the Brethren
1 Interview with the author, 16 January 2007
2 Interview with the author, 14 October 2006
3 Bruce D. Hales, 'Living Our Beliefs: the current way of life of the Exclusive Brethren', 2007, at www.theexclusivebrethren.com
4 'Profile of the Brethren' (document sent to federal education minister Dr Brendan Nelson, 31 May 2004)
5 Interview with the author, 30 January 2008
6 Bruce D. Hales, Reading, Hutt, White Book 161, p. 15, 24 April 2006
7 Reading, Sydney, White Book 161, p. 11, 18 March 2006
8 Interview with the author, 14 October 2006
9 Interview with the author, September 2007
10 Notes of Meetings, White Book 1, p. 74, January 2002
11 Bruce D. Hales, Leicester, White Book 165, 16–18 June 2006, p. 86
12 Ministry of Bruce D. Hales, Perth, White Book 94, p. 107, 2004
13 Priscilla Alderton, interview with the author, 14 March 2008
14 Notes of meetings, Bruce D. Hales, White Book 223, p. 87, 20 October 2007
15 'Profile of the Brethren' (document sent to federal education minister Dr Brendan Nelson, 31 May 2004)

16 Bruce D. Hales, Berwick, White Book 51, 26 July 2003
17 Bruce D. Hales, Reading, Sydney, vol. 14, pp. 190–91, February 2003
18 James Taylor Junior, White Book 32, p. 389
19 Interview with anonymous former Brethren member, 28 December 2006
20 Bruce D. Hales, White Book 145, p. 110, 10 December 2005
21 Interview with the author, 21 May 2008
22 Marriage Vows for Exclusive Brethren members, to be spoken on a Tuesday night meeting
23 Bruce D. Hales, White Book 161, p. 15, 24 April 2006
24 Bruce D. Hales, transcript of Business Seminar in Wagga, 5 February 2005, 'Business Seminars', P.L. Weeks and R.M. Phillips (eds), Provision Marketing, Melbourne, p. 198
25 Interview with Peter Thompson, ABC TV Talking Heads, 10 July 2006, http://www.abc.net.au/talkingheads/txt/s1679970.htm
26 Bruce D. Hales, White Book 169, pp. 11–12, 20 May 2006
27 James Taylor Junior, White Book 6, p. 673
28 Bruce D. Hales, White Book 16, Sydney, 12 April 2003
29 Interview with the author, 28 December 2006
30 Interview with the author, 8 November 2007
31 www.peebs.net

Chapter 4: The System

1 Bruce D. Hales, 'Living Our Beliefs: the current way of life of the Exclusive Brethren', 2007, at www.theexclusivebrethren.com
2 Bruce D. Hales, transcript of Business Seminar in Wagga, 5 February 2005, 'Business Seminars', P.L. Weeks and R.M. Phillips (eds), Provision Marketing, Melbourne
3 Correspondence with former Brethren member, who wishes to remain anonymous, 16 March 2008
4 Correspondence with former Brethren member, who wishes to remain anonymous, 16 March 2008
5 www.peebs.net.au
6 Anonymous contribution to www.peebs.net discussion
7 'Sophie' is a false name. Interview with the author, 24 February 2008
8 Interview with the author, 27 February 2008
9 Correspondence with former Brethren member, who wishes to remain anonymous, 16 March 2008
10 'Notes of Meetings in Sydney', J. Taylor Jnr, vol. 41, p. 212, 1965

11 Letter of James H. Symington to undisclosed recipient, 31 January 1966
12 Letter of James H. Symington to undisclosed recipient, 21 February 1966
13 Transcript of Exclusive Brethren Business Seminars, 'Stated Objectives for the Seminar Program', January and February 2005
14 Answers to questions supplied by P.B. McNaughton and Co, 29 October 2007
15 Letter of James H. Symington, addressed to 'Beloved Brethren,' 1977
16 Unifocus Limited Financial Statements for the year ended 31 July 2006, Company Registration No. 4938684
17 Interview with Quentin McDermott, *Four Corners*, ABC, September 2007 (for 'The Brethren Express', *Four Corners*, ABC, 15 October 2007)
18 www.peebs.net.au
19 Interview with Quentin McDermott, *Four Corners*, ABC, September 2007 (for 'The Brethren Express', *Four Corners*, ABC, 15 October 2007)
20 Correspondence with a recently 'out' Brethren member, who wishes to remain anonymous, 18 January 2008
21 Interview with former Brethren father, who wishes to remain anonymous, March 2008
22 Interview with the author, 30 June 2007
23 www.theexclusivebrethren.com/update/faq.htm
24 Summary Information Return of Aims, Activities and Achievements, 2006, Hughes Travel Trust, Charity Registration Number 1038566.
25 Paul's letter to the Philippians, *Holy Bible*, Darby Translation, Chapter 2, Verse 14

Chapter 5: The Alderton Family

1 Alison Alderton reluctantly agreed to tell her full story to me after I initially wrote about her in an article in *The Age* in 2006. She is ambivalent about this because she believes it will ruin any chance she has of re-establishing a relationship with her children still inside the Exclusive Brethren. Her words are taken from an interview at her home in Springwood, New South Wales, on 27 February 2008.
2 Interview with the author, 24 February 2008
3 Interview with the author, 14 March 2008
4 Priscilla's baby was born and is now a healthy adult, teaching circus performance.
5 Sophie said her children were now doing well, led fulfilling lives, and had good relationships with both their parents.

6 Letter to Alison Alderton, 22 February 2008
7 Interview with the author, 24 November 2006
8 'Believers a World Apart,' Michael Bachelard, *The Age*, 25 November 2006

Chapter 6: Albury

1 Interview with the author, 24 July 2007
2 Interview of former colleague, Dr John Hennessy, with the author, 29 June 2007
3 Warren McAlpin, email correspondence with the author, 12 March 2008
4 Interview with the author, Melbourne, 2007
5 'Sect Man Jailed for Sex Abuse of Girl', David Marr and Geesche Jacobsen, *Sydney Morning Herald*, 17 February 2007
6 Interview with the author, 22 December 2006. Neither the girls nor any of their family members can be identified for legal reasons.
7 Notes of a meeting between the mother and Bruce Hales, 17 January 2006
8 Dr Mark Craddock, letter to the editor of the *Sydney Morning Herald* (unpublished), 26 December 2006
9 Interview with the author, 8 August 2008
10 Draft Brethren press statement, 22 January 2007
11 Draft statement from the mother, 22 January 2007
12 Interview with the author, 30 June 2007
13 Interview with the author, 31 January 2008

Chapter 7: Persuasion

1 Interview with the author, 4 February 2007
2 'The writings of J.N. Darby', Letters: vol. 2, no. 294, www.stempublishing.com/authors/darby/letters/
3 Peter Costello, interview by Neil Mitchell, *Mornings with Neil Mitchell*, 3AW, 22 August 2007
4 Interview with the author, 27 February 2008
5 Interview with the author, 28 April 2008
6 Anonymous former Brethren member, interview with the author, 22 April 2008
7 Letter from Warwick John to ABC *Four Corners*' presenter Quentin McDermott, 12 October 2007
8 Bruce D. Hales speaking at a business seminar in Sydney, 2 February 2005
9 Interviews with former Howard staff members and party officials, who wish to remain anonymous, between January and April 2008

10 Interview with the author, 26 April 2008
11 Email to the author, 22 September 2006
12 Bruce D. Hales, 'Living Our Beliefs: the current way of life of the Exclusive Brethren', 2007, at www.theexclusivebrethren.com
13 Interview with the author, 7 March 2008
14 'Union Barred from Talking to Lab Staff', Angela Gregory, *New Zealand Herald*, 1 July 2004
15 *Belfast Telegraph*, 26 September 2006
16 Answer to Senator Bob Brown's Question on Notice no. 3478. Question asked 5 October 2007. Answer given 12 December 2007. (Hansard page: 132, Senate Notice Paper, 15 October 2007)
17 Interview with the author, 7 March 2008
18 Interview with the author, 4 March 2008
19 Interview with the author, 27 February 2008
20 Bruce D. Hales, White Book (undated)
21 Letter from unidentified Exclusive Brethren authors to John Howard, 28 April 2003
22 Letter from unidentified Exclusive Brethren authors to John Howard, 16 September 2003
23 Letter from unidentified Exclusive Brethren authors to John Howard, 31 May 2003
24 'The Brethren Express', *Four Corners*, ABC, 15 October 2007
25 Letter from Warwick John to ABC *Four Corners* presenter Quentin McDermott, 12 October 2007
26 Comments to the author by a spokesman for Mark Mackenzie, 23 May 2007
27 'Politics, Pamphlets and Prayers,' *Dateline*, SBS, 15 November 2006
28 Nick Redmond, 'Bound for Court', *Central Western Daily*, 10 September 2004
29 Email of candidate Reverend Robert Griffith to his supporters, 1 September 2004
30 Phone interview, 25 March 2008
31 'Hidden Prophets', *Sydney Morning Herald*, 1 July 2006
32 Australia, Senate 2006, *Official Hansard*, no. 8, p. 69
33 'Beneath the radar' group behind late pro-GOP ads, *St Petersburg Times*, 2 November 2004
34 'The Brethren Express', *Four Corners*, ABC, 15 October 2007
35 'The Brethren Express', *Four Corners*, ABC, 15 October 2007 (statement by US Brethren members Tom Holt, Don Carnwath, and Dan Holt)
36 'The Brethren Express', *Four Corners*, ABC, 15 October 2007

37 'The Brethren Express', *Four Corners*, ABC, 15 October 2007 (statement by Bruce Carmichael)
38 Peter O'Neil, 'Secretive Religious Sect Behind Anti-Gay Ads', *Vancouver Sun*, 15 July 2005
39 Peter O'Neil, 'Secretive Religious Sect Behind Anti-Gay Ads', *Vancouver Sun*, 15 July 2005
40 Nicky Hager, *The Hollow Men: a study in the politics of deception*, Craig Potton Publishing, 2006
41 David Marr, 'Hidden Prophets,' *The Sydney Morning Herald*, 1 July 2006
42 'Libs Told Brethren How to Get Votes', Matthew Denholm, *The Australian*, 5 June 2007
43 Australia, Senate 2006, *Official Hansard*, no. 8, p. 69
44 Australia, Senate 2006, *Official Hansard*, no. 8, p. 57
45 Letter from unidentified Exclusive Brethren authors to John Howard, 19 September 2003
46 Letter from John Howard to unidentified Exclusive Brethren recipients, 25 September 2006
47 John S. Hales, White Book 68, p. 216, October 1991
48 Letter from Warwick John to ABC *Four Corners* presenter Quentin McDermott, 12 October 2007
49 John W. Howard doorstop interview, 22 August 2007
50 Interview with the author, 26 April 2008
51 Howard, doorstop interview, 22 August 2007
52 Howard, doorstop interview, 22 August 2007
53 Interview with the author, 5 March 2008
54 Interview with the author, 7 March 2008
55 Kevin Rudd, doorstop interview, 22 August 2007
56 Letter from ex-Brethren member Peter Flinn, representing 30 former members, to Kevin Rudd, 25 February 2008
57 Press release from Kevin Rudd's office to the author, 6 May 2008
58 Undated White Book references

Chapter 8: Schooling

1 Bruce D. Hales, Notes of Meetings, Berwick, Australia, 26 July 2003. White Book 51
2 Interview with the author, Meadowbank School, 28 March 2007
3 Roger Kirkpatrick and Bruce D. Hales, Notes of Meetings, Berwick, Australia, July 26 2003, White Book 51

4   Warwick John and Bruce D. Hales, Exclusive Brethren Assembley Meeting, 24 July 2004
5   Brethren elders Euan Chirnside, Norman Mauger, Alistair Shemilt, and Philip Grace, 'Submission to Mr. Don Hayward M.P. Shadow Minister for Education'
6   Brethren elders Mark Nipper, Alistair Shemilt, David Thomas, and Euan Chirnside, 'Deputation to the Chief General Manager, Department of School Education, 10am Monday April 6th, 1992' (unpublished, leaked document)
7   Letter to Euan Chirnside from Don Hayward MP, Minister for Education, 16 December 1993
8   Documents obtained by the author, March 2008
9   Letter to David Thomas from Stephen Elder, parliamentary secretary to Don Hayward, Minister for Education, 31 August 1994
10 Letter to directorate of School Education Quality Programs Division, 19 October 1994, from Brethren elders Doug Burgess, Gordon Stevens, David Thomas
11 Interview with the author, 1 February 2008
12 Letter to John W. Howard, Prime Minister of Australia, 'Re: Commonwealth Funding for Non-Government Correspondence School', from Brethren elders John K. Anderson, Bruce D. Hales, Stephen C. Hales, and C. Warwick John, 25 May 2000
13 Letter to David Kemp, Minister for Education, Training, and Youth Affairs, 'Re: Commonwealth Funding for Distance Education Students', from Brethren elders John K. Anderson, Bruce D. Hales, and David W. Stewart, 31 May 2000
14 Letter to John K. Anderson, CEO, Meadowbank Education Inc., from Aurora Andruska, assistant secretary, Schools Resources Branch, Department of Education, Training and Youth Affairs, 22 June 2000
15 Jim McMorrow was the former education department first assistant commissioner when the ERI funding model was designed in the 1980s. Interview with the author, 4 April 2008
16 'Profile of the Brethren' (document sent to federal education minister Dr Brendan Nelson, 31 May 2004)
17 I am grateful to the anonymous correspondent 'Ellie', writing on www.peebs.net, who compiled some of the figures in this section.
18 Interview with the author, 29 January 2008
19 'Review of SES Funding Arrangements for Non-Government Schools: a report on an internal departmental review into the effectiveness of the

SES funding arrangements for non-Government schools', (Department of Education internal report), December 2006
20 Stephen Hales, 'Funded like Other Schools', letter to the editor, *Weekly Times*, 6 June 2006
21 Letter to Dr Brendan Nelson, Minister for Education, from David W. Stewart, 21 April 2004
22 'School Ethos and Guiding Principles' (Exclusive Brethren document)
23 Letter to Dr Brendan Nelson, Minister for Education, from David W. Stewart, 22 July 2004
24 Bruce D. Hales and David W. Stewart, Exclusive Brethren Assembley Meeting, 24 July 2004
25 Interviews and correspondence with the author in November 2006 and March 2008
26 Interview with the author, 16 January 2007
27 www.peebs.net (posting on 22 September 2006)
28 Interview with the author, 16 January 2007
29 *Parents and Students Handbook: learning to learn, a national approach to education*, Meadowbank Education Inc., 2008
30 Interview with the author, Meadowbank School, 28 March 2007
31 MET School science curriculum (unit: 'Life goes on'; sub-unit: 'Evolution')
32 *Parents and Students Handbook: learning to learn, a national approach to education*, Meadowbank Education Inc., 2008
33 Correspondence with the author, 21 January 2008
34 Bruce D. Hales, notes of Meetings at Kellyville, White Book 187, p. 51–56, 8 November 2006
35 Interview with the author, 24 February 2008

Chapter 9: The Family Court
1 Paul's Epistle to the Romans, *Holy Bible*, Darby translation, Chapter 1, verses 27 and 29–31
2 *Ex parte Paul; Re Paul* (1963) 80 WN 557. I am indebted to the Family Court of Australia for an unofficial paper, prepared by one of their officers, Family Law Cases on Religion, 15 June 2007, for much of the historical summary.
3 *Mauger v Mauger* (1966) 10 FLR 285
4 *Evers v Evers* (1972) 19 FLR 296
5 *K v K* (1979) FLC 90–680
6 *Pasio v Pasio* (1979) FLC 78–514
7 *In the Marriage of Firth and Firth, Boyer and Boyer (Interveners)* (1988) FLC 91–971

8   Account taken from the judgment of Justice Geoffrey Walsh, Family Court of Australia, Melbourne, 1 May 1981. Family law dictates that the parties to cases cannot be identified.
9   Interview with a witness, Warren McAlpin, 1 April 2008
10 Paul Guest, interview with the author, 1 April 2008
11 In the Marriage of EAG and EMG, JAA and HLA (interveners), unpublished judgment of Justice Stephen Strauss, Family Court of Australia, 5 March 1982
12 Interview with Quentin McDermott, *Four Corners*, ABC, 2007
13 Interview with the author, 27 February 2008
14 Quoted in a letter by ex-Brethren members to Australian Prime Minister Kevin Rudd, 25 February 2008
15 Ministry of John Hales, White Book 165, p. 33
16 Unpublished judgment of Justice Stephen Strauss, Family Court of Australia, 12 August 1991
17 Interview with the author, 23 December 2006
18 Louise Samways, *Dangerous Persuaders: an expose of gurus, personal development courses, and cults, and how they operate*, Penguin Australia, online edition, 2006, p. 63
19 *Litchfield v Litchfield* (1987) FLC 91–840
20 Exclusive Brethren submission to then chief justice Alistair Nicholson, 8 May 2002
21 Exclusive Brethren document, *Important Information for Senators Re: Proposed Notice of Motion by Senator Bob Brown*, 23 February 2007
22 Ministry of Bruce D. Hales, Volume 16, Reading at Sydney, Saturday April 12 2003
23 Letter to Alistair Nicholson, Chief Justice of the Family Court of Australia, from undisclosed Brethren marriage celebrants, 15 July 1991
24 Letter to Alistair Nicholson, Chief Justice of the Family Court of Australia, from undisclosed Brethren marriage celebrants, 8 May 2002
25 Exclusive Brethren submission to government's inquiry into 'A New Approach to the Family Law System – Implementation of Reforms', 13 January 2005
26 Letter to Attorney General Philip Ruddock from undisclosed Exclusive Brethren correpondents, 3 May 2005
27 Exclusive Brethren submission to the Senate Standing Committee on Legal and Constitutional Affairs, 'Comments on Aspects of the Government's 10 November 2003 Discussion Paper: a new approach to the family law system', 13 January 2005

28 Letter to undislosed Brethren recipients from Attorney General Philip Ruddock, 15 June 2005
29 Interview with the author, 7 March 2008
30 Interview with the author, 3 April 2008
31 Exclusive Brethren document, 'Important Information for Senators Re: Proposed Notice of Motion by Senator Bob Brown', 23 February 2007
32 *M v M*, unpublished judgment of Justice Robert Benjamin, Family Court of Australia, 21 December 2006
33 Hearing in the Launceston Family Court, 20 February 2007
34 Interview with the author, 20 February 2007

Chapter 10: Silencing Criticism
1 Tim Twinam interview with the author, 1 April 2008
2 US Court of Appeals for the Seventh Circuit judgment, *Chicago Lawyers' Committee for Civil Rights v Craigslist Inc.*, 14 March 2008
3 www.stempublishing.com
4 www.mybrethren.org
5 www.peebs.net (Sheela Seesahai entry, posted 31 October 2006)
6 Vermont Statutes, 12 V.S.A § 1041; Exercise of rights to free speech and to petition government for redress of grievances; special motion to strike.
7 Email interview with Professor Willem J. Ouweneel, 26 March 2008
8 www.peebs.net (13 February 2005)
9 This account comes from the website of Concerned Christian Growth Ministries at www.ccgm.org.au
10 www.ccgm.org.au/Articles/ARTICLE-0106.htm

Conclusion
1 Bryan R. Wilson (Reader Emeritus in Sociology, University of Oxford), *The Brethren: a current sociological appraisal*, 2nd rev. ed., 2000, at www.theexclusivebrethren.net/documents/academicstudy.pdf
2 Press release from Kevin Rudd's office to the author, 6 May 2008
3 John Howard, interview with Chris Smith, *Afternoons with Chris Smith*, Radio 2GB, 31 August 2006

Index

Abbott, Tony, 183, 187, 234
Aberdeen Incident, 7, 9–16, 31, 36, 38, 39, 276, 286
Abetz, Eric, 183, 204
Agnew School, 231, 232, 235, 243
alcohol, 8, 12, 37, 57, 77, 161, 237, 287
Alderton, Alison, 115–20, 122, 126, 129, 132–40, 142, 257
Alderton, Bob, 115–20, 123, 126, 127, 130, 132–9
Alderton, Priscilla, 117, 123–30, 131, 136, 138, 140, 142
Alderton, Sophie, 119, 120–3, 126, 130–2, 136, 138, 141–2
All Pumps, 53, 192
Anchor Fundraising Inc., 236
Anderson, John, 97, 99, 104, 212, 215, 226, 227
Andrews, Kevin, 180
anti-depressants, 57, 159, 165
apprehended violence orders, 49, 51, 156–7, 167, 289
Archway House, 41, 81
assembly discipline, 12, 22, 25, 30, 35, 50, 58, 60–1, 62, 65–6, 73, 77, 155, 159, 252, 290

baptism, 63
Benjamin, Justice Robert, 268, 270–1
Bible and Gospel Trust, 71, 102, 272, 279, 283–4
Bouma, Prof. Gary D., 52, 205, 206, 247
Bradnick, Robin, 86–7
Brash, Don, 2, 199–201
Brown, Bob, 68, 201, 204, 206, 209, 211
Bush, George W., 186, 196, 198, 242
business seminars, 75, 83, 85, 91–5, 181

Cadman, Alan, 184, 233
Catholicism, 18, 19, 56, 77, 230, 243, 249
Chadwick, Virginia, 221
charities, 21, 53, 72, 76, 79, 83, 98–101, 102–4, 108, 111–13, 236, 238, 295
Chirnside, (Euan) Lloyd, 205, 246–8, 249, 251
CityLink, 182
Clark, Helen, 201, 205
Clarke, David, 212
clergy, 18, 19, 20, 182

computers, 37, 58–9, 95–7, 222, 224, 232–4, 268, 276
Costello, Peter, 172

Darby, John Nelson, 8, 16–26, 27, 28, 29, 32, 37, 43, 44, 49, 63, 69, 82, 174
Delaney, Martine, 203
distance education, 181, 221–7, 230, 244
divisions, 7, 8, 14, 25–6, 27–8, 30–1, 38
divorce, 47, 50, 52–3, 166, 205, 247
Downer, Alexander, 183
Drayton, Dr Dean, 206
Dronsfield, W.R., 28
Dunlop, Kevin, 102

eating rule, 8, 33–4, 49, 56
Elect Vessel, 1, 7, 32
evolution, theory of, 217, 221, 222, 225, 240–1

family breakdown, 204, 213, 246
Family Law Act, 51, 248, 250, 264–7, 294
Fawkes, Ron, 34, 36, 137, 173, 177, 180–1
fax machines, 37, 58, 95, 97, 104, 105
Ferguson, Michael, 183
Field, Vincent, 260, 264, 288
fighting fund, 52, 77, 256–7
Flinn, Peter, 86–7
funerals, 79–80, 127

Gadsden, Alan, 84, 92
Gadsden, John, 83, 91–2, 95, 96, 98
Gardner, James Alec, 10–12, 14
Gibb, Iain, 34, 36
Glenvale School, 98, 230, 231, 232
Greens, Australian, 2, 68, 174, 189, 191, 193, 201, 202–3, 204, 209, 293
Greens, New Zealand, 201
Griffith, Robert, 193–5
Guesdon, Chris, 203
Guest, Justice Paul, 253–6

Hager, Nicky, 199–200
Hales, Bob, 177, 189
Hales, Bruce D.,
    business, 54, 81
    politics, 173–4, 177–8, 185, 190–1, 197–8, 208–210, 214, 234,
    succession to leadership, 41–2
    theology, 44, 56, 61–2
    youth, 41, 77
Hales, Daniel, 94–5, 196
Hales, John S., 35–6, 39–41, 83–92, 93, 112, 116, 148–9, 150, 177–8, 190, 207, 216, 220, 258
Hales, Stephen, 2, 53, 82, 189–92, 208, 210, 215, 226, 232
Hales, W. Bruce, 35–7, 39, 83–91, 116, 144–5
Hayward, Don, 222–3
Hennessy, Dr John, 146–9
Hewson, John, 189, 192
Holy Spirit, 31–2, 61, 70, 182
homosexuality, 47, 67–8, 151, 154, 175, 193, 194, 223
Howard, John, 41, 292–3
    election campaigns, 141, 173–4, 190–1, 193, 210
    lobbying, 1–2, 177–80, 182, 185–90, 205–6, 208–10
    school policy, 219–20, 226–31
Hughes Travel Trust, 113

Inform Advertiser, 99, 102
internet, 48, 59, 69, 96, 223, 281
Iraq war, 186, 187, 188, 193, 194

Jackson Wells Morris, 207, 289
Jensen, Lindsay, 151–9, 165
John, Warwick, 1–2, 178, 183, 184, 192, 208, 210, 212, 220, 226, 266

Kelly, Jackie, 184
Kemp, David, 225, 227–8
Ker, Madeline, 10–13, 283–4, 287
Ker, Alan, 11, 283–4, 287

Latham, Mark, 173, 189–90
Living Our Beliefs, 48, 50, 54, 75, 79, 81

Mackenzie, Mark, 2, 99, 191–2, 208, 210
'man of sin', 37, 59, 89, 233
Mantach, Damian, 202–3
marriage, 47, 52, 66–7, 194, 198, 218, 246–7, 254
Martinez, Mel, 196–7
McAlpin, Warren, 148, 149–51
McCorkell, Clive, 116
McCorkell, Tony, 151, 155–6, 207, 271, 289
McNaughton, Phil, 196, 266
Medicare, 186–8
Melrose Park School, 229, 230, 232
MET School, 226, 229–30, 232, 240
Milne, Christine, 201–2, 204
mobile phones, 37, 58, 59, 95, 98, 103, 105
Monday, Don, 104–5, 197–8, 289
Murray, Andrew, 179–80

National Assistance Fund, 100
National Office Assist, 58, 82, 96–8, 100
Nelson, Brendan, 183, 212, 232–4
Nicholson, Chief Justice Alistair, 256–7, 260, 261, 262–4

onemedifund, 101–2, 188
Open Brethren, 25, 286
'opposers', 62, 139, 278
Ouweneel, Willem J., 286–7

Patterson, Kay, 186–7
Paul, Apostle, 8, 13, 32, 33, 36, 37, 49, 61–2, 92, 114, 246–7
'position, the', 13–14, 23
Pro Vision Marketing, 92

Rainbow, Gordon, 28, 32

'Rapture, the', 14, 20–1, 22, 27, 42, 185
Raven, Frederick Edward, 27–30, 32, 82
Reith, Peter, 179–80
religious freedom, 174–5, 183, 204, 213–14, 248, 251, 267, 291–5
'Review, the', 42–3, 60, 140, 143, 149–50
Roberts, Anthony, 212
Robertson, Alan, 35
Rogers, Kenneth, 145
Rudd, Kevin, 44, 212–14, 231, 291
Ruddock, Philip, 183–4, 264–7

'saints', 20, 56, 71, 74, 90, 185, 219, 234
Samways, Louise, 9, 260
Sealey, Dr Vernon, 146–9, 151, 161, 162
Sealey, Graeme, 149, 150
Seesahai, Sheila, 278–9, 281
separation, doctrine of, 3, 8, 10,13, 16, 18, 22, 24, 33–4, 35, 37, 43, 48–51, 57, 62–3, 115, 136, 143, 145–6, 162, 213, 218, 246, 248, 254, 263
sexual assault, 35, 78–9, 128, 145, 151–4, 213
Shore, Chris, 78–9, 145, 149, 153–4, 155, 157,160, 163, 166, 168–9
shut up (*see* assembly discipline)
Silver Bridge, 105
Simmonds, Neville, 200
SLAPP lawsuits, 285, 295
Smith, Nick, 287–8
splits (*see* divisions)
'spoiling the Egyptians', 77, 110, 231
Stanton, Rosemary, 75
Sterling Inc., 105
Stewart, David, 212, 215, 217, 218, 221, 227, 233–4, 239, 240, 243
Stott, Robert, 7, 15–16
Strauss, Justice Stephen, 255, 258–60
Suggate, Bruce, 110, 153, 157, 159–70

Suggate, Darryl, 150, 162, 163, 164, 167
Suggate, Trevor, 163, 164
Symington, James (Jim) S., 89, 94, 115–16, 134, 135, 137–8, 139, 147

taxation, 38, 72, 77, 83, 93–4, 98, 100, 101, 105, 107–11, 112, 163, 181–2, 204, 213, 238, 295
Taylor, James (JT) Junior, 7–16, 31–5, 36, 37, 39, 49, 56, 57, 63, 69, 71, 77, 79, 82, 116, 117, 146, 248, 276, 283, 286–7
Taylor, James Senior, 29–32, 40, 82, 84, 88–9, 176
telemarketing, 65, 94–5, 105, 200, 218
television, 37, 48, 69, 148, 222, 224, 268
Textor, Mark, 211
Twinam, Tim, 3, 274, 275–8, 281–6

Unifocus Limited, 103–4, 105

unions, 2, 69, 76, 109, 176–7, 179–81, 190, 191, 238, 242
university, 34–5, 38, 64–5, 223, 238

Vale, Danna, 183, 212
Van der velde Gilbert, Jacqui, 218, 239–40, 241, 243

Wallis, John, 288
Walsh, Justice Geoffrey, 254–5
welfare, 47, 77, 107–10
Westmount School, 100
Whitlam, Gough, 190, 248
Willmac Enterprises, 99, 191–2, 195, 204, 207–8
Wilson, Bryan R., 19, 290–1
withdrawn from, (*see* assembly discipline)
women, treatment of, 28, 47, 50, 51, 53, 59, 66–7, 70, 74–6, 244, 292–3
Wyman, (Richard) Dick, 273–5, 276, 278, 279–80, 283